D1570405

METAPHOR AND FILM

CAMBRIDGE
STUDIES
IN FILM

METAPHOR
AND FILM

TREVOR WHITTOCK

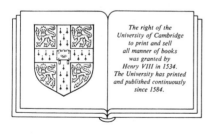

The right of the
University of Cambridge
to print and sell
all manner of books
was granted by
Henry VIII in 1534.
The University has printed
and published continuously
since 1584.

CAMBRIDGE UNIVERSITY PRESS
CAMBRIDGE
NEW YORK   PORT CHESTER   MELBOURNE   SYDNEY

Published by the Press Syndicate of the University of Cambridge
The Pitt Building, Trumpington Street, Cambridge CB2 1RP
40 West 20th Street, New York, NY 10011, USA
10 Stamford Road, Oakleigh, Melbourne 3166, Australia

First published 1990

Printed in the United States of America

Library of Congress Cataloging-in-Publication Data
Whittock, Trevor.
Metaphor and film / Trevor Whittock.
    p.   cm. – (Cambridge studies in film)
Includes bibliographical references.
Filmography: p.
ISBN 0-521-38211-4
1. Motion pictures – Semiotics.   2. Motion pictures – Philosophy.
3. Metaphor.   I. Title.   II. Series.
PN1995.W45   1990
791.43′014 – dc20   90–33652

British Library Cataloguing-in-Publication Data
Whittock, Trevor
Metaphor and film. – (Cambridge studies in film).
1. Cinema films. Semiotic aspects
I. Title
791.43

ISBN 0-521-38211-4

Contents

Acknowledgments

The sources of all quotations are cited in the notes. Special thanks, however, should go the following for permission to quote in some detail from the works here mentioned:

Simon & Schuster, Inc., for *Hitchcock* by François Truffaut, first published in Great Britain by Secker & Warburg, 1968;

the journal *Screen* for the article, "Current Problems of Film Theory," by Christian Metz;

Harvester Press for Jonathan Culler, *Saussure;*

Yale University Press for Ernst Cassirer, *The Philosophy of Symbolic Forms, Vol. 2, Mythical Thought;*

Associated University Presses for N. Roy Clifton, *The Figure in Film;*

the Macmillan Press and Christian Bourgois, editor for Christian Metz, *Psychoanalysis and Cinema: The Imaginary Signifier;*

Cambridge University Press for David E. Rumelhart, "Some Problems with the Notion of Literal Meanings," in Andrew Ortony, *Metaphor and Thought;* and

the journal *Cinéaste* for Yves de Laurot, "From Logos to Lens."

CHAPTER I
Introduction

HITCHCOCK: At the beginning of the film [*The Birds*] we show Rod Taylor in the bird shop. He catches the canary that has escaped from its cage, and after putting it back, he says to Tippi Hedren, "I'm putting you back in your gilded cage, Melanie Daniels." I added that sentence during the shooting because I felt it added to her characterisation as a wealthy, shallow playgirl. And later on, when the gulls attack the village, Melanie Daniels takes refuge in a glass telephone booth and I show her as a bird in a cage. This time it isn't a gilded cage, but a cage of misery.... It's a reversal of the age-old conflict between men and birds. Here the human beings are in cages and the birds are on the outside. When I shoot something like that, I hardly think the public is likely to notice it.
TRUFFAUT: Even though the metaphor wasn't obvious – to me, at any rate – this is truly a remarkably powerful scene.[1]

In the case of *Taxi Driver*, the theme was loneliness. Then you find a metaphor for the theme, one that expresses it. In *Taxi Driver*, that was the cabbie, the perfect expression of urban loneliness....Metaphor is extremely important to a movie.
– Paul Schrader[2]

White-light fog is used in the underwater sequence of *The Graduate* in which Benjamin, donning flippers and goggles, flees to the bottom of the family swimming pool, presumably to escape the overbearing camaraderie of his parents and their circle of friends. As the camera assumes his point of view, the world becomes a gloomy blur, shimmering but indistinct, agitated by the motion of the water and toned in a bilious, washed-out green. While the metaphor of diving reflects Benjamin's introversion and retreat, the color quality of the image indicates the psychic cost of his escapism. He has ducked away from the plastic gewgaws of suburbia but only to set himself adrift in a turbid world of ghastly color and uncertain shapes.
– James F. Scott[3]

In these passages, a director, a scriptwriter, and a film critic identify what they see as metaphors in film. Is their use of what is normally regarded as a literary term appropriate, or is it, when carried over to the cinematic context, mere license? Is "cinematic metaphor" itself a metaphor only, or do metaphors really exist in films?

Considerable hostility to the suggestion that metaphors exist in films has come from two quarters: from literary critics who consider that this extension of the concept of metaphor would empty it of all precision; and from film theoreticians who believe such applications arise from misunderstanding the true nature of the film medium. W. B. Stanford may be quoted as spokesman for the first view:

The frequent misuse of the term *metaphor* for *symbolism* demands a distinction. As S. J. Brown puts it, symbolism belongs to the sphere of *things* while metaphor belongs to the sphere of *words*. This does not mean that words cannot be things but that *metaphor* must not be used as a term for nonverbal transferences if it is to retain its meaning at all. What is one to make of this use in a cinema critique from *The Spectator* of October 4, 1935? – 'Here as a priest strikes a bell Mr. W_____ uses one of the loveliest *visual metaphors* I have ever seen on any screen. The sound of the bell startles a small bird from its branch and the camera follows the bird's flight and the notes of the bell across the island down from the mountain side, over forest and plain and sea, the vibration of the tiny wings, the fading sound' – this is symbolism, parallelism, analogy, anything but metaphor.[4]

The second view is summarized by Calvin Pryluck:[5]

A number of writers have criticized the whole idea of "film metaphor" on the partially valid basis that the photographic image in film is a literal representation of object and events. These objects and events, the argument goes, have intrinsic meanings which militate against the images being interpreted figuratively. On these grounds, Kracauer, for instance, suggested that the gods sequence in *October* would be seen as "an aimless assemblage of religious images rather than as an attack on religion."

Other writers Pryluck adduces as making similar objections are Rudolf Arnheim[6] and George Bluestone.[7]

Such views are not to be dismissed lightly. They stress the twofold drawbacks to any endeavor to apply traditional notions to new areas of experience: The traditional terms may become overextended and useless; and their employment may lead to preconceptions that hinder the recognition of the new for what it is. But what other recourse have we but to explore the unknown with the aid of the known, in the process modifying what we thought we knew and discovering what we did not expect to find? (Indeed, some regard this as the fundamental process of metaphor itself.)[8] The history of film, as much as the history of film theory, exemplifies this procedure. D. W. Griffith brought the conventions of melodrama to establish the narrative resources of the new medium, just as Eisenstein adapted the methods of Meyerhold and Kabuki theater to formulate image and montage.[9] Kracauer in developing his realist position called upon the authority of the literary critic and cultural historian, Erich Auerbach; and Christian Metz drew upon the semiotics of Ferdinand de Saussure and Roland Barthes.[10] An approach to film via the concept of metaphor, then, is not, ipso facto, to be condemned. Even if the twofold dangers mentioned cannot be totally avoided, commensurate gains might be achieved. It may be salutary to rethink the concept of metaphor within a wider context, and the use of it in the analysis of film may feed back into its application in the literary sphere. A notion thought to be so central to artistic creativity in language cannot be totally alien to artistic creativity elsewhere, and may even illuminate it. At any rate, this book will endeavor to widen the employment of metaphor by seeking to discover where and how metaphors may be legitimately attributed to films. It is hoped that this will provide insights into specific films, into the workings of "film language," and indeed into the very processes underlying metaphor generally.

Yet, the question might still be asked, why metaphor? Reasons have already been hinted at. As the opening quotations illustrate, people do frequently rely upon the term when discussing films. Often their usage is loose, and the approach has been challenged. Clarification is needed, and implications should be set out before the debate continues. Then, theories of metaphor are closely related to theories of imagination and to the processes and structures imagination employs. The study of metaphor leads off in one direction toward cognitive psychology with its interest in the mental processes underlying perception and mental categorization; in another direction toward rhetoric and strategies of communication.[11] These topics are, or should be, of cardinal interest to film theoreticians. Finally, the study of cinematic metaphor is a relatively neglected field by comparison with some others. This despite, or in part because of, those trends in film theory that have their source in modern linguistics. Although it would not be true to say that structural linguists have not propounded ideas that cast a new light on metaphor,[12] in general their treatment of the subject has been disappointing. Particularly notable has been the failure to deal with the specificity of metaphors – their uniqueness of content – and with the way metaphors, as it were, step outside accepted codes to express meanings for which the codes themselves do not allow.[13] Film semiology has been, if anything, even less fitted to tackling these issues, as I hope to indicate later in this book.[14] Cinematic metaphor, hence, still remains largely unexplored and unexplained, a challenge and a lure.

A few words need to be said about aspects of the approach adopted in this book in order to avoid any misunderstanding by the reader. First, an argument for metaphor in film needs to show that commentators *regularly* identify metaphors when attempting to explicate films. Consequently, in the sections of the book where specific cinematic metaphors are discussed, not only have I written on metaphors I myself have noted but I have also liberally cited what other film critics have said. The apparent range and variety of metaphors detected in films indicate how rare it is to find a film critic who fails to note them.

Second, on the whole I have stuck to feature films and have virtually ignored documentaries or avant-garde or experimental films. My real interest lies in features, particularly those with some genuine claim to artistic merit. Still, I hope that much of what I say applies more widely than merely to narrative films. I have no doubt, for example, that a whole book could be devoted to the way documentaries utilize metaphorical images and employ arguments based on widely shared metaphors. But that is not the book I have chosen to write.

Third, this book is as much about metaphor itself as about the figurative possibilities of cinema. Film is a way of uncovering some fundamental properties of metaphor that a restricted focus on the verbal medium of literature runs the risk of neglecting.

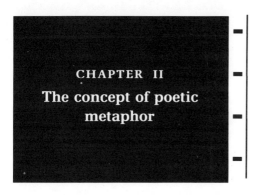

Their language is vitally metaphoric: that
is, it marks the before unapprehended relations of things and perpetuates their apprehension.

— Percy Bysshe Shelley[1]

Metaphor is usually defined as the presentation of one idea in terms of another, belonging to a different category, so that either our understanding of the first idea is transformed, or so that from the fusion of the two ideas a new one is created. This can be represented symbolically as

$$A + B = A(B) \quad \text{or} \quad A + B = Z$$

Ever since I. A. Richards proposed the nomenclature, it has become customary to refer to the original idea as the *tenor*, and the second idea imported to modify or transform it as the *vehicle*.[2]

The convocation of ideas, $A + B$, must involve some transformation; otherwise there is no metaphor. Instead there is only simple analogy, or simple juxtaposition.

Analogy is a process of reasoning from parallel cases, but with the two cases remaining separate and unchanged. A city planner might describe the traffic system in terms of the arterial network of the body; the analogy would only hold true where there are genuine parallels, and would become positively misleading should the planner confuse factors in the one category with factors in the other. Analogy is the basis of many metaphors — "similitude in dissimilitude." In particular it is the basis of that form of metaphor called simile that explicitly calls attention to an analogy.[3] "My love is *like* a red, red rose." This is *as* that. In a common type of metaphor the words spelling out the comparison are simply omitted, and the analogy is implied only. But although such similes and metaphor have something in common with pure analogy, the way they work is different. In analogy the mind

5

moves from the common factors to clinch a point or elaborate an argument. The common factors are preestablished – that is, they are generally accepted or are believed to be truly the case. Where this is not so the analogy falls down. But in simile-type metaphors the mind moves from the tenor to the vehicle and back, attempting to identify the similitude. What is there in common between the person someone loves and a red, red rose? The mind has to find meanings that will fit. The meanings so found in turn create a shift in our comprehension of the original terms.[4]

This point may be put in a different way. In analogy the connections between the subject and its parallel case are accepted literally; in metaphor the connections between tenor and vehicle are understood figuratively.

The distinction between *literal* and *figurative* is inextricably bound up with thinking about metaphor. Literal derives from being true to the letter. A literal transcript is one that accurately reproduces the words originally used. In time this fidelity of rendition was extended to two different sets of circumstances, an extension that, ironically, is itself metaphorical. "Literal" came to be applied to the recounting of events. A literal account of what happened is one that is faithful to the facts, not coloring or distorting them in any way. Second, it came to be applied to the use of language. Words used literally are words employed in accordance with the rules of grammar and to be understood in their usual or primary sense. The two applications of "literal" are, of course, interrelated, because our perception of events and our language are interrelated.

To identify a visual phenomenon as a red rose the beholder must be acquainted with the categories of redness and rose. Language gives names to most of the categories we possess. When children learn to speak, they are acquiring not only phonemes, syntax, and vocabulary but also the categories society has adopted to organize and classify and interconnect its experiences. Words in their ordinary or primary usage refer to these categories. When words are used literally the language seems most neutral, reliable, and transparent because the words accord to categories that are accepted and acceptable – ones that are handed on socially, binding the society together and making communication possible.[5]

Not all our actual experiences, however, are covered by the conceptual categories we thus acquire nor can they be represented through the literal usage of language.

Perhaps this can best be illustrated through the verbal behavior of children when they have as yet a restricted vocabulary and, consequently, a limited possession of conceptual categories. Daily they are confronted with experiences new to them for which they possess no names. What do they do when they wish to speak of these experiences? They coin metaphors. They carry over (*meta-phora*) a word they know, connected to a category they possess, to describe something for which they do not have the word or the category. Sometimes they even surprise us by coming up with a metaphor to say something for which no category has been established. So a small boy explains why it is impossible to say which part of a mongrel belongs to any particular breed by explaining that the dog has been homogenized. Such extensions of meaning, such transfers of a term out of the realm in which convention places it, are figurative uses of language. To delineate undetermined areas of experience – that is, those areas for which no set categories exist – we have to resort to metaphor.

If this account be true, evidence supporting it will be found in the history of a language. As societies change and people encounter new experiences, so we may expect to find them having recourse to language that is at first figurative but which, as the category is acknowledged and accepted, becomes literal. This, indeed, is what we find does happen. Much of the vocabulary of our language consists of words and phrases that are now dead metaphors, but which once were new mintings or wrenchings of preceding usage to describe the strange, the innovative, or the unnamed. *Skyscraper* must have once been a description expressing awe: Now it is just another noun. The perception has become categorized, the novelty has gone, and the thrill has faded.

We can now redefine the distinction between analogy and metaphor. Analogy entails literal comparison only: The categories remain undisturbed. Metaphor is figurative: Categories are compacted and broken down so that fresh meaning can be expressed. The effect of vehicle on tenor will either be to reconstruct the category of the tenor, or from the fusion of vehicle and tenor to create something for which no category yet exists.

This account leads to the suggestion that metaphors are born at a frontier of human consciousness – at a place where language with its inadequacies and our mental framework of classifications with its restrictions encounter unassimilated experiences. The difficulty of discussing what takes place on this frontier is compounded by the inescapable recognition that we cannot even discuss the nature and process of metaphor without recourse ourselves to overtly metaphorical language.

"It is proper," wrote Aristotle, "to derive metaphors ... from objects which are closely related to the thing itself but which are not immediately obvious." That is, the tenor and the vehicle must belong to categories that are neither too close to one another nor too remote. The effort demanded to span the gap between tenor and vehicle has come to be called the *tension* of a metaphor. A dead metaphor, because it has become an accepted category in its own right, is one where the tension has been lost or is residual only. Sometimes that latent tension can be revivified, as in the case of such unfortunate mixed metaphors as "No stone was left unturned in plumbing the bottleneck to the depths." Dr. Johnson's well-known objection to some of the conceits of the metaphysical poets – that they "yoked heterogeneous objects together" – exemplifies an eighteenth-century resistance to metaphors with too much tension.

Discussions of the tension or incongruity in metaphors call attention to an aspect of metaphor that has often been vehemently distrusted. May not the connections linking tenor and vehicle be arbitrary? Or even worse, may not the figurative meanings generated by metaphor be illusory? Precisely because, the argument runs, metaphor challenges the received categories by means of which we realize our experience, may metaphor not be setting up false connections and weakening our grasp on the real world? Perhaps some such fear lurked behind Samuel Parker's action in 1670 when he advocated an act of Parliament forbidding the use of "fulsome and luscious" metaphors.[6] (The obverse side of the argument is put by Wallace Stevens when he says, "Reality is a cliché from which we escape by metaphor.")[7] That metaphors may be deceitful is a perfectly rational apprehension, for even staid metaphors can have the air of playing a game of "as if" with us. It is through, however, their fanciful play of analogies that we are freed from our set habits of thought. The mind can reconceive the subject, and contemplate fresh aspects of it. This is why writers on metaphor refer to the stereoscope of metaphor, or to its multidimensional depiction of a subject.[8] Metaphor dissolves our fixed notions in order to produce fresh insights.

Thus the tension of a metaphor entails more than a gap between tenor and vehicle. It involves the effort to adjust our present and customary ways of thinking to the startling new aspects brought to light by the metaphor. Through its tension a metaphor calls into question the ordered simplicities our received categories give us.[9]

Metaphor's wrenching of language and assault on categories means it can never be employed without an accompanying emotional charge. This probably explains why metaphor is so often considered to be an emotionally expressive trope.

Rhetorical devices, since classical times, have been divided into two main kinds: schemes and tropes. In *schemes* words may retain the same meaning they have in ordinary speech, but their order is organized in a more formal manner than is usual in common discourse. In *tropes,* words are employed in senses other than or additional to those they bear normally. Words in schemes may be literal; in tropes they are always to some degree figurative. Quintilian, for example, defines a trope as "the artistic alteration of a word or phrase from its proper meaning to another."[10]

It should be borne in mind though that often schemes and tropes are combined and that schemes themselves can become the basis for metaphors. Some writers have believed, erroneously, that metaphors rely on shifts of meaning in single words only. On the contrary, metaphorical implications are most often established through larger syntactical or rhetorical units – as the dramatic verse of Shakespeare amply illustrates.[11]

There are several tropes that are so allied to metaphor that they are often classified as such. They include *synecdoche* and *metonymy*. The two figures are closely related because they both depend on contiguity, either in form or event. A literal name is substituted for another literal name with which it is customarily connected. The resultant meaning may be literal (as with "all hands to the pump"), but very often it is figurative. To say, "I suppose perfect teeth over there offered you a lift home," does more than identify a rival: It is a remark spiky with innuendos, creating a caricature.

In recent times metonymy especially has received close attention by writers on poetics. There has been disagreement as to how it stands in relation to metaphor. One view, proposed by Roman Jakobson, sees metonymy as representing a different principle of organization to metaphor[12] (a view I shall argue against later). A more traditional view (which I adhere to) is that metonymy is a type of metaphor. According to this account metaphors are of two main types: those bringing ideas together by reason of similarity or figurative analogy (e.g., simile), and those bringing ideas together by reason of contiguity (e.g., metonymy).

Now the notion of contiguity is applicable to two different sets of circumstances. First, it may be a property of objects themselves. Then the basis of the metaphor is a matter of how objects, or aspects of objects, are associated together because the linkages occur in real life. Second, contiguity may refer to the copresence of images or phrases in a poem. When such images are brought together and juxtaposed in a specific poetic context, then they can acquire figurative significance. In this case the contextual collocation rather than precontextual associations makes possible metaphoric meaning.

Where prior association rather than textual juxtaposition or similarity provides the vehicle that modifies the tenor, the tension between tenor and vehicle is normally less because the association is less unexpected. But some tension there will be, if only because the vehicle displaces or fragments the tenor. Such distortion always gives special semantic emphasis. Cumulatively this can be very powerful, and explains why metonymy lends itself to lists and catalogs in poetry: Full metaphoric tension is built up by a variety of vehicles converging from different angles on the same tenor. Anglo-Saxon riddle poems, for example, function this way.

Metonymy tends to remain within a single world of discourse. Metaphor proper on the other hand joins together a plurality of worlds.[13] Not only are terms from different categories brought together but, as we have observed, the similitudes linking them and the dissimilitudes separating them are juxtaposed. Thus even the simplest simile-type metaphor has a collocation of ideas based on disparity, as well as an association of ideas based on analogy.

This aspect of metaphor has been particularly explored by Philip Wheelwright in his seminal book, *Metaphor and Reality*.[14] He proposes the terms *epiphor* to describe the synthesis brought about by similarity and *diaphor* for the synthesis arising from the juxtaposition of the disparate elements. He sees the two processes – that of epiphor and that of diaphor – "as intimately related aspects of poetic language and as mutually contributing to the power and significance of all good metaphor."[15] Wheelwright, however, concentrates on metaphor proper. I believe that diaphoric connection can play a metaphoric role in metonymy and synecdoche as well.

According to Wheelwright epiphor is the occasion for the contiguity that makes possible the diaphoric connection. Can contiguity be provided by other means? Yes, as we have suggested, by the poetic context itself. Images do not exist in isolation, but are part of a larger discourse. Just as tenor and vehicle become more than the sum of their parts, so a juxtaposition of epithets can fuse into a larger and unexpected meaning. Take, for example, a few lines from the seven ages of man speech in Shakespeare's *As You Like It:*

Then the whining schoolboy with his satchel
And shining morning face, creeping like snail
Unwillingly to school...

Ostensibly this simply describes that moment of a boy's day when his face is scrubbed and he is packed off to school. But a profound cynicism – Jacques's, not Shakespeare's – is apparent beneath the humor. The contrast between the fresh and unbesmirched energy implied by "shining morning face" and the complaining and reluctant submission elsewhere indicated in the lines synthesizes into something more complex and disturbing: a sense that it is in the very nature of things that life should feel frustrated and confined, even by the care that seeks to nurture it: $A + B = Z$.

It could be argued that to call this an example of metaphor is to extend the meaning of the term unnecessarily widely. The point is well taken. But the dangers of not recognizing that here we have an exten-

sion of meaning, and by juxtapositions caused by metonymic collocation, are far greater.

The notion of diaphoric metaphor has been arrived at by examining
how *meanings* may be fused together to create a more complex nexus.
The temptation, if this approach is rejected, is to conceive of metaphor
as a verbal or syntactic device only. Some rhetorical accounts do just
that. But metaphor is surely primarily a semantic event. Without an
understanding of the meaning of phrases, and how the meanings interconnect, many metaphors cannot even be identified at all, and the
richness of the poetry may be underestimated. This point is so important that it warrants specific illustration and demonstration.

The example chosen comes from Wordsworth's *The Daffodils.*

I wandered lonely as a cloud
That floats on high o'er vales and hills,
When all at once I saw a crowd,
A host, of golden daffodils;
Beside the lake, beneath the trees,
Fluttering and dancing in the breeze.

According to the schoolbook accounts of figures of speech, this
stanza contains few metaphors. True, there is a simile at the beginning (though there are still rhetoricians and others who do not consider a simile to be a metaphor)[16] and "host" would be accepted as
figurative, and "dancing" as well. But from this schoolbook point of
view "floats" is not a metaphor because clouds literally float; "crowd" is
not because the word may be used of any large number of objects;
"golden" simply describes the color of the flowers; flowers do "flutter" in a
breeze; "Beside the lake, beneath the trees" is clearly a literal depiction of place.

Close attention to movement and meaning in the poem, however,
changes this picture. The simile seems simple enough, until we ask
what is being compared with what? Is the first line to be read: "I,
(feeling) *lonely as a cloud* that...wandered"? Or: "I, (feeling) lonely,
wandered as a cloud that..."? The speaker's aimless drifting across
the landscape is certainly suggested. But so is a link between his
sense of loneliness and that of the cloud: The position of "lonely" in
the line enforces it. Why should a cloud, though, be thought of as
lonely? Because it is the only one in the sky? Possibly, but that is not
what the second line emphasizes: "That floats on high o'er vales and
hills." It is the remoteness, the detachment, from the world of things
that is stressed. This separateness is contrasted with thronged involve-
ment. The third line culminates in "a crowd," and the explanation is
held over, delayed further by the intensifying exclamation of "A host,"
before the golden daffodils are discovered. The effect is to animate

connectedness, and to evoke a bond between natural objects that later lines in the poem will make more explicit:

The waves beside them danced; but they
Out-did the sparkling waves in glee;
A poet could not but be gay,
In such a jocund company.

Once the main purport of the poem is recognized – that a sense of belonging to the life of the world releases energy and joy, and saves us from the pleasant but apathetic aimlessness of detachment – it becomes clear that all the relationships detailed in the poem are to be understood figuratively as well as literally. "That floats on high o'er vales and hills" describes a mental abstractedness as much as a physical phenomenon, and prepares for the isolating moods depicted later in the poem in the phrase "In vacant or in pensive mood." Even "Beside the lake, beneath the trees," which at first seemed only literal, can now be seen as a metaphor working almost subliminally.

Syntactic or rhetorical structures and devices *do not, then, suffice to identify metaphor: The semantics of context does.* It follows from this that the investigation of metaphors in a poem is not a matter of plotting verbal signs of a special kind, but of perceiving interrelated patterns of meaning. Yet this is, in essence, the poetic process itself. Philip Wheelwright, discussing the same issue, cites Coleridge on the "esemplastic" powers of the poet and quotes T. S. Eliot's well-known remark about the way a poet's mind assimilates and fuses experiences.[17]

It is, however, largely through his engagement with language that the poet discovers and discloses such amalgamated wholes to himself. In turn the reader must start from the verbal text in order to explore the tissues of meaning inherent there. The only time it is appropriate to think of metaphor as a device merely is when attention is being drawn to a particular linguistic arrangement initiating a poetic amalgamation of meanings. Provided this is borne in mind, and the all-important significance of semantic context is never forgotten, it is possible to proceed usefully to discuss metaphor in relation to other figurative "devices." Three such devices warrant special mention if only because of the degree of overlap between them and metaphor. They are image, symbol, and objective correlative.

Ezra Pound defined *image* as "that which presents an intellectual and emotional complex in an instant of time." Several critics have noted that this is, in effect, a description of metaphor, particularly diaphoric metaphor.[18] Normally, however, image is conceived more vaguely and widely than this, as any phrase containing marked sensuous particularity. As the name suggests, it must have been visual pictures that were first thought of, but by now image has come to mean in the writings of literary critics verbal "pictures" derived from any of the senses. (When I come to write about films I shall use the term in a different but special sense, which I shall define at the appropriate time.) The classification in literary criticism is broader than that of metaphor, and it incorporates most metaphors because of their sensory appeal. Image overlaps with metaphor in another way: Both entail attitudes toward and comment on the material assimilated to them. C. Day Lewis puts it this way:

> In its simplest terms, [the poetic image] is a picture made out of words. An epithet, a metaphor, a simile may create an image; or an image may be presented to us in a phrase or passage on the face of it purely descriptive, but conveying to our imagination something more than the accurate reflection of an external reality. Every poetic image, therefore, is to some degree metaphorical. It looks out from the mirror in which life perceives not so much its face as some truth about its face.[19]

The aim of art, after all, is never to reproduce reality but to understand it: Image and metaphor are related ways of embodying significance.

Symbol may be conceived as an offshoot of metaphor that has developed characteristics peculiarly its own. Like metaphor it normally possesses a tenor and a vehicle, but its treatment of them is different. In symbol the vehicle acquires greater stress, whereas the tenor is always concealed and usually is elusive. The increased status of the vehicle is achieved partly by giving it concreteness, and partly by retaining its literal reference along with its figurative suggestiveness. In this way the vehicle is made to seem a literal example, one possibility among many, of some wider principle – as with Blake's *Tyger* where the beast in the jungle seems one case of some greater destructive energy. The wider principle is normally not specified, but the figurative senses of the vehicle adumbrate what it might be. For the symbol to be successful the vehicle must be rich in figurative connotations. These may be accumulated in two ways: first, by cultural accretion, as when an object is deeply embedded in a society's myths or has a long history of artistic usage; and second, by deliberate policy of the poet who makes the context in which the vehicle is placed foster it with figurative associations. Metaphors are normally transitory in a poem: Their effect obtained, the work proceeds to other metaphors. Symbols have greater permanence, because they are rooted in the culture, or because they are the loci of many strands in the work. This too explains why the tenor is so often elusive: Not only must it satisfy the wealth of figurative associations, but if the literal reference of the vehicle is also an example of the tenor, then the tenor too must possess a literal dimension. The difficulty of reconciling these different conditions generates the peculiar tension of symbolism. It also explains why symbolism is so often resorted to when poets are striving to express a sense of some transcendent reality, which the things of this world only figure forth.[20]

The phrase, *objective correlative*, was originally coined by T. S. Eliot, but the definition he attached to it has never proved very satisfactory. He wrote:

The only way of expressing emotion in the form of art is by finding an "objective correlative"; in other words, a set of objects, a situation, a chain of events which shall be the formula of that particular emotion; such that when the external facts, which must terminate in sensory experience, are given, the emotion is immediately evoked.[21]

This is too wide and too unspecific. Almost anything in a work of art could be an "objective correlative" by this account, the only test of recognition being the evocation of a particular emotion. It is also to be doubted whether art ever evokes emotion in so pure and isolated a way as this, untouched by thoughts, judgments, and values. Eliot's definition suffers from the defects of the affective theory of art underlying it. Although it is reasonable to reject the definition, to discard a phrase so memorable and suggestive seems a pity. But perhaps there is some more appropriate use for it. Frequently, in drama, fiction, and films, a specific object is imbued with special significance, so that every time the object reappears the meaning associated with it (including the affective meaning) is called to mind. The handkerchief in *Othello* is a case in point. This device has no name, though sometimes, and not always accurately or without confusion, it is referred to as a symbol. Objective correlative, I submit, is an apt title for such an object, and hereinafter I will so employ the phrase.

Given that a physical object handled by actors may acquire a metaphorical sense, we might ask ourselves whether other schemes and tropes besides those already mentioned lend themselves to metaphorical usage. I think all may, but I would like to call attention to a few that will turn out to be of particular importance when we come to discuss cinematic metaphor.

I will mention first *hyperbole*. This trope may be characterized as a modification established through distortion: The tenor is presented through a vehicle that is a misshapen form of it, and which stamps its own grotesqueness on the tenor.

Another trope is one we may identify by the title *rule disruption*. In this trope a syntactic form or some other recognizable code or convention (e.g., register) is broken, but in such a way that the departure from the norm requires an explanation that only a metaphorical meaning can satisfy. This type of metaphor has received much attention recently because of the interest taken by modern linguists in structures and transformations.[22]

There are no limits to the ingenuity of artists when it comes to constructing metaphors. To try and define all the conceivable ways would be pointless. But perhaps one other type of metaphor that is linked to a formal device is worth drawing attention to because of its subtle potency. Again this type of metaphor has been paid little attention by traditional rhetoric, though its practice by poets is widespread. It is achieved by what might be called *chiming* – the creation of a kind of false equivalence. In order to create a *diaphor* (i.e., a metaphorically significant juxtaposition of two different ideas), an *epiphor* (i.e., a bringing together through similarities) is constructed through what are quite arbitrary phonetic, syntactic, or semantic correspondences. Rhymes, rhythmic echoes, and puns are cases of bringing together disparate elements through some agreement in sound. It can be done grammatically through repetition of phrase structures – what is sometimes called the device of parallelism – or through quotations that deliberately juxtapose two different contexts. Sometimes it is done more for the sake of pattern than for any other reason, and then it is no more than a scheme. But it can become a metaphorical trope when the ideas are so yoked together as to interact and breed a new figurative sense. It does provide an invaluable strategy for the poet.[23]

Tropes must not, however, be thought of only as isolated devices. They function in relation to one another and to other elements in the work, which brings me to a fundamental point. In art, figurative meanings coalesce to form new constellations; patterns amalgamate to create larger structures; constituent parts are ever-combining into significant wholes. Metaphor is not only an element in this process: The process itself is one of metaphorical transformations. Art by its very nature is, as Coleridge called it, *esemplastic* – that is, metaphorical.

This must be qualified, of course, lest the claim for metaphor seem too large, or the term be extended in reference beyond any practical usefulness. Just as there are schemes, and tropes other than metaphor, for the organization of artistic meanings, so there are nonmetaphorical ways of incorporating patterns into larger wholes. Plot, theme, style, narrative point of view are some. But even these, when they entail comparisons, the recognition of similitude in dissimilitude, the illumination of one event through seeing it stereoscopically in terms of another event, can bespeak a process of making metaphorical connections. Hamlet has lost a father and, seeking revenge, pretends to be mad. Laertes loses a father and pursues vengeance recklessly, almost madly. Ophelia loses a father and goes genuinely mad. Fortinbras loses a father and assuages his pride by going off to conquer a plot of ground "wheron the numbers cannot try the cause." Are not epiphor and diaphor involved in the contemplation of these interconnections and their import? When Hermione's statue comes to life in *The Winter's Tale,* has not dramatic plausibility given place to a metaphorical enactment of the power of grace? What of the issue of blindness, physical and moral, that links subplot and plot in *King Lear?* Twentieth-century critics, explicating the complexity of Shakespeare's plays, have come to speak of them as "expanded metaphors."[24] Implicit in this is the recognition that complex works of art possess layers of meaning, and that a crucial way of bringing one layer to bear on another entails metaphorical conjoinings. Writers quite regularly structure their works by means of metaphor at every level.

Reading a poem, a play, or a novel, then, is a process of continuing discovery, as meanings breed meanings, and as figurative structures are observed to erect further figurative structures. At every stage metaphorical transfigurations lead to new amalgamations and extensions. Thus, there are inherent hierarchies of metaphorical connections within the wrought fabric of artistic works.

By the very elaborateness of its form, and by the nature of the material shaped – whether it be language or something else – the work of art calls attention to its disparity from the world outside it. Yet by the very fact that a work of art often "imitates" some aspect of the world, it also calls attention to a similarity between them. Likeness and difference. So once again when we consider the relationship of art to the reality it deals with, we are back to a metaphorical relationship. The ultimate metaphor the reader must complete for himself or herself is to comprehend how the artistic vehicle *modifies and transforms the tenor that is that reader's experience of the living world.*[25]

Different periods, with their diverse ambitions and interests, have stressed different attributes of metaphor. The principal uses ascribed to metaphor include the following:

(1) *Decoration:* This approach conceives metaphor to be an embellishment, a mere stylistic flourish laid upon plain sense. It assumes that literal meaning is more important than figurative. At best, metaphor so conceived is thought to play a trivial role only. At worst, metaphor is regarded as deceitful: It distracts people's attentions away from clear and rational thought by its arbitrary associations and confusion of categories. This attitude to metaphor derives from a rhetoric that would prescribe rules for public speaking and clear discourse, and not from a rhetoric developed as a basis for poetic expression. The philosophical theory underpinning it is positivist. In poetry that gives its central attention to literal meaning, decorative metaphors are often obliquely presented examples or illustrations of generalizing assertions.

(2) *Emotional effect:* The minimum claim that is sometimes made here is that metaphors contribute vividness and memorability to rational discourse. This is, at least, an acknowledgment that metaphor provides pictorial or sensory concreteness. But most writers on metaphor, including some who distrust its irrationality, stress the emotional power of metaphor. If this aspect has been, and on the whole will be, underplayed or sketchily dealt with in the present study it is because the emotional potency of metaphor is virtually unanimously recognized.

(3) *Concision:* This approach still places emphasis on rational and literal meaning but regards metaphor as contracting a series of complex statements into one brief figure. Critics adopting this view of metaphor do not stress the new meaning that may coalesce in a metaphor but rather attend to the components that have gone into the metaphor. William Empson's discussion of metaphor in *The Structure of Complex Words*[26] and many of his accompanying analyses tend this way. Structural linguists have given a new slant to this approach by regarding metaphor as a manipulation in the surface structure that gives rise to a series of propositional sentences in the deep structure.[27] The point that is often disputed, however, is whether all metaphors can be unraveled this way and their meaning translated back into the sum of their component parts.

(4) *Naming the unnamed:* This approach envisages metaphor as creatively compensating for deficiencies in the language. Metaphor, by presenting one object in terms of another, is able to identify certain characteristics of the first for which no terminology has been coined. Sometimes it can do this because the concept providing the vehicle encompasses distinctions that, when applied to the tenor, define new facets of it. In general, this approach goes with a view of language that stresses how dependent on metaphor it is for its development and for its acquistion of new words (e.g., skyscraper).

A variation of this use is the employment of metaphor in lieu of a word that cannot be used for reasons of obscenity, blasphemy, or political ban. By obliquity or ellipsis the responsibility for identifying the taboo topic is placed upon the reader. (In the days of the Hays Office Code, film directors were to become adept at finding metaphorical euphemisms for the sexual act.)

(5) *Naming the unnamable:* The preceding approach presupposes that certain categories do not have names, and metaphor helps to name them. This approach assumes that some experiences always will fall between or beyond categories and can only be expressed by means of metaphor. Any experiences entailing synesthesia would be relevant here. When this approach emphasizes metaphor's potency for capturing private and idiosyncratic experience, it tends toward subjectivism.

More often, however, the approach typifies idealism – the belief that there are realms of reality outside ordinary perception discoverable only by insights and revelations. The major proponent of this view in English criticism is Coleridge, and his account of the secondary imagination is virtually a theory of metaphor. Significantly, in Romantic and post-Romantic poetry there is a tendency for metaphor to merge with symbolism.

Inevitably this approach stresses the uniqueness of metaphors: What they express is untranslatable into other words.

(6) *Eliciting the readers' own creativity:* This approach stresses the effort required to find the figurative relationships that will justify the yoking together of the disparate elements. The poet has a gift for making connections and for choosing the metaphors that elicit those connections. Readers, faced with these metaphors, must discover for themselves the connections linking tenor and vehicle. In doing so they become, as it were, poets by proxy. Because potentially more than one relationship may bind tenor and vehicle, and because readers must supply the connections out of their own experience, there is a degree of freedom and fresh creation in what they do, posited by this account.[28] This theory of how metaphor functions involves a paradox. The poet manipulates the readers by setting up the metaphor in the first place, but the readers in "completing" the metaphor – that is, supplying the meanings that are needed according to the linguistic specifications of the metaphor – bring contributions from their own experience that are actually outside the poet's control. Interpreting a metaphor then entails that the readers, without falsifying the linguistic text given them, make the metaphor their own.

One extreme account of this approach denies the importance of the poet's contribution at all, and runs the risk of making metaphors meaningless by overstressing the readers' freedom to the extent of making it uncheckable license. A more logical and restrained version of this account would simply stress that reading is always a process of experiential insights, and that a great writer is one who creates a text that seems inexhaustible: Its meaning changes and grows as the experience a reader brings to bear upon it becomes more the product of a mature, informed, and wise sensibility. Indeed, that is why we attend to good critics at all – by the example and aptness of their criticism they help us cultivate such a sensibility.

Finally, let me set out what I suggest are the principal forms by which metaphors are generated:

Explicit comparison (epiphor)

Identity asserted

Identity implied by substitution

Juxtaposition (diaphor)

Metonymy (associated idea substituted)

Synecdoche (part replaces whole)

Objective correlative

Distortion (hyperbole, caricature)

Rule disruption

Chiming (parallelism)

This list (which is formularized in Chapter V) is not offered as an ideal or a complete classification of metaphorical forms, but merely as a guide to some of the most common manifestations. Indeed, if, according to the basic contention of this book, metaphor leaps over the restricted categories of our experience, *any attempt to classify metaphor itself must be regarded as misconceived*. As well attempt to net Proteus.[29]

Many classificatory schemes have been proposed over the centuries. Aristotle initiated the endeavor with a species–genus analysis, and also gave hints of an animate–inanimate classification, which some of his successors developed further. Domains of thought and dominant traits common to both tenor and vehicle are other bases that have been selected for the construction of topologies. Christine Brooke-Rose, in *A Grammar of Metaphor*,[30] summarizes these approaches and briefly criticizes them before offering her own classification of metaphors in terms of syntactic forms. Although her definition of metaphor is broad ("any replacement of one word by another, or any identification of one thing, concept or person with any other"), her grammatical categories still limit the number of metaphors she can acknowledge and do not enable her to explore adequately how metaphor can breed metaphor in poetry. A liberal treatment of metaphor carries less dangers then than a restrictively oversystematic one. It is not claimed that the formulas I have offered are complete, merely that – sketchy as they are – they will serve to open out one way of discussing metaphors and of drawing attention to them in films as well as in poetry.

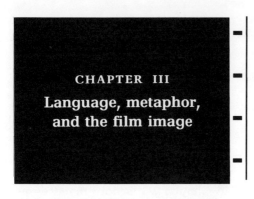

CHAPTER III

Language, metaphor,
and the film image

In the end we design the tool for the material – in the end, but never in the beginning.
In the beginning we have still to find out
the first things about the ways in which the
material is and is not workable; and we explore it by trying out implements with
which we have already learned to work
other materials. There is no other way to
start.

– Gilbert Ryle[1]

The difference between the two media, language and film, is the basis
of many objections to the notion of cinematic metaphor. For metaphor,
it is said, is primarily a linguistic concept, and film is not a language,
or at any rate does not function in the way verbal languages do.[2] Consequently, the application of a model foreign to the nature of film must
inevitably lead to distortion and misrepresentation. It is not my intention to play down such difference but rather to see how far a particular
concept, that of metaphor, can be used to illuminate the workings of a
new art, and to see how the art itself can modify and extend our understanding of the concept. In general the strategy of this book will be

1. to argue that most film theoreticians who touch on this issue have oversim-
   plified the concept of metaphor;
2. to develop a stylistics of metaphor appropriate to film;
3. to demonstrate the presence of metaphors, of various types, in a significant
   number of films; and, last but not least,
4. to put the case for a more inclusive theory of metaphor.

Because many writers have regarded the primary unit of film meaning to be the film image, and have considered that the basic difference
between language and film commences here, this seems to be a good
starting point. The simplest possible way to define the film image
would be to identify it with a single frame extracted from the film
strip. But such a definition would possess serious deficiencies. Psy-

20

chologically it is wrong. When watching a movie, we experience action, movement, and sound, not a static frame. We need to accept as images the gesture of a hand, say, or the ringing of a telephone. In order to conform then to ordinary discourse and common experience, a looser definition of film image is necessary. This suggests that the film image should be thought of as any simple object or event, normally perceived and regularly identified as a single entity, that is presented on either the screen or the sound track. Though vague, this revised definition has the merit of being truer to everyday usage. In ordinary life we do identify things this way, forming gestalts out of clusters of sensory data and labeling them according to acknowledged categories. Also it is common practice to regard as an image any artificial imitation or reproduction of something.

An acrobat's somersault, the clanging of a fire engine, a spiral staircase, or a sunset may all be conceived of and experienced as separate entities. Even a crowded landscape may be regarded as a unified whole, though were someone to call attention to a particular building the gestalt would shift along with a change in focal interest. It would shift again were the eye to be caught by the movement of a train, for the contrast of relative stillness and specific motion would lead to a reorganization of the scene. In movies, visual and aural composition may guide eye and mind, accentuating elements, bringing out contrasts, and emphasizing distinctions. A long shot with a neutral background of two men fighting in the center of the screen might register as one image – a fight; a closer shot placing the fighters near the opposite sides of the frame might be read as two images – the antagonists, or the blond guy and the dark guy. The frame held at the end of Truffaut's *The 400 Blows* (*Les Quatre cent coups*) possesses three images: Antoine Doinel, the seashore, and time frozen – for the last is also an experience supplied by the shot and stressed all the more by the contrast between this shot and those preceding it. Although composition or context may influence or even on occasion determine what we take to be the film images, normally we identify objects depicted in films in much the same way we identify real objects, and the psychology of everyday perception to a considerable degree applies.[3] Where kinesthetic or aural elements regularly accompany something, they are incorporated into our awareness of it: Thus we generally have one image of a moving car, not three (car, sound, motion). One consequence of this is that film images and real objects seem to share characteristics. In this, film images stand in a different relationship to the objects they depict than words do to their referents.

Words are usually arbitrary signifiers only: They do not normally possess qualities in common with the objects to which they refer. "A symbolic sign demands neither resemblance to its object nor any existential bond with it. It is conventional." So writes Peter Wollen, in a highly influential essay on the semiology of cinema.[4] Film images, as Wollen acknowledges, do share something with the objects they denote. They are "copies," "traces," "analogues," "doubles," or "imprints" of the objects. A number of phrases have been employed by writers on cinema to emphasize the iconic and indexical nature of film images. André Bazin, for instance, compares photography, in its mechanical reproduction of appearances, to other automatic processes such as the molding of death masks, and goes on to remark: "One might consider photography in this sense as a moulding, the taking of an impression, by the manipulation of light."[5] Thus film images testify to the *presence* of objects in a direct way that words do not. The existential link with a preexistent world outside the film is also a mark of cinema that written accounts lack. For example, all the critics' accounts of how a dancer such as Pavlova actually moved, and what the qualities of her dancing were, are grossly insubstantial set beside comparable film evidence.

This existential link between images and the objects they depict we even carry over into films we know to be in the main fictional. In a book we are aware that we can only be presented with an allusion to a dog barking; in the cinema we seem to see the actual dog and hear its actual bark. In its apparent duplication of reality, film can seem transparent, like a window on to life. It has an immediacy we normally, though often mistakenly, credit.

Christian Metz remarks:

Because still photography is in a way the *trace* of a past spectacle – as André Bazin has said – one would expect animated photography (that is to say, the cinema) to be experienced similarly as the trace of a past motion. This, in fact, is not so; the spectator always sees movement as being present (even if it duplicates a past movement).[6]

So it happens that "the movie spectator is absorbed, not by a 'has been there,' but by a sense of 'There it is.'"[7] There is some truth in this, but it does need qualifying. Metz is clearly thinking of visual rather than aural reproduction. If we are unaware of the mechanical source of reproduced conversation and sounds, we are likely to take them for something actually occurring just then. When we are conscious the sounds emanate from a tape recorder, do we still think of them as belonging to the present and not the past? When was this recorded, we ask, making clear our sense of the pastness of the recorded events. In my experience the same holds true for video playback of home recordings. Only if we become engrossed in the content of what has been recorded do we begin to have the illusion of nowness. It is the function of art to obtain that engrossment, and in doing so to make the presence of what is being played back more important to us than the link the material has with past circumstances and their capture on audio- or videotape.

So it is with films. We go to view them prepared to give them the credence that fiction demands, the willing suspension of disbelief that entry into that autonomous world requires. The darkened auditorium and the hypnotically bright screen help achieve this, as do credits, titles, and other conventions of cinematic narration. But our apprehension of fiction is tinged still with a sense of the authenticity of film images, of their bespeaking the existence of objects with a directness that verbal narration does not quite possess. In discussing the phenomenology of film images, we must consequently take into account not only the circumstances in which they are displayed but also the mental sets audiences bring, which condition how they receive what they witness.

The transparency and the immediacy experienced in the film image are related in other important ways to the psychology of perception. That sense that the visual and aural configurations of the film image are imprints of aspects of real objects affects how we take them and encourages us to identify them in much the same way within the mind. Sensations, whether from an object or its "trace," are grouped and sorted into appropriate categories. Indeed, we are not even aware we are doing it. On the screen we see a twenty-foot close-up, and immediately identify it as something we are accustomed to seeing, an ordinary telephone. We integrate the cinematic conventions of changes of angle and proportion with the schemata we possess for recognizing objects in the real world as we identify what we are viewing. Thus, though cuts from one shot to another may bring abrupt changes of angle and size, as observers we scan each image according to perspectival assumptions, and adjust our interpretations accordingly. Our minds discover solidity, proportion, and spatial dimension in images projected on one plane. Indeed, the technology of cinema developed film toward this end, and still endeavors more and more to find ways of matching the film image with what it is an image of: Color becomes more accurate, monophonic sound gives way to stereophonic and quadrophonic, and experiments with 3-D continue. So doing, technology serves the primary imagination rather than the secondary.[8] The results are transparency and immediacy in the film image itself.

For all these reasons, film images are felt to possess great designative authority – they seem to affirm the ontology of the objects they render. Yet some drawbacks offset these advantages. The very specificity of their designation would seem to make it difficult for film images to acquire abstract or general significance. It is this particular dog or that unique face they depict. How can they express the conceptual when their manner of referring is always so concrete? Their ontological plenitude binds them to their referents, making it difficult for them to be assigned a conventional or symbolic purport. Yet without such dimensions of meaning, similar to those inherently possessed by words and phrases, how can images be combined so as to convey something more than the sum of their designations? Finally, does not each image seem to exist with much the same status as any other? Are not all equally literally there?[9] If this be the case, how can there be the possibility of figurative utterance without levels of discourse and rules for reading them?

Considerations such as these, which acknowledge the special nature of film and call attention to its difference from language, are to be found in the writings of many film theorists who question the possibility of cinematic metaphor. Christian Metz, for example, summarizing Jean Mitry's views on metaphor in the second volume of Mitry's *Esthétique et psychologie du cinéma*,[10] writes:

The filmic "metaphor" does not merit the name at all, in that it lacks two essential features (p. 24): in a metaphor, the resemblance between the two terms – i.e. the common element or term of comparison at the centre of the metaphor – is not made explicit; we speak of "a pencil of light" for instance, not of light "as thin as" a pencil. In what are claimed to be filmic metaphors on the other hand, the two terms are co-present on the image-strip, so that their resemblance is inevitably "made explicit" (taking this to mean that it is emphasised visually and therefore it is not an implied resemblance). For example: the famous "metaphor" which opens Charlie Chaplin's *Modern Times* showing a shot of a flock of sheep preceding the image of a crowd descending into an underground station – here the common element (the idea of gregariousness, impression of sheeplike behaviour) if not exactly specified, is at least clearly shown. The idea of "thinness" is carried over from the pencil to the light in such a way that when it arrives at the second term, the first is no longer present; i.e. when we speak of a pencil of light the pencil is in some sense absent. Up to a certain point (a fact which needs to be stressed), the metaphor is an operation of substitution in which the thing compared (the ray of light) takes the place of the thing it is compared to (the pencil). In filmic metaphors the two things are aligned side by side (the crowd and the sheep) and the phenomenon of transfer of meaning is much less clear-cut. The crowd remains a crowd, the sheep, sheep. The association of the two simply provokes the effect of a "symbolic leap" from one to the other which on the purely semantic level, can acquire a comparative value (i.e. the spectator associates an idea of sheeplikeness with his vision of the crowd); it may sometimes even acquire a metaphorical value (if for example, the audience happens to respond to the crowd as if it were a flock of sheep). The author speaks of a "comparative" or "analogical" relationship in the second (pp. 381–383). But both cases involve a symbolic juxtaposition and not a metaphor; whereas the theoreticians who talked of a "metaphor" here were using the word in a purely metaphorical sense (p. 25).

In the same way comparison proper, i.e. comparison as a formal procedure (not to be confused with a purely semantic effect of comparison) is impossible in the cinema (p. 24). Film does not have the word "like."[11]

A belief that the designative authority of filmic images is of primary importance dogs the discussion here. There is neglect of other factors concerning the meaning of film images, a neglect that this chapter will partly attempt to remedy.

The passage also reveals other assumptions held by many writers on metaphor in film: for instance, that the crux of the matter is the juxtaposition of shots – that cinematic metaphor, if it exists at all, depends upon montage. This view too can be challenged. Most significant of all, however, is the somewhat narrow view of metaphor itself – as always entailing an implied similarity; as the preceding chapter has demonstrated, this view assumes a highly inadequate definition and only accounts for a small proportion of metaphors. There is, furthermore, in the passage an uneasy passing to and fro between the film images and how they are taken, exemplified by such phrases as "the crowd remains a crowd," and talk of "the purely semantic level." Indeed, it is common to find such shifts of level between signifier itself and how we mentally make sense of it in all discussions of metaphor. Perhaps we need a strategy to deal with this tendency.

In modern physics the principle of complementarity has been established, whereby two different models may be applied to the study of the same phenomenon in order to achieve completeness of description. Light, for instance, is thought to consist of particles to account for some aspects of its behavior, and of waves to account for other aspects. A similar approach might be useful in discussions of metaphor. On the one hand we have a mental process that creates a synthesis of disparate ideas; on the other hand we have manipulations of signifiers in a medium that it would seem both records and passes on that synthesis. When I. A. Richards, for example, discusses metaphor, he draws explicit attention to this feature:

The traditional theory noticed only a few of the modes of metaphor; and limited its application of the term *metaphor* to a few of them only. And thereby it made metaphor seem to be a verbal matter, a shifting and displacement of words, whereas fundamentally it is a borrowing between and intercourse of *thoughts,* a transaction between contexts. *Thought* is metaphoric, and proceeds by comparison and the metaphors of language derive therefrom.[12]

Each account complements the other, and relies upon it in order to be complete. The artist cannot communicate his vision, indeed most commonly could not even arrive at it, without a medium – whether it be words, paints, or the audiovisual images of film – and devices the medium makes possible. The artistic fabrication utilizing that medium would be uninterpretable, however, unless the spectator's own mind were capable of mental processes analogous to those of the artist. One account emphasizes psychology, perception, and experience; the other the medium, techniques, and figurative devices. But we are not discussing two different things; rather we need two accounts to explain the one thing. The first account we may term *an imaginative theory of metaphor*, to draw attention to its links with Coleridge's explanation of the esemplastic powers of the mind.[13] The second may be called *a rhetorical theory of metaphor*, to stress its connections with classical descriptions of linguistic tropes.

Modern essays on metaphor tend, on the whole, to adopt an imaginative theory and explore its implications. Two such theories are worth adducing here, because they have bearing upon our investigation into metaphor within the cinematic image itself. G. D. Martin, in *Language, Truth and Poetry*, argues that language generally, and metaphorical language particularly, cannot be understood unless the mind draws upon experiences not derived from the verbal data.

When [Robert] Lowell writes of "yellow dinosaur steamshovels," the actual appearance of dinosaurs and steamshovels has to be contemplated and compared in imagination. We have to picture both tenor and vehicle, and fit them over each other, "picturing" both at once. Similar remarks can be made about Allen Tate's lines "long shadows of grape-vine wriggle and run / Over the green swirl." Hence the sense of reality and solidity that an image like this provides. The connotations that link tenor to vehicle are a set of visual experiences that cannot be reduced to mere language. The link is experiential, not just linguistic.[14]

A few pages later Martin calls the mind "a machine for making connexions," and supports this by quoting Eisenstein on montage.[15] Martin coins the word *interplicit* to describe the effects of superimposing disparate ideas and contexts:

When a term is extended into a new context, or used as a metaphor, it forces into consciousness – or at least into the fringes of consciousness – certain connotations, makes them "interplicit."[16]

Here we see a writer on literary metaphors taking for granted as the basis for metaphor precisely those factors that Mitry assumes would rule out Chaplin's metaphor from being a metaphor. Martin's comment also may be seen as reinforcing my point earlier that in the cinema we always fill out the solidity of the images we see by drawing on our own experience of objects and events.

Martin B. Hester, in *The Meaning of Poetic Metaphor*, also stresses the superimposition of ideas in the experiencing of metaphor, but turns to Wittgenstein's seminal discussion of *seeing as* in *Philosophical Investigations* to set out his account. Hester writes:

Metaphor involves... the intuitive relation of seeing as between parts of the description.... [it] involves not only a tenor and vehicle, to use Richards' terms, thrown together in a sentence, but the positive relation of seeing as to between tenor and vehicle.[17]

Later, he asserts that "seeing as is an irreducible intuitive experience-act. It is categorically impossible to reduce seeing as a set of rules or criteria."[18] Again,

The metaphor establishes a relation but also reveals a relation.... Our smaller minds can only apply the word "similar" after a greater mind has led us to the experience of seeing as. Seeing as defines similarity, not vice versa.[19]

The focus here is clearly on an imaginative, rather than a rhetorical, account of metaphor. It also seems to be consonant with our definition of metaphor adopted in Chapter II.

Whereas all metaphor entails a seeing as, however, the converse does not hold: Not all seeing as involves metaphor. Diction or tone, for example, may direct a reader to see as heroic or ridiculous a series of human actions, but neither diction nor tone are normally classified as metaphor. The drawing that can be seen now as a rabbit, now as a duck, that Wittgenstein uses to introduce his discussion of *seeing as* is scarcely an example of metaphor either. What is missing in these cases is *interplicitness:* the mutual influence of disparate ideas or contexts upon one another, the interaction of old and new meanings together. Metaphor is a process of interplicit seeings as. Reducing interplicitness to a set of rules or criteria again may be impossible, but our sense of its presence or absence gives us some sort of criterion for when we have a metaphor and when we do not.

Although artists normally only discover metaphorical connections in the very act of working their material (in whatever medium they have chosen), the experience of seeing as may precede the decision to employ a medium. Because of the degree of spatial thinking entailed in seeing steam shovels in the aspect of dinosaurs, the thought could well have occurred before its formation in words; it is also conceivable that the perception could be expressed otherwise, say in a drawing instead of a poem. An imaginative theory of metaphor then allows for the possibility of insight preceding utterance, and allows for different media giving their own form to that insight. If this applies to the issue of making film images too, then attempts to reject the notion of cinematic metaphor will be hard to sustain.

How do we know that there is an experiential difference between perceiving yellow steam shovels and perceiving yellow dinosaur steam shovels? There must be a difference because, as Wittgenstein answers, "I *describe* what I am seeing differently."[20] This may hold for words, or drawings, but would it be equally valid for films? Does not the camera record objectively, producing merely a "trace" of the object in front of the camera? Will not the film when projected merely show yellow steam shovels? But movie cameras do not take pictures themselves; someone always uses them to take pictures. Emphasis on the "automatic" way film records reality is misleading because it conceals the human participation. Human ingenuity developed the process of filming, and human thinking decides how and what to film. If they are dissatisfied with what was captured on celluloid, human beings alter it or film it again. If they are surprised by something unexpected found there, and they think it carries unintended meanings, they can choose to develop or suppress those meanings. In the making of films, there are no "neutral" shots – they always carry a significance over and above that of being mere reproductions of that which was filmed.

So if a director wishes to film yellow dinosaur steam shovels, and when he comes to look at the rushes all he sees are yellow steam shovels on the screen, then he will feel something went radically wrong. He did not film the objects *in the aspect of them* he wanted.

This is all very well, it might be said. But suppose the artist has an idée fixe that steam shovels look like dinosaurs. Might he not believe that is how they appear in the rushes, although no one else is seeing them that way? Might not the existential link between film image and what it is an image of lend itself to such a situation? In this regard, film is different from literature or drawing. Artists working with words or with inked lines are forced to compose their own description of the object; the arbitrary link between medium and objects (as well as the medium's techniques, rules, and conventions) ensures this. For filmmakers, the inherent "twinning" relation of film image to filmed object may be deceptive: These artists may think they have rendered something *seen as* when they have only succeeded in showing it as *seen.* Even if this logical possibility were granted, however, it would be of no consequence. The metaphor would remain unknown and uncommunicated, inaccessible to all but the private introspection of the particular filmmaker. If there are such would-be metaphors in films, they remain outside the scope of discussion, for critical debate cannot deal with what is totally private and internal, only with what is public and manifest to others. Rarely, however, are filmmakers so solipsistic. Normally they are concerned about communicating. Filmmakers, having rendered the object as they perceived it, will expect others to see it similarly. If they discover that others do not, they must acknowledge their failure, which is the failure to present the object in the aspect that they desired to show it. Filmmakers must make another attempt – that is to say, they must employ their filmic craft to obtain a different depiction. "Seeing an aspect and imagining are subject to the will," writes Wittgenstein. "There is such an order as 'Imagine *this,*' and also: 'Now see the figure like *this.'* "[21] Filmmakers must contrive to find the appropriate image, and by its appropriateness it will instruct the spectator how to see the filmed object.

What this line of thinking is leading us to is an acknowledgment that the coining of film images is not a passive process, but an *actively creative one that can incorporate metaphorical connections in the very images themselves.*

Let us pursue this line further, starting this time with another remark by a film theoretician. In an interview Yves de Laurot speaks about possible cinematic metaphors, and he makes the assumption – which as we have just seen may be a perfectly justified one – that insight can precede utterance. "The filmmaker," he asserts, "makes metaphor because he has to, out of an inner necessity: there is no other way to project his moral vision upon the reality his consciousness has shown him to exist."[22] The example de Laurot chooses to illustrate this is of seeing a bank as a temple.

[Metaphor] is a *manner* of seeing the bank as a temple. Specifically, the angle we do employ for the camera, the hushed footsteps, the shafts of light falling through the window in a certain way, the manner of photographing the teller's bar – it is a matter of framing, composing, pacing, sound, rhythm, tonalities. The result is that through the visible, we render the *invisible:* the true essence of the bank is a temple, in this or any other capitalistic country. The "invisible" is an emanation, an overtone of the real truth beyond the spurious appearance. The appearance is only a bank, but the real truth is that it is a temple. All this without *explicitly* saying it, without masterminding the audience. The miracle of the "wishful viewer" happens: that is to say, the viewer creates, co-creates, the metaphor himself. Nobody *tells* him, "this is like this"; he arrives at the conclusion himself.[23]

This example confirms a number of points we have already made. It brings out, for instance, the link between the artist's conception and the spectator's cocreation of it. It posits the film image as mediating between the two. Making the image is not assumed to be merely a matter of "automatic" copying but accepted to be a matter of craft, skill and sensibility: "framing, composing, pacing, sound, rhythm, tonalities." By such means the object is transformed within the film image: It is described differently. Metaphor is encapsulated within the very film image itself.

Film, like literature, possesses rules and conventions that have evolved through the practice of the art, and which have come to condition the latent expectations with which the spectator scans and interprets the image. The filmmaker, intentionally and intuitively, employs these. We need only recall here how position within the frame, central or peripheral, changes the aspect of the image and instructs us how to read it. Film depends on many such intrinsic "codings."[24] They make the filmic "imprint" something other than the object it reproduces: They imbue it with new significances. Thus the very organization of the film image – something quite unavoidable – is one reason why the image inevitably is to some degree a *seeing as*. Also, despite the apparent mimetic density of the image, it is still only a thin and partial selection of what is available to be experienced in reality. Any real object or event possesses an ontological plenitude that defies total reproduction. No film image, for instance, can ever denote more than chosen aspects of an object or event, and then directly only those aspects that are visual, auditory, or kinesthetic. Even to depict an actual bank, with no further intention than to show it literally, a filmmaker will be forced to rely on synecdoches: the entrance, the vault, the teller's bars, the rustle of notes, and so on. What is selected can never be more than aspects of the object filmed.

To explain how in the film image *seeing as*, which is a mark of all film images, can become on occasion full cinematic metaphor, it is necessary to break down into its components the types of meaning a film image carries. The first of these we may term the *designation* of the film image.

An image, through being an "imprint" of some aspect of the object, identifies the object. That is, the image *denotes* the object. To say this is to imply more than a simple perceptual recognition: In identifying the object the spectator mentally posits the whole for the part, for the aspect, shown. His own knowledge enables him to supply properties it possesses. He fills in. An image of a telephone supposes it might ring; an image of sails tells of a ship and its sailors.

In addition to such cognition, based on assimilated categories of human knowledge, the spectator brings to his identification of the image a tenuous network of associations: memories, connections, emotional overtones. Some of these will be personal, but the more important associations from the filmmaker's point of view will be those that are cultural and belong to the public domain. These are the *connotations* he can call upon when he makes the film image.

The designation of the image then comprises both its denotation and its connotations. The dual nature of the film image offers scope for metaphorical manipulation.

Let us go back, for illustration, to the metaphor of a bank as a temple. The image, or the cluster of subsidiary images that establish the primary image, must denote a bank. But in its aspect or parts of its aspect it will also denote a church. Consequently, a second set of connotations associated with churches are enabled to modify or interact with the first set, bringing about a new synthesis, an altered comprehension. In other words, it is the interplicitness of double designation that converts *seeing as* into metaphor.[25] *A* is *B*. It is important to emphasize, however, that the filmic metaphor is created by more than the spectator's perception of the film image: It draws on his prior experience of the objects themselves, and requires his active "co-operation."

Anything that establishes double designation within the film image lends itself to cinematic metaphor. Mise-en-scène can be as much a source of metaphors within the image as movie photography. Chaplin's miming is a good illustration of this, as the following commentary by Rudolf Arnheim testifies:

> If the scene [of Charlie as the starving prospector] in *The Gold Rush* showed nothing but a starving man wolfing a cooked boot, it would be no more than a grotesque caricature of poverty. The excellence and forcibleness of the scene consists in the fact that in depicting misery the contrast of riches is given simultaneously by the most original and visually striking similarity of this meal to that of a rich man.
>
> Carcass of the boot = carcass of a fish
>   Nails = chicken
>   Bootlaces = spaghetti
>
> Chaplin makes the contrast painfully clear to the eyes of the spectator by demonstrating the similarity of form of such objectively different things.[26]

One might also instance the scene near the end of *8½* where Guido is dragged off by both arms to his calamitous press conference: His efforts to escape mimic those of a recalcitrant child.

Double designation when supporting a metaphor implies the co-presence of tenor and vehicle. But how do we know which is the tenor and which the vehicle? It will be recalled that one of the objections leveled against the notion of filmic metaphor was precisely this, that all images are equally literally there, whereas it was said that in verbal language this was not the case. (As Metz said, "when we speak of 'a pencil of light' the pencil is in some sense absent.") Metaphor within the film image gives us a partial solution to this problem. The stronger denotation, the one more fully present, will normally identify the tenor; the weaker or more suggested denotation will be that of the vehicle. In the cited examples, the bank, Charlie's boot, and Guido the man are clearly primary; the *seen as* denotations are secondary and so figurative. In these instances the objection is shown to be invalid. In more ambiguous circumstances the issue is resolved in another way.

An equivocal shot, say, may open a sequence: We may not know whether the scene is meant to be taking place in a bank or a church, the denotative aspects being so open to dual interpretations. But as the sequence unfolds it becomes clear that the action is taking place in a bank. The bank then becomes the tenor because it belongs to the level of main continuity. The custom, in film as in literature, is to situate the tenor in the plane of discourse or narration. If difficulties arise, it is usually a sign that we are faced with a more extended or complicated trope, such as allegory or double metaphor. In general, however, this rule of thumb is reliable and unproblematic. It also has relevance in montage metaphors, as we shall see.

We have not, however, completed our analysis of meaning connected to the film image. Every film image acquires meaning over and above its designation by reason of its being placed in a context among other images. This further component of meaning we may call the *signification* of the image.[27] For example, an image may denote a yacht, and supply a host of connotations ranging from luxury and leisure to independence and adventure. In a specific film, however, through it being linked to a particular character and his sexual problems, it might come to signify a surrogate for the women with whom he cannot have satisfactory relations. The filmmaker chooses and places an image in relation to other images precisely in order to obtain such a specific signification. At this level film approaches most nearly the symbolic conveyance of meaning found in verbal language. But the degree to which film may be treated as a language system is problematic and an issue still disputed by film semioticians and their critics.

Words are granted a possible range of usages by social contract, as it were. Context, which includes syntactic position and semantic situation, as well as the occasion of the utterance itself, makes clear with what specific meanings a word is being used. Generally, film images are not symbolic in this sense because their denotation is not conventional but mimetic. The exceptions to this are in the nature of visual clichés – for instance, the calendar with its leaves blowing over, which in many Hollywood films became a sign for the passing of time, or a shot of the Eiffel Tower, which says the action is now set in Paris. They remain the exception rather than the rule, and are artistically displeasing. Normally, film images are iconic neologisms. As Pier Paola Pasolini remarked: "A dictionary of film images does not exist. There are no images classified and ready for use. If by chance we wanted to imagine a dictionary of images, we would have to imagine an *infinite dictionary,* just as the dictionary of *possible words* remains infinite."[28]

The infinity of possible film images is more akin then to the number of possible sentences in a language than to the actual word count of any particular spoken language. But sentences seem more geared to rendering conceptual thought than are film images, particularly so when we are considering only the designations of film images. The deficiency, though, can be remedied by combining film images into significant clusters. The recognition of this led to speculations as to whether there might not be a syntax underlying the linking of film images. Many early writers on cinema spoke with confidence about a grammar of film (e.g., Raymond Spottiswoode). Later writers have discerned the lack of rigor in these attempts, but the lure of a linguistic model has always been strong. Christian Metz, for example, followed Jean Mitry in criticizing naïve applications of linguistic models, but himself devoted much effort to investigating whether there were more appropriate tools to be found in the general theory of communication derived from the semiology of Ferdinand de Saussure,[29] even though the sine qua non of Saussure's whole system is that the signs he discusses are arbitrary and not iconic.[30] The semiological emphasis on codes has led to various classificatory attempts such as Noël Burch's endeavors to define the number of relations possible between succeeding shots.[31] Even if these were to be regarded as "syntactic" structures of a kind, they would still fall far short of demonstrating that cinema possesses a full grammar.

In general, the soundest conclusions would seem to be those expressed by Jean Mitry, who considers that film images acquire meaning through their siting in a carefully controlled system of implications. That is, the *signification* of film images depends more on the artistry of the organization than on the formal rules of a strict syntax – more on a developing rhetoric than on a fixed grammar. As with poetry, conventions may evolve, and subsequently may be appealed to, modified, or even rejected. The fundamental language of film, such as there is, is the "language" of artistic composition itself. Such circumstances do not militate, however, against cinematic metaphors springing out of the *signification* of film images; indeed, they may even facilitate them doing so, which will be evident when we consider what is involved in defining the context of the film image.

Since the advent of the sound film, dialogue and oral narration, for instance, have become an inherent part of the cinema. Even the so-called silent movies depended on a recourse to musical accompaniment. To ignore this reliance on sound is to place undue emphasis on the visual and can lead to the fallacy that true cinema is what is seen only, not what is seen and heard. Film has its own special visual properties, but it incorporates all the formal properties of speech and music as well, giving them new resonances by bringing them into relationship with the moving pictures. It follows that film inherits from other arts – music, drama, fiction, dance, painting, and photography – many of their artistic forms and conventions. The arts of narration, rhythm and counterpoint, spatial design, and iconic allusion are as much the potential of cinema as is visual montage. Whether at any given time one of these elements dominates depends on the overall intention and organization of the film. Yet they all may contribute to forming the context of the film image. They may all collaborate in establishing the signification of any given image.

This is so obvious, it would scarcely seem worth saying. What is extraordinary, however, is how often film theorists forget it or ignore it.

Take, for example, Mitry's comment quoted earlier in this chapter: "Film does not have the word 'like.'" Of course film possesses the word "like," just as it possesses any other word the director cares to use. Such a remark could not have been made, even as a momentary lapse, but for the deeply embedded preconception that certain properties are innately more cinematic than others. It points to a prejudice against the "literary," which in its own way is quite as distorting about film as any naïve linguistic model. If we are to understand the signification of film images and its role in generating some cinematic metaphors, then we must be prepared to consider all relevant factors and not rule out some in advance because they are deemed "uncinematic."

Initially, signification was defined as the component of an image's meaning acquired through the context in which the image is placed. An image, however, may also acquire signification by the manner in which it is presented. An illustration from language may help to clarify what is intended here. A number of synonyms denote the same object, but each synonym will give it a different complexion. This is amusingly demonstrated by such mock conjugations as, "I am firm, you are stubborn, and he is pig-headed," or "Animals sweat, men perspire, women glow." Film, of course, does not possess formal sets of synonyms equivalent to these. But an object may be filmed in a number of different ways. A variety of images thus are available to designate the same object. Which image is selected and how it is composed can radically change its purport and value.[32]

All the elements of cinema that affect the image can be utilized to create such film "synonyms": camera placement, lenses, framing, filters, lighting, camera speed, type of film stock, and so on. Film manuals usually devote a large amount of space to setting out the techniques for taking shots, spelling out the different effects to be achieved by them. Their precepts can only be generalities because each image is unique: Meaning will be governed to a considerable degree by the relationship between that which is shot and how it is presented. For example, speeded-up motion *generally* renders the action comic. But F. W. Murnau uses speeded-up action in *Nosferatu* to depict the supernatural mystery of Nosferatu's coach; and Stanley Kubrick uses it in *A Clockwork Orange* to distance and stylize the depiction of Alex's sexual energy and behavior. The manuals clearly are right to attach such importance to the image's presentation. Much of the meaning and power of a film derives from the aptness and potency of its images. So much has been written and published on this, there is little need to labor the point further, except to note the extent to which the signification in a film's images helps define the style, tone, and attitude of a film. Precisely because a film does not possess a full syntax that helps structure the way we are to interpret things, other means of integrating the material take on added importance. Getting the film image right is the true sign of artistic control.

Signification becomes the basis for a metaphor within an image because a tension that demands a figurative resolution has been set up. There is, perhaps, a clash between the object filmed and the manner of its filming. Or between how it has been filmed and more expected ways of filming it. For example, in *The Third Man* Carol Reed employs a number of tilted shots. The spectator is aware that these are a departure from normal shots and that presenting things so askew implies something about the loss of moral balance in the postwar black market ruins of Vienna. A more complex shot from *Citizen Kane* calls attention to the misleading nature of the film image that is presented us. Kane, Leland, and Bernstein gaze at a photograph of the *Chronicle* staff displayed in a window. The camera moves in on the photograph and then, by means of a scarcely observable lap-dissolve, presents the audience with an image they take to be merely further rendition of the same still photograph – until Kane moves into the picture, and it is seen to be a movie image of the same people who were previously working for the *Chronicle* now posing for a photograph with their new employer. The trompe l'oeil is witty, but it also makes some serious points in a figurative way. For Kane the *Chronicle* staff does not exist as real people but only as an image that helps increase the circulation of his newspaper. Film claims to show the truth, but constantly deceives: This consorts with a core theme of the film, reiterated in many ways throughout, that reality is ultimately unknowable and all our modes of probing it are partial, misleading, or ineffectual.

The cinematic metaphors just described belong to the general category of distortion metaphors. Hyperbole and caricature are the best-known subspecies of this type, and they too have their equivalent in cinematic images. Fred Astaire, in *Royal Wedding,* is so full of joie de vivre that he dances up the walls and along the ceiling. Peter Sellers's president, in *Dr. Strangelove,* is such a liberal intellectual that he even possesses a head that is egg-shaped. But in Raoul Walsh's *The Roaring Twenties* there is a shot of the urban skyline that suddenly dissolves to the ground before our eyes: This seems neither hyperbole nor caricature but rather the visual embodiment of what many experienced at the time of the Great Crash of 1929 when what seemed a solid economic world collapsed overnight. It is also, however, a good example of a cinematic metaphor of the distortion type.

The other major type of metaphor based on the film image itself is that involving metonymy. This type of metaphor, though, is difficult to achieve through the single image. The reason is that metonymy is so endemic to film that it normally loses any figurative implications. The screen frame so arbitrarily includes and excludes, selecting one part and lopping off the rest, that audiences become accustomed to reading the part for the whole. A gloved hand pushes the door open, stealthy footsteps cross the dark room – the sinister intruder is conveyed by such details. But if what has to be filled in has a perfectly literal status, one cannot claim there is metaphor here. Semantic emphasis, even where selection and fragmentation draw upon subtler workings of the imagination than the intruder example provides, is not enough. There has to be, for metaphor to occur according to our account, a juxtaposition of alien categories or contexts that generates a new, interplicit solution. Metaphors of the metonymy type can occur in films, but they need a clustering of metonymies, or a combination of metonymy with some other factors (such as quotations that allude to an alien context) to be successful. Repetition is another way of giving a metonymy sufficient emphasis to establish it as a metaphor of the substitution type. Robert Bresson, whose art is very elliptical anyway, often resorts to this type of metaphor: In *A Man Escaped* (*Un Condamné à mort s'est échappé*) the frequent close-ups of Fontaine's hands become expressive of the mortal will to escape, so that we may appreciate how the unseen but immanent grace of God may work together with that will. This metaphor, however, depends for its effect on its place within the total context of the film. Although metaphors of the metonymy type have their source in the mode of presenting the film image, they rely to such a degree on combination with other elements that they could just as easily be classified under metaphors created through montage.

In this chapter we have noted that many, if not most, discussions of cinematic metaphor, whether positing its existence or attempting to deny it, have assumed that cinematic metaphor if it exists at all will be created by the relating of one image to another through editing. We have tried to show that cinematic metaphors may be found within the film image itself. In doing this we have broken down the meaning of the film image into key constituents. The next step is to consider how film images may be organized into larger significant groupings, and to see how that organization further assists the creation of cinematic metaphors.

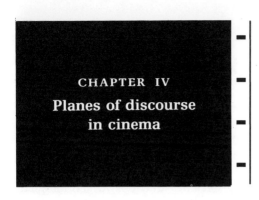

[Cinematic narrative] assaults the audience
with impressions; it raises and casts off
metaphors so rapidly that the conscious
mind can barely perceive them; it affects us
like some agile yet penetrating notation.
— Eric Rhode[1]

The core of many objections to the existence of cinematic metaphors is that films do not possess different levels of discourse. All images are literal representations, it is suggested, and therefore have the same signifying status. Because metaphors involve shifts in levels of meaning and rely on defined linguistic rules for performing these shifts, and because these conditions are not present in films, it follows that cinematic metaphors are not possible.[2] We have challenged this view at the level of the film image; now we need to extend our refutation of it.

A reason we have already advanced for regarding such objections as invalid was that they are based on a restricted understanding of metaphor: Not all literary metaphors are identifiable through syntax alone. Metaphor is a concept belonging to hermeneutics: The perception of metaphorical meaning we showed to be an issue of interpreting interplicit significances. There is, however, another fallacy at the root of objections to cinematic metaphors. They ignore the (logical) distinction between signifier and signified.

Ferdinand de Saussure posited that all signs consist of an object or event that bears the meaning (the *signifier*) and the meaning itself (the *signified*).[3] Because two signifiers are copresent, however, it does not follow that their signifieds are copresent in exactly the same way — even if it is claimed that cinematographic signs are primarily iconic and indexical (i.e., are traces of an original object with which they share some likeness). As we showed in Chapter III, the meaning of a film image consists not only of its denotation but also of its connotations and significations. Consequently, two signifieds may belong to quite different planes of discourse: One can easily be literal while the other is figurative. (This will be illustrated later by examples.) To bring out some of the implications of this remark, more needs to be said about the way contexts create signification.

Metaphor is not the only element in artistic discourses that belongs largely to the domain of hermeneutics. Indeed, the very essence of art is that it creates meanings by venturing outside customary rules of communication. This has long been known, but because semiology has so influenced film theory in the last few decades, a semiological restatement of this feature of art may be apposite here. In his book on Saussure, Jonathan Culler draws a distinction between what he terms "explicit codes"[4] and others less defined and definable:

> Codes of the first type are designed to communicate directly and unambiguously messages and notions which are already known; the code simply provides an economical notation for notions already defined. But aesthetic expression aims to communicate notions, subtleties, complexities which have not yet been formulated, and therefore, as soon as an aesthetic code comes to be perceived as a code (as a way of expressing notions which have already been articulated) then works of art tend to move beyond this code. They question, parody, and generally undermine the code while exploring its possible mutations and extensions.[5]

Three pages later he develops this further:

> Many semiological systems are complicated, however, by the fact that they rest on other systems, particularly that of language, and thus become "second order" systems. Literature is one such system: it has language as its basis and its supplementary conventions are conventions about special uses of language. Thus, to take a simple example, the rhetorical figures such as metaphor, metonymy, hyperbole, synecdoche can be seen as operations of a second-order literary code.... Traffic signs do not violate the code of traffic signs, but literary works are continually violating codes. And this because literature is fundamentally an exploration of the possibilities of experience, a questioning and deepening of the categories in and through which we ordinarily view ourselves and our world. Literary codes have an important role in that they make possible this questioning and deepening process, just as rules of etiquette make it possible to be impolite. But literary works never lie wholly within the codes that define them, and that is what makes the semiological investigation of literature such a tantalizing enterprise.[6]

Culler's remarks on literature can just as well be applied to other arts. Painting, for example, could well be said to draw upon "second-order systems" by calling upon literary associations or by making iconographical references to social customs or religious lore. Consequently, any elucidation of a painting cannot restrict itself to the visual form alone, or to the brush techniques that produced it, but must take into account cultural allusions and grasp the implications of their interplay. Semiology's aim is to set out systematically the factors that enter into such interplay. But, as Culler's comments imply, such systematization is a losing game, since art constantly violates systems as well as employs them. Art will always be several steps ahead of the system makers. Further, for those who care about art – rather than about semiology – what is so fascinating is not what the artist draws upon, but *what he fabricates out of it,* the rich nexus of meanings and new experience he renders available. This is why ultimately the exploration of significance in the arts lies with alertly discerning viewers and readers, not with semiologists.

I have quoted the passages by Culler, however, written in the language some film theorists are accustomed to, in order to stress the complexity of the process whereby we make sense of film images. The signification of the film image will be the product of many factors: its juxtaposition with other images, its role in the thematic or narrative development of the film, its relation to the conventions of cinematic or other arts, its place in social beliefs or customs, even its cultural and historical siting. Whether a film image is to be understood literally or figuratively will be an emergent property of such factors.

In Chaplin's *Modern Times,* for instance, the Gamine (Paulette Godard) and the Tramp are resting on a pleasant, suburban sidewalk. The fond farewells of a young wife and her husband leaving for work make Charlie conscious of his own and the Gamine's homeless condition, and he daydreams of them together in their own house. The images depicting this clearly have a different status to preceding ones – they form part of a wishful reverie. When Charlie wipes his hands on the curtains, the comedy springs from a clash of conventions: A man's home may be his castle where he may do as he pleases, but we also know a middle-class home can only be kept neat and tidy if certain modes of behavior are prohibited. When Charlie gets milk for their meal by opening the kitchen door and milking a passing cow, the suburban convenience of milk on the doorstep is given ludicrous bucolic shape. Our laughter at these incongruities arises from a response to the interplay of second-order references; but the satire, which criticizes the tramp's naïveté while at the same time revealing how extraordinary and inhibiting are some middle-class expectations, cannot be reduced to them. More germane to our immediate purpose, this example illustrates the way signifieds may differ in levels of meaning. Anyone who argued for the literalness of the film images adduced here could only do so by stifling his natural response as a twentieth-century filmgoer.

Cinema is an art medium that adapts freely and easily the conventions of other arts, turning them to its own purposes. Drama, fiction, dance, painting, architecture – the range of reference accessible to cinema is infinite. The same holds for film's allusions to other cultural modes and patterns of behavior. The only limitation placed on a film's allusions will be the comprehension of the audiences for whom the film is made: For audiences must be able to pick up these references, and not be puzzled or misled by them. This is why audiences often miss a great deal in a film made for another nation, even though film is often thought of as having high international currency. Boleslaw Sulik, for example, in his introduction to Andrzej Wajda's published film scripts, explains a number of references in *Ashes and Diamonds* (*Popiól i diament*) that non-Polish audiences are certain to miss. These include filmic allusions to a painting by the Polish impressionist, Chelmonski; to Polish proverbs; to a song sung by the Polish Second Corps, which suffered heavily in the fighting for the Cassino Monastery; and to a symbolic poetic drama written at the beginning of the century by S. Wyspiansky.[7] This film is certainly not exceptional in the degree to which it employs "second-order systems."

Cinema on the other hand can scarcely be said to possess what Culler refers to as a "first-order system." We have already shown, in Chapter III, how it lacks a set vocabulary – also a syntax. What is sometimes pointed to as marks of a syntax turn out on further inspection to be cinematic conventions open to change and modification. At one time flashbacks were signaled by a close-up or a dolly-in to the face of the person remembering, followed by a slow dissolve to a sequence foggy at the edge of the frame. Nowadays, and certainly since *Hiroshima, mon amour,* all this is dispensed with: Straight cuts can be employed. At one time jump cuts were regarded as ungrammatical: Now they are commonplace. In art the one rule is that there are no rules, or rather that the assertion that there is a rule acts as an open invitation to artists to defy it, violate it, or shape it to some other purpose.

As these reflections remind us, any comments on the forms of cinematic metaphor must be tentative. How audiences respond to cinematic tropes depends on their education, experience, and expectations. What at one date may be felt to be obscure and unsuccessful, several decades later may be lucid and modish. At any given time it is not possible to foresee what rhetorical strategies may be taken for granted in years to come.

The nature of the argument I have embarked upon makes this caution pertinent. I am suggesting that many metaphors function through the signification of film images. Further, that signification is created not only by filmic context and the organization of that context but, more important, by life as people live and conceive it. Consequently, as the lived and living world changes, so the types of metaphor that films employ will change. Comments on film metaphor inevitably derive from those that have been or currently are being employed: Generalizations so arising will inevitably need modification as time passes. To take just one illustration regarding factors that might affect the issue, consider what is happening as people's access and resort to films change. For most of cinema's history, films have been made primarily for release on short runs in movie theaters. There were limited opportunities for repeated viewings by any except those making the films. The closer study of films outside that circle began as film societies, and later university courses, brought films back for repeated showings. The sale of films to television revived many old films, otherwise buried in vaults and forgotten. Students with access to editing benches could run a film backward and forward examining it frame by frame. Videocassettes are in the process of making this resource widely available. People own films as they own books, something they can dip into or peruse whenever they wish. What effects on viewing will such changes have? What on film content and style? Will it result in the making of films with more marked poetic density, more elaborate tropes and self-conscious imagery? Who can say? Speculation about future changes in filmmaking and film viewing practices serves, though, to highlight how films hitherto have been experienced.

Films made primarily to be grasped in one viewing inevitably share some of the characteristics of plays intended to be seen only once in the theater. Both have to capture the audience's interest and sustain it. Hence film's emphasis on narrative, which so often is structured dramatically with mounting climaxes, reversals, and discoveries. Hence also the attention to changes of pace and dynamics: Films must avoid monotony and orchestrate concentration. Filmmakers, however, faced (and still face) two problems not so intensely experienced by dramatists. First, given the enormous – and rising – costs of filmmaking, audiences have to be attracted en masse.[8] Inevitably this means cinema audiences are more heterogeneous than theater audiences. Second, the nature of the medium, with its abrupt changes of scene, angle, proportion, and focus, its disruptions of space and time, inherited special difficulties relating to continuity. Both situations involve problems of communication, and much of cinema's history may be read as efforts to overcome these problems. The use and promotion of popular genres, the reliance on stereotyped situations and stock characters, and the development of an easily understood iconography were ways of melding disparate assemblies of people into comprehending audiences.[9] The establishment of certain habits of filming and editing, such as cutting on movement or preparing for a change of scene by a reference in the dialogue, provided ways of minimizing breaks in literal continuity for them.

Inevitably, figurative levels of meaning were subordinated to narrative thrust. Either audiences had to be prepared for the figurative reading of images so that cinematic metaphors did not throw them into confusion; or the metaphors had to be presented in such a way that, should they be missed or misread, the continuity of the film would not be disturbed. The first method took time, involving as it did the development of a certain sophistication in audiences. But toward the end of the silent era there is evidence of its viability. The talkies, however, brought regression as difficulties in recording and synchronizing sound created new continuity problems, and speech offered simpler ways for explicating the narratives. There were exceptions to this trend, of course – Cocteau might be cited here – but the exceptions usually were made for and appealed to more selected audiences. In the 1960s and 1970s, however, some filmmakers began making a greater demand upon audiences, and films employing overt cinematic metaphors became slightly more common. The directors one might cite here are such figures as Bergman, Fellini, Antonioni, and Resnais.

But the second strategy has really prevailed throughout most of the history of the cinema in the West. By the use of metaphorical devices in an almost wholly unobtrusive way, audiences could be enabled to follow the action without distraction, while still being almost subliminally or unconsciously affected by cinematic tropes. We must appreciate, therefore, that in western mainstream cinema the metaphors employed tend to be embedded in nonfiguratively presented material, and that metaphorical and literal levels of meaning are made to coexist to a far greater degree than is the case in literary modes. Particularly is this true of metaphors within the shot.

One of the special properties of film is its ability to present a variety of images concurrently. Prose, though not poetry, generally retails things in a linear manner, describing first this before passing on to that. In a film one panoramic shot can encapsulate what it would take a novelist pages to set out in words. Painting can show coincident occurrences, but only statically. Drama can render simultaneity, but only to a limited degree: Stage settings are relatively constant, and if contemporaneous action is parceled out to different actors or groups of actors, there is the danger of dividing the audience's focus of attention. Film, however, constantly sets people, objects, and milieux within the same frame. The mobility of the camera permits variety of viewpoint, freedom of composition, and rapid changes of focal interest. Normally the presence of whatever is within the shot is taken literally: Those things are there, we feel, because they are contiguous as they would be in real life. But the filmmaker can give some of the objects or events depicted within the shot a metaphorical function, without in any way detracting from the probability of their appearance there.

The filmmaker can also choose whether to accentuate the metaphor, or to keep it discreet. In *Citizen Kane,* Kane takes Susan (Dorothy

Comingore) with him to live in Xanadu after her attempted suicide. Shots of the two of them in the mansion reveal aspects of the domain Kane is building for his wife: the huge fireplace, the massive furniture, the great staircase. The effect is more than literal or even metonymic: It is emphatically a metaphorical depiction of what their relationship has become. Kane and Susan have grown to be voids apart, and have become diminished and imprisoned in their own isolation.

Let us contrast this example with another. John F. Scott has suggested that the first shot introducing Ethan Edwards (John Wayne) in *The Searchers* incorporates a cinematic metaphor:

A dust trail tells us there is a rider approaching, but the first long-lens shot of the horseman is dominated not so much by this figure as by the butte behind him, richly red in the early sun and towering above the desert as a symbol of ruggedness and isolation. The association of the rider with this tower of strength (yet ironically an immobile and inflexible strength) is both inevitable and intentional.[10]

Conceivably on hearing this comment the response of many ordinary cinemagoers who have seen the film might be astonishment: It would never have occurred to them to view an aspect of the landscape figuratively like this. The metaphor, if it be one, is certainly not emphatic in the way the one in *Citizen Kane* is.

Orson Welles leaves us in no doubt that the milieu is to be read metaphorically: The trope is signaled by various reiterations. From the opening shot of the film the expressionist style prepares the audience for figurative associations. The Xanadu set in the scene under discussion has been constructed to dwarf the actors, the empty spaces are exaggerated by the wide-angle lens, the sound track gives a booming echo to the voices, and the dialogue further points to the analogy with Susan saying, "Forty-nine thousand acres of nothing but statues. I'm lonesome." Not much chance of missing the metaphor here. John Ford's shot in *The Searchers,* however, can be taken quite literally. There is no special marking.[11] But the shot subtly conditions one's attitude toward Ethan Andrews. After repeated viewings, the appropriateness of it, the link between rider and background, is likely to be more manifest. The metaphor's effect seeps in – it is not thrust upon one.

In *Citizen Kane* the figurative level of meaning is dominant, although it is not at odds with the nonfigurative – as some cinematic metaphors can be, such as the bedframe which changes color in Antonioni's *The Red Desert* (*Deserto rosso*)[12] – and the literal-minded in the audience can still make sense of the sequence. In *The Searchers* the literal level is overtly dominant, and the figurative suggestions are experienced rather like an overtone. Between these extremes of the emphatic and the virtually subliminal are to be found those cinematic metaphors that coexist with literal presentation and do not disrupt narrative continuity. We can also see how the existence of such metaphors was a strategy that social circumstances and the problems of communicating across a wide spectrum of people urged upon filmmakers.

In suggesting that the types of metaphor just described are endemic in cinema, we are still faced with some theoretical uncertainties. Can metaphor be as unobtrusive as it is said to be in *The Searchers* and still be a metaphor? Does there not have to be present some tension generated by the clash between literal and figurative meaning, or caused by the discrepancy between tenor and vehicle? Where is the "resistance" that has been said to be necessary for metaphor – that resistance so aptly described by William Empson when he writes: "It seems to me that what we start from, in a metaphor as distinct from a transfer, is a recognition that 'false identity' is being used, a feeling of 'resistance' to it, rather like going into higher gear, because the machinery of interpretation must be brought into play . . . "?[13]

The answer to this perplexity is that metaphors work in a variety of ways, and even in literature metaphors just as unobtrusive as this we are speaking of are not uncommon. The reader may care to look back on the discussion of Wordsworth's *The Daffodils* to see how this could be. Some metaphors demand that the machinery of interpretation be put into motion immediately; others call for it only after their effect has been contemplated for a while. Once again we are looking at an objection that derives from too narrow a view of what metaphor is and of the ways it may manifest itself.

An allied misgiving arises, not in connection with the unobtrusiveness of this type of metaphor, but in connection with the degree of literalness copresent. Can a metaphor coexist with so predominant a degree of literal meaning, and still be a metaphor? Again, much the same sort of answer may be turned to in order to pacify this doubt. Surely there is no reason why we should not regard such devices as metaphors so long as we can perceive figurative layers of meaning alongside the literal. *The Daffodils* again can be pointed to as a paradigm case, as can much of Wordsworth's poetry. And in the case of *The Searchers,* what John F. Scott's analysis reveals is that the metaphor derives from the pathetic fallacy whereby we associate human qualities with nonhuman objects, a type of transference fundamental to many metaphors.

Another cinematic illustration of an unobtrusive metaphor consorting with or embedded in literal material, however, might have raised quite a different call for justification. Some cinematic metaphors are very like what William Empson calls "Mutual Metaphors"[14] – though he does not consider them to be true metaphors at all. He thinks them to be distinct in principle from metaphors proper, and claims he only chose this term because so many people still feel the process underlying their working to be metaphorical.

Empson defines a mutual metaphor as a comparison between two ideas that produces a third more general idea, but of a kind that reduces the first two to the status of examples or illustrations. Tenor and vehicle are thus placed on the same footing and, if I interpret him correctly, have become literal examples of the more general idea. He claims that mutual metaphors are often to be found in the refrains of ballads, and gives the following as illustration:

She leaned her back against a thorn
  (Fine flowers in the valley)
And there she has her young child born
  (And the green leaves they grow rarely).

About these lines Empson says:

The effect of the contrast is not simple; perhaps it says "Life went on, and in a way this seems a cruel indifference to her suffering, but it lets us put the tragedy in its place, as we do when we sing about it for pleasure." And you might say that the birth of the child and the growth of the plants are treated as both natural, so that in a remote way they are both compared. But the flowers in the valley and the girl on the hill *are both meant to be really there;* she will illuminate them as soon as they her. The likeness, I think, comes in if at all as a faint Mutual Metaphor, so there is no need to call the thing a Metaphor as such *even when further meanings are extracted from it.*[15]

Innumerable parallels to this illustration can be found in films. I do not think the example quite illustrates what Empson claims it does, however; I believe it can be demonstrated that certain principles of metaphor are applicable here just as they are in analogous cinematic cases.

The ballad Empson quotes is about a mother who kills her illegitimate child.[16] In Chapter III we noted that we customarily accept the tenor as belonging to the plane of narration or discourse. Surely this is what we do when we read or hear this ballad. It is the mother's story that is being told: It is she – her actions, her feelings, her response to the pressures upon her – that the narration is about, and consequently the tenors of any metaphors in the tale will relate to her and her story. Furthermore, whatever metaphors there are in the ballad cannot be seen in isolation but must be read in relation to the full context activating them. The refrain, for example, recurs throughout the ballad, its meaning becoming richer and denser with every repetition.

Smile na sae sweet, my bonie babe:
  (Fine flowers in the valley)

And ye smile sae sweet, ye'll smile me dead
(And the green leaves they grow rarely).

In the second stanza the refrain has become a vehicle to convey the beauty of the child and the lustiness of his growth. The suggestions present in the previous stanza are not discarded, but are held in relation, polyphonically as it were. This is so throughout. The final stanza of the poem stresses the wickedness of the mother's action, and intimates how inexorable are the laws that will punish her – as inexorable as the laws of nature that make the plants grow.

O cursed mother, hell is deep,
(Fine flowers in the valley)
And there thou'll enter step by step
(And the green leaves they grow rarely).

By this stage the meanings of the refrain are too compressed for it to be possible to set them all out. But it may be noted that at the end of the ballad life, far from seeming cruelly indifferent to the woman's suffering, is recognized as the ground of instinct and joy, of natural morality. Life, as the great source of our being and spiritual salvation, is rightly celebrated in choral harmony. The plants, as the vehicle or as a series of interlayed vehicles, have functioned dynamically to express what only metaphor can express so concisely and with such density.

A less complex example of a situation where two objects "are both meant to be really there," and yet where one of them can be shown to function as the vehicle of a metaphor, is to be found in the first line of the ballad:

She leaned her back against a thorn...

That the mother should bear her child by such a tree tells us that she had to bear it alone, away from friends and helpers, out in the open. But had another tree that grows in the wild been selected it might have told as much. What would have been lost is the metaphor, for the choice of thorn suggests a connection between the pains of birth and the fierce barbs of the tree. This is what David Lodge calls a metonymy become metaphor,[17] and is a clear case where literal presence does not exclude metaphorical import.

David Lean's *Oliver Twist* opens with a similar metaphorical image. Oliver's mother-to-be is seen wending her way across a stormy landscape. In the foreground the branch of a thorn is silhouetted against the sky, the barbs made vivid by flashes of lightning, clearly figuratively depicting the pains of childbirth coming upon her. The metaphor is impressed upon us by the manner in which it is presented.

For more delicate examples of metonymy functioning as metaphor, let us take again a John Ford film. In *The Quiet Man* Sean Thornton

(John Wayne), an American boxer, returns to Innisfree in Ireland, the place where his family lived before they emigrated to America. An early shot in the film shows him shortly after his arrival in a wood of tall trees. The strong vertical column of the man is echoed by the vertical trunks of the trees surrounding him. The expression on his face, as well as the beauty of the scene, present his keen pleasure in being there. The height and age of the trees affirm that they have been long-rooted in this soil. Thus they carry a metaphorical suggestion about the land itself, Thornton's relationship to it, and his motives for returning. The country's culture is old: Its customs and lore go back deep in history. What Thornton is seeking is his ancestral roots. For he has none himself. Though tall and strong like the trees, he has lost a living connection with his origins. The mainspring of the plot will turn on this alienation, and it will be the source of many of the film's darker ironies. Thornton will marry Mary Kate Danahar (Maureen O'Hara), but not accept her traditional view of marriage with the importance it assigns to the woman's dowry. He thinks her demand for her dowry is monetary only. His misreading of her motives derives from his loss of contact with his heritage, and it nearly destroys their marriage. Thornton's first glimpse of Mary Kate occurs in a shot almost immediately after the one just described. She is seen barefooted, herding a flock of sheep – that is, she is *seen as* a figure in a pastoral. This aspect of the shot is so marked that it suggests an essential element in Thornton's response to seeing her. He wishes to find an idealized woman in an idealized landscape. (The dialogue reinforces this: Michael og Flynn [Barry Fitzgerald], on being asked if the person Thornton saw is real, replies, "Nonsense, man, it's only a mirage brought on by your terrible thirst.") The later shot modifies the earlier, hinting at the naïve romanticism coloring Thornton's search for his roots.

Not all this will necessarily be apparent on the first viewing of these shots. It requires events later in the story to demonstrate how false Thornton's view of Innisfree is, and what are the factors that bred it: his mother's nostalgic accounts of Ireland when as a newly arrived immigrant to America she was struggling with hardship, poverty, and indifference; his own alienating labor in the Pittsburgh blast furnaces; and the guilt he carried for killing an opponent in the ring. Indeed, the sensuous beauty of these shots virtually invites the audience to identify with Thornton's view and itself indulge in romantic fancies – except that these are increasingly criticized as the film proceeds to set Thornton's idealizations against the tensions and undercurrents of life in what is admittedly a highly stylized Innisfree.[18] Only on a second or third viewing of the film, then, is the full metaphoric import of these two shots likely to be appreciated.

What these examples show is that cinematic metaphors do not have to be overt comparisons – as with, say, Kerensky and the peacock in Eisenstein's *October;* they may derive their being from subtler interplays and by less disruptive introductions of the modifying vehicle. Ford achieves his metaphors here by means of composition and allusion, and by the siting of his images in a dense network of discourses.

In its use of a stylized rural setting to deal with issues of cultural conflict, and with the theme of the ideal in conflict with the mundane, *The Quiet Man* clearly belongs to an old genre – that of pastoral comedy. It is in the tradition of *As You Like It.* The reference to Shakespeare's fine comedy reminds us what an intricate web of modes, styles, conventions, and allusions may be knit together into an artistic whole. It would be a crass member indeed of the audience who believed that, because all the characters were portrayed by living actors on the stage, all the Shakespearean characters had to be credited in the same way or with the same degree of actuality. Some are stock, romantic figures, others pastoral stereotypes (both straight and burlesqued), others social types caricatured for comic or satirical purposes. The Duke, Orlando, Corin, Silvius, Phebe, Jacques, Audrey, and Ganymede all belong to different planes of dramatic reality, and while all are comingled, they demand of us and receive different levels of acceptance. *As You Like It* is, to use Jonathan Culler's term, a masterpiece of "second-order" organization. So too is Ford's *The Quiet Man,* and it too makes a multiple layered demand upon the audience's attention. The interplay of levels affords opportunity for evocative cinematic metaphors. The denial of such metaphors then, on the grounds that in films all images are "equally there" is more than an obtuseness about the existence of rhetorical figures: It represents a refusal to attend to the subtleties of cinematic artistry.

CHAPTER V
Varieties of cinematic metaphor

"Metaphor" is a loose word, at best, and we must beware of attributing to it stricter rules of usage than are actually found in practice.

— Max Black[1]

The student of visual effects does well in taking metaphor seriously, for they must tell us something of the way our experiences are categorized.

— E. H. Gombrich[2]

To attempt a definitive taxonomy of metaphors, whether literary or cinematic, is futile. How can a figure, which functions by sabotaging category boundaries, itself be bounded? No system will hold it. Yet, even to survey the multifarious forms metaphor can take, some ordered procedure is necessary. A method has to be adopted, if only to organize the material to be examined and to crystallize problems. Table 1 presents ten general formulas corresponding to the list in Chapter II of what seemed, with reservations, to be the principal forms generating metaphor. These formulas will serve as a basis for studying the variety of cinematic metaphors.

The use of the formulas, though, should not be taken to imply that any cinematic metaphor conforming to one of these formulas is necessarily equivalent to a literary metaphor of that (or some other) type, or that the one may be translated into the other. There is no reason to suppose that the effect of cinematic metaphors may be captured in words without loss, any more than there is for believing that verbal metaphors are reducible to literal exposition. Employing the formulas, abstract and general as they are, presents some kind of test of those formulas, and readers may like to consider to what degree their application proves strained or fitting.

What is being investigated are specific occasions when figurative

Table 1. *Metaphoric formulas*

A is like B	Explicit comparison (epiphor)
A is B	Identity asserted
A replaced by B	Identity implied by substitution
A/B	Juxtaposition (diaphor)
Ab, so b	Metonymy (associated idea substituted)
A stands for (ABC)	Synecdoche (part replaces whole)
O stands for (ABC)	Objective correlative
A becomes A or $\mathscr{A}$	Distortion (hyperbole, caricature)
$ABCD$ becomes $AbCD$	Rule disruption
$\dfrac{(A/pqr)}{(B/pqr)}$	Chiming (parallelism)

meanings are deemed to be present in films, and by what strategies those meanings are made manifest. We are thus pursuing here a rhetorical account of cinematic metaphor: We are concerned with tropes and figures. But, as the last chapter showed, some cinematic metaphors may be so unobtrusive, so subliminal, that their very existence may become matters of dispute. It is best when studying rhetorical devices to concentrate on those that proclaim themselves to be such or those that the filmmaker seems to be declaring are such. In the theater actors speak of "pointing" a line or phrase when it is necessary to ensure that the audience does not miss it. In a similar fashion certain cinematic metaphors may be regarded as "pointed": These we will designate marked metaphors. We can imagine them as being situated at one end of a sliding scale, at the other end of which will be placed unstressed and subliminal metaphors. This chapter will focus primarily on marked metaphors, often considering not only how they function but also how the "pointing" is done.

Explicit comparison (epiphor): *A* is like *B*

Our first category raises immediately the issues of medium and pointing. It has more than once been asserted – dialogue apparently being forgotten or not considered sufficiently cinematic – that film has no equivalent for the word "like."[3] Therefore, is it possible to have purely nonverbal tropes based on explicit comparison in cinema?

A clue to the answer lies in recognizing the role of *like* (or its equivalents) in a literary simile. The word instructs the reader to note the similarity between two ideas. Because the two ideas derive from different categories or different realms of discourse, the similarity normally entails search and it is more easily discovered in some cases than in others. On rarer occasions, with what have been termed *negative metaphors,* the whole point of the instruction may be to emphasize the dissimilarities rather than the similarities.[4] An instruction, however, may be conveyed without overt verbal statement. A husband may say to his wife, "Time to go," or he may tap her on the arm, look at his watch, and then the door. A directive to seek for similarity just as easily can be conveyed without recourse to words. The film in effect nudges the spectator, indicating, "Watch out, this is like that."

There seem to be three main strategies for accomplishing this:

1. Two objects with some shared aspect, or some well-known affinity, may be placed markedly side by side.
2. Some inherent common feature of each may be stressed by the way the objects are presented cinematically.
3. A similarity not inherently present in the objects themselves may be constructed by the way the objects are presented cinematically.

In type 1 mise-en-scène is more important than the filmic presentation. The similarity will be a preexisting visual one, or will be based upon some preexisting schema or a literary cliché. Chaplin's cut from a flock of sheep to a crowd descending into an underground station in *Modern Times* belongs here. Generally this is the least interesting type of explicit comparison because it does not often involve new insights.

As the comparison becomes subtler or more novel, and the way of presenting it cinematically becomes more important, type 1 shades into type 2. The next example, for instance, is created by camera movement and angle of vision as well as by mise-en-scène. In Fellini's *8½,* Guido (Marcello Mastroianni) is in the station awaiting the arrival of his mistress. The train enters the station, steaming powerfully toward the camera, its mass increasing until it stops. Carla (Sandra Milo) does not emerge from a coach on the side of the train we can see, so Guido crosses in front of the engine to the platform on the other side, the camera trucking with him. When Carla finally comes she steams toward Guido (whose viewpoint is ours) in much the same way as the train had, the actress's mien exhibiting something of the same sense of an irresistible force bearing down upon us.

Two examples from films by Stanley Kubrick may be cited to demonstrate explicit comparisons created primarily through filmic means. The title sequence from *Dr. Strangelove* presents apparent documentary shots of a nuclear bomber being refueled in midair by a tanker aircraft. The melody on the soundtrack, "Try a Little Tenderness," impishly overrides the documentary purport, inviting us to see the two planes as symbiotic mammals, thus comically introducing at least one of the major themes of the film – how man's technology may grow to take on a life of its own. In *2001: A Space Odyssey,* by means of matching the movements and by a shock cut, Kubrick explicitly compares a bone employed by primitive ape-man as a weapon and then thrown up in the air to a spacecraft of the future.

The second example is of special interest. Commonly a cut with matching motion is employed to make an unobtrusive join. Here, because initially the disparity between the objects seems so great, the effect is not unobtrusive but startling. The leap in time is across millennia. Yet the marked visual similarity forces one to ask what else the two objects have in common. Both bone and spacecraft, we realize, are products of our evolution as a tool-using creature. The cinematic simile encapsulates a sense of our ever-increasing technological sophistication but also its obverse: Perhaps for all our technological progress we have not evolved spiritually at all, and the same primitive motives and instincts that enabled the ape-man once to make a weapon of a bone now drive us to manufacture space-age hardware. Some of these meanings, it is true, accrue because of the context in which the simile is placed. But the simile has an important role in enunciating them. The example also demonstrates how suggestive an explicit comparison can be, and how its meanings are not restricted to the expression of shared semblance only.

Identity asserted: *A is B*

Whereas explicit comparison directs attention initially to a resemblance or set of shared similarities, asserted identity generally implies that the essence of something is not what we normally take it to be, but something quite different. In *A Midsummer Night's Dream,* Helena no longer quite seems the straightforward trustworthy friend Hermia once took her to be, but has shown herself to be a duplicitous person, skinny rather than attractive and tall, who likes men to dance around her. The phrase "painted maypole" expresses Hermia's now vision of Helena. The previous figure we discussed, explicit comparison, is a relatively restrained trope, as it invites the contemplation and weighing up of two things in relation to one another. Asserted identity is a more forceful figure, often accompanied by a strong emotional charge; by means of it something we thought we knew is suddenly overcast by an alien category or concept.

There would seem to be three main ways in which film can identify one thing with another:

1. By context, which forces the audience to see *A* as *B*. (The context is often an emotionally charged one.)
2. By distortion of *A,* either in the mise-en-scène or in the process of filming, so that it appears to be another object, *B.* (This may be distinguished in theory, if not always easily in application, from metaphors of the distortion

type by the fact that here the distortion is employed to make *A* seem something else, belonging to an alien category, and not just a caricatured or grotesque version of itself.)

3. By presenting certain selected features of *A* that it holds in common with *B*, but presenting them in such a manner that there may be some genuine doubt as to whether it is *A* or *B* we are looking at.

Again some examples may clarify and give more substance to these somewhat abstruse distinctions. Let us begin with two illustrations of how context can identify one thing with another.

In Hitchcock's *Psycho,* Marion Crane (Janet Leigh) has absconded with money from a client, but after a conversation with Norman Bates (Anthony Perkins) in the motel she recognizes the folly of her action and resolves to return the money. Having made this decision she goes to take a shower. Because we have been party to Marion's temptation, guilt, struggle, resolve, and repentance, it is impossible not to feel that her washing herself is more than a physical deed, that it is indeed an act of spiritual cleansing. Robin Wood remarks on this: "We see Marion under the shower, and her movements have an almost ritualistic quality; her face expresses the relief of washing away her guilt."[5] As a consequence of the act of identity that we make, when Marion Crane is murdered in the shower our sense of shock is all the greater: We perceive a terrible moral gratuitousness in the crime.

Next a more lighthearted illustration. In Robert Hamer's *Kind Hearts and Coronets* Louis D'Ascoyne Mazzini (Dennis Price) describes his beginnings and says of his parents, "They were poor, but they had five happy and harmonious years, before my arrival sent Papa to join the heavenly host." A shot of the widow wheeling a pram is accompanied by the florid tenor voice of the father leading "the heavenly choir" – an aural identification that mocks common pieties, as does many another genial barb of wit in the film.

Kubrick's wit is more astringent, as evidenced in *Dr. Strangelove.* Two examples of it conveniently illustrate how filmic effects may be the source of many identity-asserted metaphors. On several occasions the employment of a fish-eye lens to depict members of the B-52 crew, particularly the black bombardier (James Earl Jones), curves the instruments of the aircraft about the distorted shapes of their helmeted heads, making the men themselves appear to be merely components of nuclear-warfare technology, so changed from human form are they. At the climax of the film Major T. J. "King" Kong (Slim Pickens) releases the bomb, which has stuck, and then rides upon it earthwards: a cowboy waving his western hat and whooping on his plunging bronco. There is probably a further level of identification here as we think of an irrational mankind being borne along by its technology to inevitable self-sought destruction.

A somewhat hackneyed example of type 3 metaphor is that of dancers photographed from directly above, à la Busby Berkeley, so that they appear to be flowers or sea anemones or whatever. If the shot is just a momentary change of angle while the dance is mainly presented straightforwardly, then it is more like a simile; if, however, the shot is extended, and the choreography is designed for the overhead angle, then we are likely to have a full assertion of identity. A more complex example of type 3 comes from Antonioni's *Blow-Up*. The photographer (David Hemmings), taking fashion pictures of the model Verushka, tries to capture the look he wants by suggestively exciting her with his own body and with the camera. As the session mounts in intensity with his cries, his straddling her, and the convulsions of their movements, the behavior of the two takes on increasingly the look of an act of fornication. The metaphor is significant in the film because, apart from what it reveals about the character of Thomas, it raises the issue of the degree to which the photographer himself manufactures what he snaps and is himself ravished by what he takes.

Substitution: *A* replaced by *B*

In verbal metaphors based on substitution, a new term, from an alien domain, replaces the customary term. The process in language is aided, not hampered, by syntax, which itself is in part a set of rules for substitutions: A sentence remains grammatical so long as it is an adjective that qualifies the noun and a noun that governs the verb, and so forth. Metaphorical substitution normally stretches semantic rules, not syntactic ones – or else it would become a rule disruption type of metaphor. The constancy of the syntactic order provides a framework for semantic substitution. But cinema, as we have seen, has no equivalent to linguistic syntax. How then can the filmmaker indicate there has indeed been a substitution? His task, it would seem, is rendered harder and not easier by the freedom of film to show many things and to leap in an instant from one to another. An audience, in order to recognize the substitution, must have an expectation of what should appear so that they can perceive something has been put in its place. Because the image that has been omitted is normally the tenor of the metaphor (or the means whereby the tenor is identified), it is of paramount importance that the missing object be called to mind. Such an awareness must be based either on a pattern established by the film itself, or on a pattern known to be linked to an actual state of affairs. In the first case, however, the pattern must not be too formal for then we would be presented with an instance of rule disruption rather than of substitution. What are most common are shifts in the mode of discourse, or else surprising turns in the narrative line.

Again examples may clarify what is meant. In musicals, a character might wish to express her feelings for the person she loves. Instead of speaking, she expresses these feelings through dancing. This is not exactly a disruption of a pattern because it is in the pattern of musicals to have such shifts. But it is the substitution of one mode for another and consequently can bear metaphorical import. In Herbert Ross's *The Turning Point*, when Emilia (Leslie Brown) makes eyes at the young Russian star Yuri (Mikhail Baryshnikov), she envisages their love in a brief fantasy sequence where they dance alone in the studio with only the mirrors to observe them. The imaginary pas de deux (from *Romeo and Juliet*), which substitutes for how the pickup probably occurred in the studio, then dissolves into the actual adagio of their lovemaking, their bodies twisting and gyrating still to Prokofiev's music through to the climax of her final port de bras across his naked back. A substitution metaphor shades into an identification metaphor to reveal how for Emilia the intense experiences of dance and of love have become intermingled.

Another example, where one mode of presentation is substituted for the one we expect, occurs in William Wyler's *The Best Years of Our Lives.* The returned air-force veteran (Dana Andrews) climbs into an old disused bomber, and there recalls some of his missions. Normally such memories would have been, in the 1940s when the film was made, depicted by means of a flashback sequence. Wyler presents it instead through use of the score and by means of moving the camera and changing the angles of shooting. The effect is to suggest, more powerfully than the customary mode of narration could have done, the overmastering irruption of the past onto the present.

In Satyajit Ray's *Pather Panchali* there is very simple, though extremely effective, aural substitution. When the father (Kanu Bannerjee) returns home after a long absence, with presents for the children, he learns that his daughter is dead. We see him utter a cry of lament, but what we hear on the sound track is the wail of a flute. The father's grief is at once distanced and universalized.

Surprising twists in the narrative can bring about replacements for what we had anticipated seeing, and these too can generate substitution metaphors. In *The Best Years of Our Lives,* on the first day of his return to civilian life, the father (Fredric March) remarks how good it is to be back in civilization. This is followed by a shot of raucous and barbaric jazz in a nightclub where, it turns out, he and his wife have now gone to celebrate his return. Through the effect created, the editing conveys the man's shock at how the civilization he yearned for has changed beyond recognition. John Boorman's *Point Blank* provides another illustration. Walker (Lee Marvin) returns intending to take revenge on his wife and her lover who both betrayed and shot him. On arrival at the wife's house Walker bursts into the bedroom, and fires bullet after bullet into the empty bed. The substitution of a bed for the human target Walker sought delineates his vengeful obsession and its sexual origins. It also makes the violence more real and intense for the audience.

Walker's hatred, his wife and her lover being absent, is transferred to the bed. Such transference is a fundamental characteristic shared by us all, and provides the mechanism for many substitution metaphors. Because of our interest in A, when it is replaced by B we regard B as a substitute, and transfer back from B qualities that modify A. In Polanski's *Knife in the Water* (*Nóż w wodzie*) the boy and the wife finally make love. As the couple in their embrace disappear below the frame of the screen we are left looking at the dropped sail of the boat, prone and flapping in the breeze. We see in it the sexual grappling and spasms we cannot directly observe.

In this last instance, movement out of the frame while the camera stayed on an appropriate object created the transference. It could be done, however, by other means – camera movement itself, or the pulling of focus, or by a dissolve or some other editing linkage.

Film lends itself to transference because of the variety of elements copresent within shots and sequences. The director, however, must control and manipulate the audience's shifts of attention. How elaborate and calculated such manipulation can become is demonstrated by Hitchcock's discussion with François Truffaut of a sequence from *The Birds*. The scene spoken of illustrates how emotion can be presented obliquely by transference from one element to another. For instance, from sound (including silence) to visual action.

TRUFFAUT: When Jessica Tandy discovers the farmer's body, she opens her mouth as if to scream, but we hear nothing. Wasn't that done to emphasise the sound-track at this point?

HITCHCOCK: The sound-track was vital just there; we had the sound of her footsteps running down the passage, with almost an echo. The interesting thing in the sound is the difference between the footsteps inside the house and outside. Did you notice that I had her run from the distance and then went to a close-up when she's paralysed with fear and inarticulate? There's silence at that point. Then, as she goes off again, the sound of the steps will match the size of the image. It grows louder right up to the moment she gets into the truck, and then the screech of the truck engine starting off conveys her anguish. We were really experimenting there by taking real sounds and stylising them so that we derived more drama from them than we normally would.

For the arrival of the truck, I had the road watered down so that no dust would rise because I wanted that dust to have a dramatic function when she drives away.

TRUFFAUT: I remember that very clearly. In addition to the dust you even had the smoke from the exhaust pipe.

HITCHCOCK: The reason we went to all that trouble is that the truck, seen from a distance like that, moving at tremendous speed, expresses the frantic nature of the mother's moves. In the previous scene we had shown that the woman was going through a violent emotion, and when she gets into the truck, we showed that this was an emotional truck. Not only by the image, but also through the sound that sustains the emotion. It's not only the sound of the engine you hear, but something that's like a cry. It's as though the truck were shrieking.[6]

We began our illustrations by referring to dance, so let us close this discussion of substitution metaphors with another dance reference. Many of Fred Astaire's numbers are metaphorical for reasons previously mentioned. One number, however, also illustrates how the impossible can be substituted for the possible, and how a metaphor can be created out of a transgression of a natural law. In Stanley Donen's *Royal Wedding* Astaire dances up the walls of his room and across the ceiling, apparently totally defying gravity, in a witty expression of choreographed elation.

Juxtaposition (diaphor): *A/B*

There has been a tendency in the past for film theorists to regard juxtaposition as the main basis for cinematic metaphors. The reason was that editing was thought to be the source of metaphors, and editing encourages freedom of juxtaposition. Probably Eisenstein, in his earlier accounts of montage, influenced thought in this direction. But, as his later emphasis on vertical as well as horizontal montage reveals, metaphors generated by juxtaposition can occur just as frequently within shots as between shots. (A fuller consideration of Eisenstein's views will be found in Chapter VI.)

Juxtaposition entails contiguity in time or space. But contiguity does not necessarily entail juxtaposition, because objects in life, as well as in films, are often contiguous quite fortuitously. Juxtaposition has to be regarded as a *significant* contiguity – one that establishes a special relationship between *A* and *B*. Again, not all significant relationships will be metaphorical since many can be explicated in literal terms. To take an example from Eisenstein on montage: A close-up of a grave plus a close-up of a woman in mourning may lead us to assume she is a widow, but the deduction involves no intermingling of categories, and consequently the juxtaposition does not result in a metaphor. Films often rely on such collocations, and audiences have become adept at seeing implications and making connections.[7] These are more often literal than figurative. Indeed, literal relationships are the more easily posited precisely because they do not involve the stretching or modifying of categories. This being so, we need to explain how a filmmaker cues the audience to exert the extra effort required to hunt for a figurative meaning.

One further consideration. Juxtaposition as the basis for metaphor implies that the objects are not related through similarity or substitution (for then we would have the other types of metaphor already discussed). Yet the one object must be reconceived in terms of the other. What provides the significant linkage between them? Often it turns out to be an incongruity felt between *A* and *B,* which becomes the source of their mutual interplicitness.

There would seem to be four main strategies whereby the filmmaker can ensure that juxtaposition generates a metaphor:

1. The audience is preconditioned to anticipate metaphors.
2. Something in the manner of presentation itself serves to signify that a particular juxtaposition is to be interpreted figuratively.
3. No satisfactory literal explanation presents itself, so that the audience is forced to look for a figurative explanation. In practice this usually means that the continuity of the narrative has been markedly disrupted.
4. A literal explanation is acceptable, but there is something sufficiently resonant about the juxtaposition to invite further search for figurative implications.

For the audience to be prepared for metaphorical readings, the film (or that section of the film) must declare itself to be "poetic" in genre and style. Overtly surrealistic films, experimental or underground movies, zany comedies, or dream sequences in otherwise naturalistic films provide cinematic occasions when audiences will accept figurative rather than literal reasons for links between things. Sometimes these occasions are cued by the circumstances of release, as for example when an experimental film is shown at a college of art. Often the filmmaker himself provides cues early in the film. The notorious shot of an eye being slashed by a razor at the beginning of Buñuel's *An Andalusian Dog (Un Chien andalou)* may be seen as performing such a function. Lindsay Anderson and David Sherwin's *If...* is primarily a literal narrative until the fight in the café between Mick (Malcolm McDowell) and his girl (Christine Noonan). Their snarling at one another like wild animals can still be taken as play, but when their wrestling bodies suddenly become naked the film indicates a shift to another (more subjunctive?) style. So when later the chaplain (Geoffrey Chater) pops up out of a drawer in the headmaster's cupboard, the audience is more adapted to responding in the right way to the zaniness of this action juxtaposed against a traditional scene of a headmaster admonishing a recalcitrant pupil.

An example of type 2 strategy can be found in John Boorman's *Point Blank*. Shots of Walker (Lee Marvin) striding down a wide corridor are juxtaposed against shots of his wife. Although a literal interpretation is plausible – Walker is on his way to find her – the manner of presentation suggests much more than this. The repetition of the intercutting, the strident rhythm of the music over the cuts, the extended time Walker remains in the location of the corridor – all these act as markers indicating that the sequence is also to be read as a metaphorical depiction of the guilt haunting Walker's wife, her sense of an inexorable vengeance pursuing her.

Nicolas Roeg's *Walkabout* opens with a blank brick wall occupying the screen. The camera trucks to the right to reveal a crowded urban scene. After a montage of city shots, the shot of the blank wall is repeated, and the camera begins to truck right again. But on this occasion the scene that is juxtaposed against the edge of the wall is the wilderness of the Australian outback. The first time, though the audience will have felt metaphorical overtones in the emphasis on the brick wall, the juxtaposition of wall and city scene is explicable in literal terms. The second time a literal explanation is ruled out, and we have a case of a type 3 juxtaposition metaphor. When the shot is repeated yet again, to reveal now the father's car parked in the outback, the audience is being pushed to recognize the man's despair at his urban existence and to appreciate the melancholia that leads him to a final and total rejection.

In *The Red Desert (Deserto rossa)* Michelangelo Antonioni resorts to the fourth type of strategy we have outlined in order to portray the neurotic feelings of his central figure. Giuliana (Monica Vitti) is seen against a wall that has large blotches of paint spattered upon it.[8] Because of her position she is both linked and juxtaposed to the blotches. Although their presence has a literal explanation – colors are being tried out before the room is repainted – the striking nature of their irrational shapes, set against the trim figure of the woman, suggests the presence of an emotional disturbance in Giuliana that belies her outer calmness. Antonioni often employs striking shapes for the purpose of juxtaposition metaphors. The use of the strange mushroom-shaped tower at the beginning of *The Eclipse (L'eclisse)* provides another example.

Metonymy (associated idea substituted): *Ab* so *b*

In his book, *The Modes of Modern Writing: Metaphor, Metonymy, and the Typology of Modern Literature,* David Lodge suggests that both metonymy and synecdoche are tropes that entail condensation through deletion: "A rhetorical figure, rather than a précis, results because the items deleted are not those which seem logically the most dispensable.... this illogicality is equivalent to the coexistence of similarity and dissimilarity in metaphor."[9] Because the very processes of filming – selecting camera angles, focusing, and framing – entail selections and rejections, film is inextricably tied to metonymies of a sort. But it is what Lodge calls the "illogicality" of the selection that makes a cinematic metonymy a full trope. Consequently, where such "illogicality" occurs, a tension – equivalent to the tension in metaphor proper – should be discernible. Calling to mind the items omitted would indicate they are not the items most naturally deleted. Further, the item selected is seen to possess an apt suggestiveness that goes beyond mere reference to the object it replaces. By such means the metonymic object brings a new matrix of thoughts and feelings into existence.

Of course, as tropes both metonymy and synecdoche are subspecies of substitution metaphor. But where in pure substitution metaphor the imported item comes from a domain utterly alien to that of the tenor, in these tropes the item selected not only belongs to the domain of the tenor but also possesses an association with the tenor. We can also make a distinction arising from how that association comes about. In some cases of metonymy, for instance, it may have been created by an actual state of affairs – just how things are connected in the world in which we live. A metonymy drawing upon such an association we might term a *received* metonymy. But in other cases the association may be created during the course of the film. This we might term a *contextual* metonymy.

In Godard's *Vivre sa vie* (*My Life to Live*) the sexual transactions with clients are indicated by showing Nana (Anna Karina) reaching for a metal coat hanger. Although its link with the acts of prostitution is clear – a prostitute has to undress to some degree, and might well hang up her clothes – this item is selected for repeated emphasis, and it is not one of the more obvious actions one would associate with the practice of prostitution. The "illogicality" of its selection is what makes this metonymy striking, and an appropriate figurative correlative for dehumanized and unerotic sex.

The previous example relies on received associations. In Fellini's *La strada* the film itself creates the link between Gelsomina (Giulietta Masina) and her song. Some time after he has deserted her and apparently forgotten her completely, Zampano (Anthony Quinn) hears someone singing the song, and he seeks its source. In part the figurative tension here is supplied by the manner of presentation. When Zampano first hears the song, there is some mystery as to where it originates. The sound track provides the song with no atmospheric locale – as though the source could be interior, inside Zampano himself. Even when he finds that the woman hanging out washing has been singing it, this feeling persists. The news of Gelsomina's death only serves to reinforce the sense that miraculously a part of her lives on in the callous and unloving Zampano. The washing flapping on the line in this sequence may also be read as a metonymy with unobtrusive metaphorical implications. In its white purity the washing proffers an association with the innocence of Gelsomina, and reminds us of her desire to lead a complete married and domestic life with Zampano – a possibility he has irredeemably destroyed.

Synecdoche (part replaces whole): *A* stands for (*ABC*)

Much that has been said about metonymy applies to synecdoche: It involves compression through deletion; the figurative meanings generated by it derive from the "illogicality" of the deletion made; our view of the whole is conditioned by the value we place on the associated part. Synecdoche, however, is nearly always *received:* There is not quite the scope for *contextual* synecdoches that there is for contextual metonymies. Any film abounds in synecdoches, but they are overtonal rather than marked. To obtain a marked synecdoche the incongruity of the part selected must be great; alternatively, special emphasis has to be provided through the means of presentation. Very frequently both synecdoche and metonymy are themselves combined with other types of metaphor, and function in a subordinate capacity.

An example from Godard's *Vivre sa vie* (*My Life to Live*) illustrates how the movement of the camera may be used to mark a synecdoche and call attention to its figurative implications. Nana is negotiating with a photographer late at night in a bistro. She is trying to get him to let her have some money; to bed her he is using the bait of offering to take publicity pictures of her, which will help her get film roles. As they negotiate the camera pans across from one to the other, but at the peak of the swing the frame on that side only bisects the figure. Such repeated exclusions of all but part of one figure serve to suggest that neither character fully exists as a person for the other but only as a means to a personal end.

James Monaco cites another Godard scene as an example of synecdoche: "Juliet Berto in Godard's *La Chinoise* (1967) has constructed a theoretical barricade of Chairman Mao's 'Little Red Books', parts that stand for the whole of Marxist/Leninist/Maoist ideology with which the group of 'gauchistes' to which she belongs protect themselves, and *from* which they intend to launch an attack on bourgeois society."[10] But to my mind the major trope here is explicit comparison, created by the constructed barricade; the role of the synecdoche is subordinate, though essential for the full meaning.

Objective correlative: *O* stands for (*ABC*)

This may be regarded as a special type of contextual metonymy. In a film a specific object becomes associated with a particular character, or with some event or situation pertaining to that character. As with metonymy, the device is a means of condensation, but it is largely the aptness of the object rather than the incongruity of what is deleted that makes for a successful objective correlative. Although the figure could be subsumed under metonymy, the extensive use in films of props – that is, in theatrical parlance, small objects that an actor may carry on or off the stage, and which he will give significance to by handling – probably justifies the classification of it as a trope in its own right. Props in films need not even be confined to small objects. Buster Keaton, by his handling of it and the relationships he establishes with it, certainly converts a whole train into a prop in *The General.* The train also acquires direct metaphorical significance at various points in the film, as when it objectifies Johnny Gray's obsessive one-track-mindedness by transporting him unseeing through two armies.

A more typical example of objective correlative is to be found in Polanski's *Knife in the Water* (*Nóż w wodzie*). During some of the scenes in the cabin, the husband (Leon Niemczyk) listens to a sports match on radio by means of an earplug. Although this is given literal motivation – he is a sports commentator, and his wife objected to the sound of the radio – in context this correlates with and exemplifies his self-centeredness, which makes him oblivious to the feelings and needs of others. This film also provides an excellent illustration of how an objective correlative differs from a symbol, but may also shade off into one. The boy (Zygmunt Malanowicz) carries the knife of the title, largely as a badge to give him some sort of status. But the knife also as the film proceeds acquires sexual connotations. In part these are traditional, in part they are suggested and reinforced by various events throughout the course of the film. Thus the knife becomes a full symbol, and does not remain a metonymy like the radio's earplug. Indeed, it may be taken as a paradigm case of what constitutes a symbol within a film. More ambiguous, however, are the games played by the two males in *Knife in the Water:* the picking up sticks, the hand wrestling, the tricks with the knife, and so on. Each one in itself is perhaps simply a metonymy for the rivalry between the two. But considered as an underlying pattern constantly being reasserted, the game playing may be read as a full symbol for a biologically inescapable competitiveness in man.

Let us return to the objective correlative with one further example – though again one not without some overlap with a different kind of trope. Consider the five broken teacups seen by Mrs. Brenner (Jessica

Tandy) in Hitchcock's *The Birds* when she finds the dead farmer. I suggest these should be read both as a metonymy and as an objective correlative. They function as a metonymy because they imply the damage done by the birds that have attacked the house, and they hint at some further unspeakable destruction. But because they correlate with Mrs. Brenner's tense fragility, glimpsed in the desperation of her endeavors to preserve a domestic and unchanging home life, the broken teacups also act as an objective correlative for the deep-seated anxieties now surfacing in Mrs. Brenner.

Distortion (hyperbole, caricature): A or $\mathscr{A}$

Distortion implies a deviation from what is normal. If all the letters in this sentence are the font they are, then A is a distortion, whereas if all the print were like A then that letter would not be a distortion. This truism is set down because it bears upon something problematic. Where perception of visual or aural material in a film is concerned, what constitutes a distortion? It cannot be simply from what we perceive in ordinary life, because most film images deviate from that. The lens of the camera does not capture in a scene quite what the eye alone would see; recorded sounds are not as directional and are more selective; the level of amplification is probably greater; black-and-white film stock translates the world into shades of gray; color stock does not accurately reproduce the world's colors; wipes, dissolves, pans, indeed the screen frame itself, have no place in everyday vision. Yet all these can come to be accepted as part and parcel of a movie that we feel does not travesty what we see. (It is even possible to watch a Cinemascope film projected without the required anamorphic lens, as I have, and come to forget after a while that the human figures on the screen are grossly elongated.) What is natural is what the mind accepts as natural. Conventions and cinematic devices can easily become so transparent we forget they are present. Distortion then must be understood as a deliberate deviation from what is expected in a specific context.

Even when we are aware of distortion, its calling attention to itself does not necessarily point to the presence of figurative meaning. It may be part of a cinematic convention (as with dissolves). It may be merely a way of drawing attention to certain literal features (as with slow-motion studies of birds in flight). Or it may be the way of *marking* the presence of another type of metaphor – as in the example from *Dr. Strangelove* mentioned earlier where a fish-eye lens was used to achieve an identity-asserted metaphor. For a true metaphor of the distortion type the mutated image must create a perspective of the object such that our sense of what category it belongs to is affected.

Distortion metaphors are common in films because of the variety of means available to the filmmaker for manipulating the appearance of objects. Again, though the distinction is perhaps largely a technical one, we may distinguish between mise-en-scène distortions and filmic ones. The first are organized before rolling the camera; the second are achieved by the camera (through employment of particular film stock, lenses, camera speed, etc.), or afterward in the laboratory or the cutting room. Mise-en-scène distortions are more likely, however, to be deviations on ordinary perception; filmic ones to be deviations from the expected mode of presentation.

Metaphors of the distortion type based on mise-en-scène range from the expressive sets of Robert Wiene's *The Cabinet of Dr. Caligari* (*Das Kabinett des Dr. Caligari*) to the moody lighting effects of American film noir.[11] A comic distortion metaphor, with a sting to it, occurs in Chaplin's *The Great Dictator* when even the microphone recoils before Adenoid Hynkel's malevolent denunciation of the Jews.

Filmic distortion metaphors include the following. The acrophobia of "Scottie" Ferguson (James Stewart) in Hitchcock's *Vertigo* is rendered through the vertiginal shift of perspective in the shot of the stairwell (attained by the camera simultaneously zooming and dollying in opposite directions). John Frankenheimer employs a fish-eye lens to depict the helpless panic of his protagonist (Rock Hudson) in *Seconds* when, in the climactic scene, he is wheeled off for medical recycling. (This differs from the use of a similar lens in *Dr. Strangelove* in that here the distortion itself is the vehicle of the metaphor; in Kubrick's film it is technology that becomes the vehicle.) In *The Miracle Worker* Arthur Penn employs a combination of slow motion, jump cuts, and enlarged graininess of film stock with its hazy pointillism to evoke the defective eyesight of Annie Sullivan (Anne Bancroft) and the anguish of her memory of her brother's death.

One final observation. There is a type of distortion metaphor based on a radical viewpoint or an obsessive selection that by screening out a more balanced presentation of the subject effectively distorts it for metaphorical purposes. I am thinking for example of how films sometimes treat the milieu so as to create figurative overtones. In *Metropolis* scenic design presents a picture of the city as a slave camp for workers; in *Taxi Driver*, through selection and lighting particularly, the film in key sequences portrays the city as a libidinous version of hell.

Rule disruption: *ABCD* becomes *AbCD*

The effect of rule disruption is to make the spectator think, even if only unconsciously and for a fraction of time: Why was I given that instead of what the established code requires? If the implicit answer to the question entails figurative meanings, then we have a rule-disruption metaphor.

In literature such metaphors are comparatively easy to point to when they derive from a breaking of syntactic rules, but can be more difficult to put one's finger on when they arise from ruptures in less formal and more tacit codes. Because films have no firm and established syntax, this difficulty must be acknowledged. But all arts, including the cinema, select and arrange material in patterns of varying degree of formality and informality, and such patterns easily acquire the status of tacit conventions. In cinema the patterning would seem to fall into four broad types:

1. prefilmic conventions brought in from other arts or from social customs;
2. filmic conventions acquired in the shifting course of film practice;
3. *schemes,* or formal organizational patterns, specifically set up by the filmmaker as a means for structuring a particular film; and
4. unconscious motifs or patterns that, while the filmmaker did not deliberately and foreknowingly put them there, still influence the organization of the film.

As the last category makes clear, within and between these various kinds of structuring the degree of artistic deliberateness will vary. Spectators too will probably differ in their sensitivity to these patterns, and consequently in their sensitivity to any flouting of them. In this discussion, however, we need merely concern ourselves with marked metaphors – that is, with rule-disruption metaphors that are deliberately and consciously constructed and where there is evidence that the spectator's attention is being drawn to them.

A good source of examples to illustrate this type of metaphor is the work of Alfred Hitchcock – he is such a deliberate craftsman and so ingenious in the games he plays with audiences' expectations and in his manipulation of their responses. Many of his disruption metaphors relate to an overall menace in his films, to the fear that beneath the bland surface of life chaos and horror lurk.

Let us begin with an amusing example but one that invariably produces gasps from audiences. In *To Catch a Thief* Mrs. Stevens (Jessie Royce Landis) stubs out her cigarette in the yoke of a fried egg. The action astonishes with its grand disregard for the niceties of table manners and epitomizes the vulgarity of pampered and self-indulgently wealthy people. In *Strangers on a Train* the unbalanced murderer, obsessed with his schemes, is set apart from ordinary people by his being the only stationary head at a tennis match where all others are panning theirs to and fro with the ball. Finally, let me revert to a scene mentioned before, the shower murder in *Psycho.* It has been argued that, because audiences are accustomed to identify with the star of a thriller and feel confident that whatever happens the star will not be killed off, when relatively early in *Psycho* they witness the murder of Marion Crane who is played by a star actress (Janet Leigh), they experience extreme disorientation. This disruption of complacent assumption, combined with the disruption of another cherished pattern – that someone who repents and washes off her guilt should not be harmed – works to create a disturbing sense of the gratuitousness and insecurity of our existence.[12]

Chiming (parallelism): $\dfrac{A/par}{B/pqr}$

This figure could be said to be a cross between two tropes, namely those of juxtaposition and explicit comparison. The joke about Christmas as a season of "alcoholidays" illustrates how it functions.[13]

$$\left. \begin{array}{l} \text{alcoHOL} \\ \text{HOLidays} \end{array} \right\} \text{alcoHOLidays}$$

A quite arbitrary similarity or parallelism becomes the opportunity for a juxtaposition of two ideas. The similarity might be accidentally available in the material (as where the overlap is an arbitrary alphabetical one), or it might be manufactured by the artist (by his constructing a rhyme scheme, analogous grammatical patterns, or whatever) for the purposes of a metaphorical collocation. In the marked form of the trope, we are confronted with deliberately constructed analogies or parallelisms. A formal pattern intentionally sited in the manner of presentation – rather than simple contiguity in space or time as in a straight juxtaposition – becomes the impacting agency. The device can, in fact, be constructed in quite an elaborate fashion.

I would suggest that the following metaphor from *Psycho*, noted by Robin Wood, is of this type:

Much of the film's significance is summed up in a single visual metaphor, making use again of eyes, occurring at the film's focal point (the murder of Marion): *the astonishing cut from the close-up of the water and blood spiralling down the drain, to the close-up of the eye of the dead girl, with the camera spiralling outwards from it* It is as if we have emerged from the depths behind the eye, the round hole of the drain leading down into an apparently bottomless darkness, the potentialities for horror that lie in the depths of us all, and which have their source in sex which the rest of the film is devoted to sounding. The sense of vertigo inspired by this cut and the spiralling movement itself, are echoed later as we, from high above, watch Norman carry his mother down to the fruit cellar.[14]

Another illustration of chiming metaphor is to be found in the still from John Huston's *The Treasure of the Sierra Madre* (Fig. 1). Here the visual composition sets up a series of analogous structures that, through the juxtaposition of their differing components, obliquely enact the balance of forces present in the dramatic narrative. A stranger (Bruce Bennet) comes upon the gold mine made by Dobbs (Humphrey

Figure 1. A fine balance of triangular conflicts: *Treasure of the Sierra Madre*, dir. John Huston. Photo courtesy of National Film Archive / Stills Library, London. © 1948 Warner Brothers Pictures, Inc. Renewed 1975 United Artists Television, Inc.

Bogart), Curtin (Tim Holt), and Howard (Walter Huston), and asks to be cut in on the deal. Should they accede, or should they kill him? Essentially the four men are linked by a series of triangles (the tent in the upper right corner repeating and emphasizing the triangle motif):

One triangle is in the foreground and is based upon the squatting figures, the eye focus of the characters reinforcing this by making our gaze follow Dobbs's in the center to Howard and then to the stranger in the lower left corner.

A second triangle surrounds Dobbs, its points located by Curtin, Howard, and the stranger.

A third triangle is more vertical, and puts Howard outside it.

The establishment of three powerful formations like this, without a commitment to a predominant one, reflects the currents of the conflict. The stranger, as the intruder who causes the crisis, is the apex of all three triangles. The first triangle excludes Curtin and puts him furthest away: He is weakly indecisive about what should be done. Howard mediates between the first two triangles because what he chooses will decide whether the intruder will live or die: His role is reinforced by having the two figures focus on him. Dobbs is central, which makes him a powerful figure, but this power is subdued by his oblique stare at Howard and by his being diminished in relation to the two who are higher from the ground than he is; he is also diminished in relation to the stranger who is nearer the frontal plane of the screen. The line of the tent also stresses a strong diagonal from the stranger through Dobbs's face to Howard's. Howard is also thrusting forward, the mass of the tent giving him more weight, while a vertical established by the flame of the fire and the coffee pot points upward to his face: These too reinforce the crucial nature of his role. Thus through contrasts created by means of compositional parallels, the tensions of the scene are made visually manifest.

This completes our survey of the main types of cinematic metaphors. It does not pretend to be complete, because it is a central contention of this book that a definitive taxonomy of cinematic metaphor is not possible. But what seem to be the regular or recurrent forms that generate metaphors have been looked at and illustrated. The examples that have been cited have been chosen with the intention of clarifying and giving specific substance to comments that otherwise might seem too abstruse. More examples might have been offered, but it seemed wisest not to try the readers' patience too much. (I have yet to find, for instance, anyone who admits to reading Christine Brooke-Rose's *A Grammar of Metaphor* right through.) Anyway, readers should by now be able to put forward their own candidates for the types of cinematic metaphor.

Some examples, though chosen to illustrate particular classes of metaphor, might well be interpreted in ways that indicate they should be placed in a different category. This should not worry us too much. We do not discern metaphors in order to categorize them but in order to profit from what they have to offer us: density of meaning intensely experienced. We knew the scheme adopted was at best a rough-and-ready one, as any taxonomy provided by a rhetorical theory of metaphor has to be. It will always fall short in mapping the subtleties of artistic function. Though inadequate, it does perhaps perform the service of apprising us of some strategies artists employ, and consequently of alerting us to watch out for future applications of them. Rhetorical accounts of metaphor, however, need to be supplemented by what was called in Chapter III an imaginative account of metaphor. That will be attempted in Chapter VII, "The mind's eye." First, it may be worth casting a look at some other attempts that have been made to set out a theory of cinematic metaphor – to see what we can learn from them of issues that a theory, and in particular an imaginative theory, of cinematic metaphor needs to address.

Only connect.   — E. M. Forster.[1]

In books on cinema innumerable references to cinematic metaphors are to be found, although most frequently they are identifications of particular metaphors rather than discussions of the existence of cinematic metaphor per se. Some of these references to specific metaphors are mentioned in this book, but those used represent but a small fraction of the number that could be cited. In general, film critics and commentators take it for granted that films abound with figurative constructions, and are not restrained in pointing them out. Attempts to develop theories as to how such metaphors are constructed, or what constitutes a cinematic metaphor, are by contrast all too few. Particular attention should be drawn, however, to the brief accounts attempted by such disparate writers as Ejxenbaum, Gianetti, Huss and Silverstein, Durgnat, and Tudor.[2]

But there are three authors whose writings, I believe, deserve specific examination. The first and most important of these is Sergei Eisenstein; indeed, given his importance it would be negligent not to look at what he has to say. His explicit comments on metaphor may be few, but the idea of metaphor permeates many of his critical essays on cinema theory, and guides much of his practice as a director. Further, the creative work has given rise to significant critical disputes about the viability of the kind of metaphors he sought to employ. The other two authors I shall be discussing, N. Roy Clifton and Christian Metz, are writers whose commentaries on cinematic metaphor appeared in the last few years – indeed they were only published after much of this present book had been drafted. Their inclusion has the advantage of setting my own arguments about cinematic metaphor in the context of recent but markedly different approaches.

Sergei Eisenstein

Eisenstein's theory of montage is itself, in part anyway, a theory of metaphor. Therefore, before considering what Eisenstein has to say specifically on metaphor, an overview of his utterances on montage is desirable. Inevitably this will entail simplification. Eisenstein's thinking developed and changed over the years, and in his endeavor to be eclectic he often expressed contrary or conflicting ideas, or hit on brilliant suggestions that were never fully followed up or incorporated in a coherent system.

The purpose of film, Eisenstein believed, was not to reproduce the mere external features of the world, but to communicate the artist's seminal experience of reality and his understanding of its significance. To achieve this an artist must so select and structure his work that an audience, on seeing it, would come to share his vision, and indeed be able to perceive, think, and feel as he had. At times Eisenstein makes this sound as if the director begins with a clear-cut idea, which he manipulates the audience into accepting by the way he fragments and reconstitutes his filmic material. In such passages – and in certain sections of his own films, it must be said – Eisenstein lays himself open to the charge that he conceived of film as a tool for disseminating propaganda. But essentially this is not what he intended. Eisenstein believed in art and saw the artist as a person who could elicit in his audience a creativity similar to his own.

The strength of montage resides in this, that it includes in the creative process the emotions and mind of the spectator. The spectator is compelled to proceed along the selfsame creative road that the author travelled in creating the image. The spectator not only sees the represented elements of the finished work, but also experiences the dynamic process of the emergence and assembly of the image just as it was experienced by the author. And this is, obviously, the highest possible degree of approximation to transmitting visually the author's perceptions and intention in all their fullness, to transmitting them with "that strength of physical palpability" with which they arose before the author in his creative work and his creative vision.[3]

Communication of this kind would not be possible unless artist and spectator shared a common imaginative faculty. Eisenstein assumed that they did. At the basis of montage lay, he asserted, "the same vitalizing human qualities and determining factors that are inherent in every human being and every vital act."[4] What is important is the internal creative act, the mind's apprehension of significance, attained by innate powers that enable the mind to combine disparate elements into meaningful wholes.

The process is not solely an intellectual one, however, for feelings and sensations are also involved. Eisenstein often places his emphasis differently, in some essays stressing the cognitive character of the creative experience, in others the emotive. In general, he appears to have assumed an interconnection, the intensity of emotions making possible qualitative leaps in thought, and new thoughts exciting fresh feelings. But the key to understanding Eisenstein is the recognition of the link he saw between the inner world of experience and the aesthetic forms employed to communicate that world. Eisenstein reasoned that the rules and methods underlying the construction of a work of art must correspond to the laws and structures underlying the creative processes of the mind. In an important essay he made this explicit.

Inner speech, the flow and sequence of thinking unformulated into logical constructions in which uttered, formulated thoughts are expressed, has a special structure of its own. This structure is based on a quite distinct series of laws. What is remarkable therein, and why I am discussing it, is that the laws of construction of inner speech turn out to be precisely those *laws which lie at the foundation of the whole variety of laws governing the construction of the form and composition of art-works.*[5]

A study of how the creative mind works will furnish "an inexhaustible storehouse, as it were, of laws for the construction of form."[6] Thus Eisenstein's theory of montage is at one and the same time both formalist and psychological.

In early writings Eisenstein conceived these laws as being in essence dialectical. Doubtless he was encouraged in this by that trend in Marxist doctrine that affirms correspondence between the dialectical nature of the material world and the dialectical nature of thought itself. In later essays, however, the strict dialectical formulation is played down and more importance is given to the *organic:* "The law of building the work answers *the law of structure in natural organic phenomena.*"[7] This may reflect a development rather than a change of conception. In discussing the dialectic of montage Eisenstein had described how the "collision" of elements on one plane gives rise to a synthesis upon a higher plane. Organic wholeness might be envisaged as an architectonic extension of this principle, so that it consists of a hierarchy of qualitative transformations culminating in an ultimate and all-embracing unity.[8] Certainly Eisenstein often thought of cinema in this way, as an evolutionary synthesis of all previous arts, and consequently considered his own explanation of montage to be a fundamental account of how all the arts worked. (Indeed, in his own work and his own way, Eisenstein quite as much as Wagner or Diaghilev sought to establish the paramountcy of the *Gesamtkunstwerk.*) But an organic theory of art allows for greater subtleties of form and expression than a dialectic theory can encompass, and it may be too that the shift in Eisenstein's emphasis was influenced by practical experience, both as filmmaker and as teacher in the State Cinema Institute in Moscow.[9]

Montage, as initially defined, concerned the juxtaposition of shot with shot. It is possible to trace an expansion of the concept until it comes to include almost every possible filmic organization, whether within or between shots. In the essay "Word and Image," for instance, some of the preparation an actor undertakes in creating a role becomes montage. The actor will imagine a number of pictures embodying the theme he has to enact, select those that are most evocative, refine them of all "but the decisive and determining properties," and finally combine them "with the purpose of bringing to life *the initiating image of the theme.*"[10] Not only is montage not restricted to editing and combining images, it has become virtually the search in any area of filmmaking for some "objective correlative" – in Eliot's sense – which will evoke the appropriate feeling or thought in the spectator. Elsewhere, by introducing the notion of "vertical montage" as well as "horizontal montage," Eisenstein further widened the concept: Vertical montage opens the way for the significant juxtaposition of all elements coexisting within the shot, such as sound and visuals, color and line, actors and decor. Even juxtaposition may not be essential for montage. Quite early in Eisenstein's career, and certainly explicitly acknowledged after he saw the performances of a visiting Kabuki company, is the idea of "transfer," whereby one theme can be expressed through different elements of staging. Thus a journey might be depicted through mime, then through scene change, then through music. Cinema, even more than theater, lent itself to such a "grand total provocation of the human brain."[11] Further modes of formal complexity are made possible when musical paradigms are introduced into film structuring, as Eisenstein comes to do when he begins to write of "counterpoint," "polyphony," "the tonal dominant," and "overtonal montage"[12] in connection with the treatment of visual rather than aural material. It is difficult not to feel that the general concept of montage is in danger of collapsing under the weight brought on by its own inclusiveness.

It is important to remember, however, the ambitious nature of Eisenstein's project. Not only did he wish to enunciate the principles governing a new art form, he was convinced that they would reveal the fundamental laws of all aesthetic construction and would scientifically illuminate the creative processes of the human mind itself. Given the magnitude of the task he set himself, ultimately critics of Eisenstein's theories may well judge them as not complex enough rather than take the view that they are overcomplicated.

Some of the ideas adumbrated here certainly bear upon issues we have found it necessary to discuss in relation to metaphor. Eisenstein's notion, for instance, of correspondence between artistic form and "inner speech" makes a more extreme claim than our earlier suggestion that a principle of complementarity is needed to account for both the rhetorical structures generating metaphors and the processes by which we interpret them, but the problem it is attempting to resolve is not unrelated. His discussions of dialectic structures and of the hierarchical basis of organic form are relevant to explorations of the "esemplastic" nature of metaphor, and to the possibility that metaphor plays a central role in the overall organization of an artwork. But to what extent did Eisenstein explicitly relate montage to metaphor, and to what degree is his theory of montage to be taken as an account of figurative structures in cinema?

Eisenstein's frequent assertion that the juxtaposition of two shots could produce a whole greater than the sum of parts might seem to align montage with the *diaphoric* type of metaphor. In "Word and Image," for instance, Eisenstein claims that "two film pieces of any kind, placed together, inevitably combine into a new concept, a new quality, arising out of the juxtaposition."[13] But the example he gives raises doubts as to whether the resultant meaning need be metaphorical at all. "For example," he writes, "take a grave, juxtaposed with a woman in mourning weeping beside it, and scarcely anyone will fail to jump to the conclusion: a widow."[14] The conclusion is arrived at through recourse to a common and established set of associated ideas, and is itself as literal as the ideas that gave rise to it – as we noted in Chapter V. Something further must be present in a juxtaposition if figurative meaning is to be the end product. (We might also query whether any two shots will inevitably produce a new concept: Some conjoinings may be so arbitrary that nothing but confusion ensues.) It was not, of course, Eisenstein's intention in this particular essay to argue that montage was necessarily metaphorical: His prime concern was to show how an effective selection of detail can coalesce in a unified concept, and to suggest that film editing was much like poetic composition in this regard. But in one essay at least he did argue that montage can generate tropes. The essay, seminal to our discussion, is "Dickens, Griffith, and the Film Today."

In it Eisenstein contrasts the editing of D. W. Griffith, which he considers representational and literal, with Soviet montage, which he claims is essentially figurative.[15] Soviet cinema, he declares, discovered the montage trope. Simile and metaphor are possible in film, but they are found "in the sphere of *montage juxtaposition*, not of *representational montage pieces*."[16] He criticizes Griffith's attempts to render Walt Whitman's lines, "Out of the cradle endlessly rocking... uniter of here and hereafter," by filming Lillian Gish rocking a cradle. This fails he thinks because, first, it is only an isolated picture, existing without integration in a total structure of thought; second, it is too "lifelike" and therefore insufficiently abstracted for the image to fulfill its intended purpose.

Eisenstein takes the "naked woman" in Dovzhenko's *Earth* as illustrating the same errors. Again incompatibility of material and too much naturalism defeat the filmmaker's aim.

The spectator could not possibly separate out of this concrete, lifelike woman that generalized sensation of blazing fertility, of sensual life-affirmation, which the director wished to convey of all nature, as a pantheistic contrast to the theme of death and the funeral!

This was prevented by the ovens, pots, towels, benches, tablecloths – all those details of everyday life, from which the woman's body could easily have been freed by the framing of the shot, – so that representational naturalism would not interfere with the embodiment of the conveyed metaphorical task.[17]

The argument that follows this has curious kinks and turns. Eisenstein considers that the defects of American editing arise from their ideological limitations. The Soviet filmmakers in the early days of silent movies, on the other hand, had the works of Marx and his successors to show them the way to true synthesis. Thus their epoch, "sharply ideal and intellectual," found in the "juxtaposition of shots an arrangement of a new qualitative element, a new image, a new understanding."[18] This overemphasis on intellectual meaning, however, pushed them into excesses (though the examples he cites, from October [Oktiabr], seem to be described more with pride than with regret). He then takes off on a tangent to discuss metaphor in language, and concludes that primitive metaphor stands at the dawn of language. "It is not surprising, therefore," Eisenstein writes, "that the period of the birth of articulate montage speech of the future had also to pass through a sharply metaphorical stage."[19] The excesses were a necessary step on the way to discovering the true nature of cinema language.

Thus the secret of the structure of montage was gradually revealed as a secret of the structure of emotional speech. For the very principle of montage, as is the entire individuality of its formation, is the substance of an exact copy of the language of excited emotional speech.[20]

Here we see emerging Eisenstein's conviction that artistic forms have close correspondence to primitive inner mental laws, although the latter part of the essay moves toward a restatement of an organic theory of art. Early cinema erred in placing too much emphasis on juxtaposition and "contemplative dissection," instead of "an emotional fusion in some new quality."[21] Eisenstein is vague as to what precisely this new quality is, but his concluding remarks suggest that he conceived it as "a unity of a higher order – a means through the montage image of achieving an organic embodiment of a single idea conception, embracing all elements, parts, details of the film-work."[22]

Although the essay is hardly a model of consecutive thought and unambiguous definitions, it is extremely suggestive in the way it touches on many of the problems relating to cinematic metaphors. For our purposes certain crucial points may be abstracted from it:

1. Because of the representational nature of film, juxtaposition of montage units alone may not be successful in producing viable metaphors.
2. The units have to be suitably stylized through lighting, framing, and so on, for the purpose of metaphor, so that the spectator is guided in his reading and integrating of them.
3. The principles governing the selection and stylization of the units should derive from the overall unity of the filmmaker's conception.
4. The meaning expressed must not only be an integrated one, but must represent a new quality, an extended dimension of significance – that is, it must be figurative, not literal.

Interestingly, hostile criticisms of Eisenstein's film practice often allude to just such points. Siegfried Kracauer, for instance, takes his stand upon the representational nature of film. He complains that Eisenstein's use of "objects as signs or symbols voids the shots of them of their inherent meanings." He regards the intrinsic representational character of images as being so at odds with figurative communication that spectators may be left with "an aimless assemblage" rather than with a significant trope.[23] John H. Fell sees the problem rather as one of integrating levels of discourse. Employing metaphor in films is rendered difficult by "our commitment to illusionistic narrative," and he goes on to argue that the cross-cutting between Kerensky and the peacock in *October* disrupts the seeming reality of a reenacted event: "What is a peacock doing in the Czar's palace?"[24] Eisenstein's stylization of his images has often been denounced as mere "mannerism," the most notorious expression of this charge being made by the director of the Soviet Film Office when he stopped the making of *Bezhin Meadow (Bezhin Lug)*.[25] The inadequacy of the filmmaker's conception has also been regarded as responsible for the deficiencies of Eisenstein's montage metaphors. It is felt that the comparisons are made in a crude and heavy-handed way, and are too often dependent on prefilmic stereotypes (e.g., as vain as a peacock). The generating ideas, far from being fertile and exploratory, or breaking down our hidebound categories, tend to be simplistic and doctrinaire. Peter Harcourt, for instance, cites the Kerensky sequence – rightly in my view – as an example not only of political oversimplification but also of moral falsity for the way it invites a smug response.[26] Charles Barr argues that, since Eisenstein's aim is always propaganda, there is no genuine exploration of issues by him, and consequently there cannot be any by the spectator. "The spectator 'interprets' but there is no genuine freedom of association." Unification is achieved "only in a mechanical way, and there is only one correct solution. The very last thing Eisenstein really wants us to do is to evaluate for ourselves, or even experience for ourselves, what we are shown."[27]

These criticisms may call into question aspects of Eisenstein's success as a filmmaker, but in doing so they reinforce the validity of the points already adumbrated, showing Eisenstein's awareness of how these issues are all interconnected and cannot be considered separately. In this Eisenstein is, in his theory at any rate, less one-sided than his critics: Kracauer, for instance, clearly emphasizes the representational nature of film at the expense of other possibilities, whereas Eisenstein recognizes that counterpulling tendencies have to be reconciled and transcended. Although I share some of his critics' doubts about certain of his actual montage metaphors, I am inclined to blame their relative failure on Eisenstein himself — enthusiasm for the revolution in some of these instances carried him away from his duty as an artist and he chose to honor political dogmas instead of a critical openness. But he is not the first or the last artist-theoretician whose practice does not match the artistic goals he himself has formulated. His theoretical speculations remain seminal and challenging.

The centrality of the issues raised by Eisenstein will become more apparent if we consider in more detail what was only touched upon before — his remarks about the concept of inner speech. It is in the essay "Film Form: New Problems" that Eisenstein sets out the claim that the same laws that govern inner speech are those behind the form and composition of artworks.[28] He also attempts to delineate some of these laws. A contrast is established between what might be termed ordinary discursive thought (i.e., speech that has been logically formulated) and inner speech, which is at the stage of (what Eisenstein calls) "image sensual structure." It appears that Eisenstein envisages this mode of thought as belonging to an earlier stage of mankind's cultural evolution, though — since there is no absolute divide between us and so-called primitive societies — modern man has not left it behind in his development. But the observation of it in earlier societies, where it manifests itself in norms of custom and ritual behavior, helps us to make explicit some of its fundamental principles, thus more clearly enabling us to see how these also apply to artistic techniques underlying our own artworks.

In "early thought processes"[29] there is no clear distinction between part and whole. If one receives an ornament, for instance, of a bear's tooth, it signifies that the whole bear (or, what amounts to the same thing, the bear's strength) has been passed on to one. Eisenstein comments, "No one, having received a button off a suit, would imagine himself to be dressed in the complete suit. But as soon even as we move over into the sphere of artistic constructions, the same *pars pro toto* begins immediately to play a tremendous part as well."[30] He proceeds in this connection to cite the scene in *Battleship Potemkin* (*Bro-nenosets Potemkin*) where the throwing overboard of the ship's surgeon is signified by a shot of his pince-nez dangling in the rigging. Thus this cinematic synecdoche is related to the psychological principle that makes it possible.

Similar parallels are drawn between artistic practice and other psychological manifestations. For example, the demand in art that all elements must sound the same key (illustrated by *King Lear* where the inner tempest echoes the tempest on the heath) is based on more atavistic yearnings for correspondences. Such yearning is illustrated by a practice of the Polynesians, who at the time of childbirth arrange for all things nearby to be untied and open so as to ease the passage of the child into the world. Another psychological principle is that of taking image as object. This may be observed in the "regressive" behavior of the girl who tears into fragments the photograph of her unfaithful lover; she is reenacting the magical operation of destroying someone by destroying their image. (Indeed, how often in films have we not seen a person's self-loathing depicted by the smashing of the image in the mirror?)

Of course, Eisenstein was not alone in taking peoples "still at the dawn of culture"[31] as representatives of nonlogical, nonrational modes of seeing connections. The reports and observations of anthropologists, such as Lévy-Bruhl, on the "savage" mind, had stimulated much interest and speculation. Allied discussions were not uncommon. Sigmund Freud's notion of myths being the "precipitates" of unconscious processes as expounded in *Totem and Taboo* and elsewhere is an obvious example. In 1925, Ernst Cassirer had, in the second volume of *Die Philosphie der symbolischen Formen*,[32] attempted a systematic study of the symbolic modes of thought present in primitive myth. Much in Cassirer's volume offers a remarkable parallel to Eisenstein's contentions. A passage, where Cassirer discusses the false analogies "legitimated" by the logic of mythic thinking, shows this.

The typical contrast between myth and cognition can be shown in the category of similarity no less than in the categories of the whole and the part and the attribute. The articulation of the chaos of sensory impressions, in which definite groups based on similarities are picked out and specific series are formed, is, again, common to both logical and mythical thinking; without it myth could no more arrive at stable configurations than logical thought at stable concepts. But the similarities of things are, once again, apprehended in different directions. In mythical thinking any similarity of sensuous manifestation suffices to group the entities in which it appears into a single mythical "genus." Any characteristic, however external, is as good as another; there can be no sharp distinction between "inward" and "outward," "essential" and "nonessential," precisely because for myth every perceptible similarity is an immediate expression of an identity of essence.... For where we see a mere analogy, i.e. a mere relation, myth sees immediate existence and presence.... The thing is present as a whole, as soon as anything similar to it is given.[33]

Indeed, in reading this the reader may well have been reminded of what was said in Chapter II about the construction of chiming metaphors – that is, those metaphors where some arbitrary similarity of rhyme, alliteration, or assonance is utilized to yoke two quite disparate ideas. Why do we so often feel, say, that a rhyme links in some significant and not accidental way two crucial words and their referents? Is there not about this some element of serendipity, perhaps even of primitive magic?

Certainly Eisenstein, in connecting inner speech with what is primitive or regressive, came to ask a question that seems to arise directly from such considerations. Is art, he asked, "nothing else but an artificial retrogression in the field of psychology towards the forms of earlier thought processes?"

In the answer he gave, Eisenstein was to insist that art must penetrate "layers of profoundest sensual thinking" while combining this with its opposite, highly conscious understanding and striving. I shall not at this point pursue the implications of Eisenstein's answer – that will be postponed until Chapter VII. Suffice to say now that Eisenstein's answer demonstrates once again that, in his turning to the cinema as the art that combined in one the most expressive properties scattered among the other arts, he came to demand of the film artist an integration of personal dedication with an impersonal intellectual quest; and that he attempted to show, by his example as by his teaching, how creativity could go hand in hand with a sound exposition of artistic principles.

N. Roy Clifton

N. Roy Clifton is a Canadian who, for many years, kept a record of the tropes and schemes he had observed in films. His subsequent published study, *The Figure in Film*,[34] containing as it does some sixteen hundred examples drawn from more than seven hundred films, is the most thorough demonstration of cinema's use of rhetorical devices yet attempted. The existence of a wide range of rhetorical figures – many of them, as I argued in Chapter II, themselves metaphorical or serviceable to metaphor – is proved beyond any shadow of doubt.

At the beginning of his book Clifton acknowledges that "a figure cannot be treated in isolation from other figures" and goes on to say that "this will remind the reader that an image may combine several figures, or be seen as different figures from different viewpoints."[35] Bearing this disclaimer in mind, Clifton proceeds systematically to

identify particular cinematic tropes and schemes, while frequently noting that there may be other categories into which the illustrations
might be fitted, depending on how they are read. This strategy seems
viable, and it has rewards. Even where the examples cited might be
challenged by someone who feels that the link between that category
and a particular film sequence is questionable, the illustrations themselves are full of interest, are concisely described, and are well expounded. Most, however, seem not only apt but they serve to show
how permeated films are with rhetorical constructions.

The following is given as an illustration of Clifton's method. Under
the subheading, "Anastrophe – The Unusual in Film – Angle," he first
explains the term:

Anastrophe is an unusual arrangement, an inversion of what is logical or normal, in literature of the words of a sentence, in film of the image, in angle, in
focus, and in lighting. It comprises all forms of technical distortion. It is
clearly a figure to be used rarely, and it is not always certain if it has the effect intended.[36]

Clifton then asks, "What could be more unusual or inverted than
showing someone upside down?" He considers several scenes where
the image is rendered topsy-turvy. I cite one of these:

Again, in the *Ballad of a Soldier* (Grigori Chukhrai), one of two signalmen is
killed, and the other runs, pursued by a German tank. In a down air shot, the
camera pans with tank and man, and at one point the scene turns, placing the
ground up, the sky bottom right, the chase continuing. Is it the disoriented
panic of the man fleeing wildly without plan, or the manic mind of the tank
driver, pursuing one man, when he should be addressing himself to the destruction of companies, when, in fact, he could shoot? A bizarre act seems to
call for an anastrophic treatment.[37]

Clifton attempts to retain as far as possible the distinctions recognized by classical rhetoric in the figures he examines, while bending
them where necessary to the specifically cinematic. His endeavor to
keep the figures distinct as far as possible deserves respect, and it
contrasts with the tendency that might be detected in my book to con-
flate many figures under the grand protean heading of metaphor.[38]
Thus, where I have subsumed cinematic simile under the wider functioning of metaphor, Clifton maintains the distinction.

Basically, he considers cinematic simile to consist in the drawing
attention to a likeness amid difference:

To create a simile is to choose or abstract from one total event a single characteristic it shares with another. Then differences between the events, however
great, are ignored. The greater they are, indeed, the more striking the simile
becomes.[39]

Like myself, Clifton recognizes this must entail a "marking" of the figure in some way.

The director must have an eye for the narrow lune of likeness where things that are highly unlike overlap and thus abstract a new class of things, defined as having this trait in common. He must also be able to shoot or edit them in such a way as to make this common trait so clearly visible that the word "like" leaps to the viewer's mind.[40]

An example Clifton provides of how such directorial marking may come about is the following, which also serves to illustrate the distinction he feels exists between simile and metaphor proper.

When we see the peasant Khymr, head hanging down, asleep on the driver's seat of a water tank, and the horse in the shafts down on its knees, head also drooping, the director is clearly saying, "Like teamster, like horse," we add the word "like" and make it a simile (*Happiness*, Aleksandr Medvedev).[41]

Here the two sides of the figure exist in equal balance as it were, and are separable. Whereas in metaphor proper, Clifton contends, "the two members blur into one, the image and the meaning beyond being taken in at the same moment, as if the image had lost its own identity and could only convey the figurative meaning contrived for it."[42]

Whether a figure be a simile, a metaphor, or some other trope, Clifton holds the view that the audience is involved in the creation of the figure. He considers it clear from examples he cites that "the viewers themselves must make the metaphor: they are given cement and gravel, but they must mix the concrete."[43] What "making the metaphor" means is not really explained, although perhaps the multitude of examples do offer some kind of ostensive definition. Clearly, however, some form of cocreation is envisaged. The director provides the means, but the connections must be made by viewers themselves. Those who cannot do this – well, it is just their hard luck. Further, Clifton prefers figures that make demands on us, and he seems to think poorly of metaphors that can hardly be missed, so little is left for one to do.[44] Generally, he goes by his own intuition and assumes that if he detects a metaphor, the chances are that the director put it there. He does acknowledge, however, that on occasions different viewers might make something different of the same sequence. He also recognizes the need to place some restrictions on the personal freedom to make what one sees mean what one wishes. Thus he writes,

I merely assume that as a director has deliberately assembled what we see in the frame, and the order in which the frame comes before us, if what I find appears to be a figure, I am justified in *giving whatever meanings an average viewer would.*

There are two qualifications to this. First, it must be clear from the context there was no reason for shooting or editing the image the way it was done, other than metaphorical. Second, if the style of the director's work as a whole does not run to metaphor, it would be rash to find a metaphorical intent in a single scene.[45]

This is about the nearest one finds in Clifton's book to the statement of a hermeneutic principle. In general, he eschews theoretical discussion, and such rules as he advocates tend to be straightforward and pragmatic. The book is not necessarily the weaker for such a common-sense approach. Indeed, much of the book's merit lies in the dialectic exchange it continually invites: The reader must, from example to example, enter into a silent dialogue, asking questions such as, "Is that figure really there? Is that what it signifies? Is that how it fits in?" Disagreement can often be as stimulating and illuminating for the reader as agreement. It is to the credit of the book that it looks with lively intelligence at images and draws the reader into doing the same.

Having said that theorizing is not a major interest of the book, it may seem then somewhat carping if I take up some points of theory for comment. I do so, however, because the issues thus raised have bearings on arguments I engage in elsewhere in this book.

First, I would like to take up Clifton's use of the term *image,* for his decision to use it the way he does affects what he says about the structure of metaphors. Clifton sees a need to keep his usage of image clearly distinct from its usage in the study of literature, where it has long been employed as a synonym for trope. Therefore he writes that, "Film consists of arrangements, not of words but of images. The word 'horse' is decoded by the mind on its way to the image *horse;* in film there is no word, only image.... in this book the word is used only for the pattern projected on the screen, black and white or colored."[46] But there are some disadvantages to defining it so. For one thing, sounds are also part and parcel of films, and aural stimuli have as much right as visual ones to be considered images. Then the discussion here (and elsewhere) omits a consideration of how an image relates to its referent. This point is important, as often there is a tension between the image we actually see on the screen and the object it is an image of. For example, when a swirling dancer is filmed from above, the image that appears is as much of a flower as of a human performer. The distinction between object and image raises questions, delineated elsewhere in my book, about the film image as a sign, and what it shares and does not share with verbal signs. The failure to take such considerations into account leads to undesirable consequences when image is used as a term defining one side of a metaphor.

Cinematic metaphor has two parts, according to Clifton: "an image on the screen, and some event or idea compared with it, together giving a visible form to an attitude or comment."[47] Actually, what this sentence affirms, while denying it, is that metaphor has three parts, not two. Metaphor is tripartite in structure, not dualistic. There is (1) the image; and (2) some event or idea compared with it – these first two parts might be said to constitute the *interpretans* of the metaphor; and then (3) the attitude or comment – the *interpretand,* as it were. The absence of due attention to part 3 in the original statement leads to confusion when Clifton proposes a term of his own as the name for part 2. First, Clifton cites I. A. Richards's coinage of terms to describe parts 1 and 2: "The event in the narrative with which the tenor deals he calls the *tenor,* the comparison that carries the comment he calls the *vehicle.*" But to cite no more is to misrepresent Richards, for he goes on to say that the meaning of a metaphor arises from the interaction of tenor and vehicle. He emphasizes that the meaning is not normally to be identified with the tenor alone – nor, for that matter, should it normally be identified with the vehicle alone.[48] When Clifton comes to propose his own terms for the two parts of a metaphor, this admonition appears forgotten. Having already suggested that *image* should constitute one half, he suggests that the term naming the second half should be *gloss,* and he explains the term and his reasons for choosing it as follows:

> The other part or extreme [of a filmic metaphor] embodies the director's attitude, or his gloss or comment on it. Of these three, I suggest "gloss." "Gloss" (from the Greek) is a word of explanation inserted in a text, or a comment on, or interpretation of it; and "gloss" (from the German) is a surface luster added to an object. In both cases the original remains, but the gloss has added enrichment. The gloss is also a glass, through which we see the image differently; or a glaze to color an image that could exist without it. All these are ways of saying what a metaphor does, being as it is an image on the screen, enriched by a gloss or glaze added by the director.[49]

It might be thought from this explanation that Clifton's gloss added by the director was equivalent to Richard's borrowed idea, or the vehicle. But when Clifton illustrates his usage with examples, it becomes clear not only that there is some inversion of the terms but that he uses gloss to refer both to the tenor and to the meaning created by the interplay of tenor and vehicle. I quote only the first of his three illustrations.

> When her lodgers realize that Mrs. Wilberforce will certainly confess to the police her nonexistent guilt, and implicate them, they sit glumly around the room. Louis makes the decision: he snaps open his springknife, and throws it at the tabletop, where the point of the knife embeds in close-up. The image is the embedded knife, but the gloss is clear: Mrs. Wilberforce must die (*The Lady Killers,* Alexander Mackendrick).[50]

Now if I read Richards aright, an account using his terminology would go something like this: The tenor of the scene – that is, the event in the narrative, the principal subject – would be the resolve to kill Mrs. Wilberforce. The literal way to present this would be for the character to say, "I think we have to kill her," or words to that effect. Instead of a verbal statement, an action is substituted: the borrowed idea, the imagined nature, in other words, the vehicle.[51] The meaning of the metaphor, depending as it does on interaction, is more than the idea "Mrs. Wilberforce must die"; expressed also are the ruthlessness and violence implicit in the decision.

From what I say it would follow that Clifton, in the use of his terms, is confusing *interpretand* with aspects of the *interpretans.* This is regrettable, particularly as *gloss* has an admirable suggestiveness. I think it is specially apt to describe those sequences where a landscape, say, is made to seem menacing or romantic by the glaze of music that has been superadded to the image. But unless Clifton's terms can be made consistent with Richards's, his usage is likely to create muddle.

Fortunately, having coined his terms, Clifton does not employ them often, the range of his illustrations with their accompanying commentaries not being restricted in any way by them. Most of his observations do not depend on them, and derive instead from untendentious and free-ranging perception.

A case in point is Clifton's sensible treatment of dead cinematic metaphors. These metaphors have lost their charge, and we are apt to forget they are metaphors until some clash in context temporarily revives their latent force, not always to the film's advantage. Most up and down shots Clifton considers to be dead metaphors. He is also very interesting on the closing of a door as a subdued metaphor whose figurative suggestiveness directors ignore at their peril. (Reading what he had to say, I was reminded of Coppola's excellent use of it in *The Godfather, Part II* where the Don [Al Pacino] shuts his wife out of the house when he has found her visiting their children, and we are made to realize with horror that he is not only closing the door on his wife but is cutting himself off irrevocably from all life-giving relationships.)

It is, perhaps, worth noting that when Clifton offers his own list of dead metaphors (i.e., figures he has seen so often that they are now clichés), they fall into distinct categories. I list some of them, but using my own typology:

1. birds that rise in the sky after death, the flight of the soul (*The Passion of Joan of Arc*) – juxtaposition metaphor;
2. the windblown sheets of a calendar pad, the passing of days (*Scarface*) – in part synecdoche (because the calendar is associated with time), in part substitution (because the wind fluttering the leaves implies days swept along);

3. people who seem confined in body or mind seen through the geometry of gates or fences – juxtaposition metaphor;
4. newspapers rolling off the presses standing in for the millions who read that news – metonymy.

In this last case, any metaphorical meaning is lost unless something about the way the papers themselves have been filmed illuminates an aspect of the readers themselves. Richards's criterion provides a useful rule-of-thumb method for detecting whether a metaphor has become so dead it is virtually a literal statement: He says, "If we cannot distinguish tenor from vehicle we may provisionally take the word to be literal; *if we can distinguish at least two co-operating uses, then we have metaphor.*"[52]

There is a wealth of material in the pages of Clifton's book, and the book is a delight to dip into. By bringing such a wide range of cinematic figures before us for our scrutiny, Clifton has made a significant contribution to film studies.

Christian Metz

In the fourth, and longest, section of his book *Psychoanalysis and Cinema: The Imaginary Signifier*[53] Christian Metz turns his attention to the study of metaphor and metonymy. Where, in general, N. Roy Clifton wishes to show how rhetorical categories are relevant to the study of cinematic figures and tropes, Metz sets himself a more ambitious task. As he considers it both hopeless and arbitrary to apply the rules of one system (classical rhetoric) to another (cinema), he therefore believes what has to be done is to discover the underlying principles that must apply as much to film as to verbal texts.[54]

Metz advances one specific reason for thinking classical rhetoric to be inadequately equipped for the analysis of cinematic figures. While acknowledging that classical rhetoric has down the centuries been concerned with the examination of rhetorical constructions that are by no means restricted to single words, treating as it often does with what appears in phrases or whole sentences,[55] Metz argues that for us today rhetoric has become merely a catalog of word-based figures.[56] This emphasis on the word then, rather than on wider segments of meaning, makes it impossible, for example, for classical rhetoric to deal with such cinematic figures as the flock-of-sheep image at the beginning of Chaplin's *Modern Times*. (It should, perhaps, be noted that, despite references to I. A. Richards and Stephen Ullman, Metz seems largely unaware of the extensive work done on metaphor by British and American scholars. It seems also a pity that he could not have been acquainted with Paul Ricoeur's *La Métaphore vive,* which appeared the same year as his own book, for Ricoeur devotes considerable attention to the way metaphor functions in larger units, and he draws finely on the classical tradition of writing about metaphor.)

Rejecting classical rhetoric as a useful source, Metz turns to other realms of thought – first, as he has in previous publications, to linguistics, and in particular to the type of linguistic thought associated with Ferdinand de Saussure and Roman Jakobson. Certainly a new impetus to the discussion of metonymy was given by Jakobson[57] when he argued that different types of aphasic disturbance suggested that the mental mechanisms underlying metaphor and metonymy were distinct. In the same influential publication he surmised that the distinction between metaphor and metonymy might be seen as related to the distinction made by linguists between syntagmatic and paradigmatic organization.[58] Metz spends some time discussing this supposition.

Although Metz finds interesting the homology between on the one hand metonymy–metaphor and on the other syntagmatic–paradigmatic, he concludes that the dualisms are not to be conflated. The main reason he advances goes something like this. Syntagmatic ordering relates to contiguity in the plane of discourse (i.e., how words stand beside one another on the page); and paradigmatic selection, though semantic, relates to positional similarity in the plane of discourse as well. By contrast, metonymy and metaphor depend on contiguity or on similarity in the "referents" of the words. (That is, we use *crown* for a monarch because monarchs actually wear crowns; and we can coin the metaphor because ships cutting furrows in the waves do actually look like ploughs throwing aside the earth.) It should be noted, however, that in using the word *referent* Metz means by it "real or imaginary" things signified by the words. In employing this particular argument Metz is not saying anything new or startling. Indeed, I. A. Richards, to take one example, said many years ago that metaphor was "a borrowing between and intercourse of thoughts" and not just "a shifting and displacement of words."[59] Richards, however, qualified this later in the same series of lectures by taking up the issue of words being "the meeting points at which regions of experience ... come together," thus making apparent that no easy separation of verbal and semantic levels is possible. Metz is more interested, however, in holding to a clear-cut division between what is in the "plane of discourse" and what is not. For one thing, it gives him the opportunity to construct a classificatory scheme. Employing the four sets of terms, he is able to set up what is, in effect, a taxonomic table:

Metaphor + Syntagmatic presentation	Metaphor + Paradigmatic presentation
Metonymy + Syntagmatic presentation	Metonymy + Paradigmatic presentation

(It is I who have set it out in tabular form to make what he says apparent in a simple glance.) Having drawn up these compartments, though, Metz does very little with them. He certainly does not attempt any sorting out of cinematic figures by means of them. This may be due in part to Metz's intention of concerning himself more with "operations" than with "localised metaphors or metonymies that could be isolated."[60] It may also be due in part to Metz's skepticism – at times amounting to virtual denial – of taxonomic categories. He speaks, for example, of "the taxonomic illusion"[61] that something cannot be fitted into more than one compartment. Throughout the essay Metz emphasizes the way concepts overlap, intersect, collaborate, interact, even merge. These assertions, however, are contiguous with equally assiduous endeavors to demonstrate how various binary divisions may be employed in conjunction to formulate complex taxonomic schemes. (I shall illustrate this point more fully later.) The coexistence of somewhat incompatible attitudes makes it difficult at times to know where Metz is aiming to go, or what he thinks will be achieved should he arrive.

Metz's strategy of keeping apart the plane of discourse and the plane of reference has another consequence. It leads him later to claim that it is most unusual for the signifier itself to be altered by a semantic idea or admixture of ideas. An example of such an alteration is what, in English, is known as a portmanteau word – for example, "workaholic." Metz sees this as something quite special, unlike the workings of metaphor or metonymy at all. "There hardly exists," he asserts, "a concept of metaphor or metonymy in which these figures affect the phonic or graphic element of words."[62] This can only be received with astonishment by English-speaking readers, at any rate, well accustomed to Shakespeare's puns, Herbert's and e. e. cummings's graphic tricks, not to mention the way the sound is regularly made to echo the sense by the thrust in poetry of rhythm and rhyme. A book on how poetry works – such as, say, Winifred Nowottny's – demonstrates beyond question that such indeed is the language as poets use it.[63] When then Metz goes on to say, "The present day partisans of the binary approach have moreover never attempted to make the connection: alliteration, apophony and the like are simply not mentioned. The task was in any case impossible because these figures have nothing to do with the referent...,"[64] we can only wonder what literary criticism he has been reading. Has he perhaps put completely out of his mind Jakobson's famous (some might say infamous) dictum that: "The poetic function projects the principle of equivalence from the axis of selection to the axis of combination"?[65] Anyway, this hiatus in Metz's thinking would suggest that he is not aware of how prevalent both distortion and chiming metaphors are. Metz also seems to be of the opinion that cinema alone distorts visual images – ignoring how distortion forms the basis of many metaphors in the plastic arts, ranging from the sly tricks of caricatures to Picasso's deployment of aggressive sexual imagery in many of his later etchings.

Still, whatever the shortcomings to be found in Metz's application of linguistic ideas to the analysis of metaphor and metonymy, the enterprise is clearly a rational one. Difficulty is really encountered, however, when Metz enters the other dimension of his argument, the application of psychoanalytic ideas. In part this is because of the status of these ideas, and the degree to which we are expected to accept them as unquestionable verities. Gaps in reading, as with Metz's lack of acquaintance with British and American scholars and their work on metaphor, are forgivable: Not even the most erudite scholar can claim to have read everything. But where some ideas are highly controversial, and we find no references to critics of those ideas, we may suspect an active censorship is at work. Metz is steeped in Freud's work, and in the commentary on and extension of that work by Jacques Lacan. But there is virtually no reference to rival schools of psychoanalytic thought (such as Jung's), and certainly none to the not insignificant body of critics who have called into question the scientific validity of Freudianism, or have asked for some evidence of the efficacy of psychoanalytic therapy as a means of curing the mentally sick. Metz demands his readers be as committed to the Freudian venture as he is. Indeed, Metz's aim is to advance the insights of Freud into new areas. Psychoanalysis is not merely a tool to be used and discarded, but an indispensable mode of understanding. It is not marginal to Metz's enterprise: On the contrary, it is the very heart of it.

This creates problems for those critics or scholars – probably most of us – who do not wholly take on trust the Freudian corpus, and who are even skeptical about claims parts of it make. (I find my own skepticism has been much invigorated by scrutinizing Metz's book.)

Often when reading a writer on art who employs Freudian ideas, the validity of those ideas in their own right does not become an issue.

We recognize that the writer is trying to illuminate the object of his attention by examining it in the light of an imported model. It is a form of "seeing as." The literal truth or falsity of the vehicle, the model brought into play, is not a matter for dispute. Thus there is no need to challenge terms such as *the pleasure principle* and *the reality principle* when reading some of Lionel Trilling's literary criticism,[66] any more than there is to concede existence to the Olympian gods when we come upon a critic who talks about artistic works exhibiting "Apollonian" or "Dionysian" qualities. But if we are taken by the lapels and told we must burn incense at some shrine to Apollo or join the Bacchic dances on the heights of Cithaeron, we may well feel that something more than the granting of imaginative sympathy is at stake.

Let me give an example of what I mean apropos of Metz. In one section of his book, "Disavowal, Fetishism," Metz produces an argument of the following nature. First he reminds the reader of Freud's linking of fetish and fetishism with castration fears. While summarizing Freud's views, and pointing out that Freud took them very literally, he goes on to call attention to Lacan's notion of "the scenario of castration" as an essentially "symbolic drama in which castration takes over in a decisive metaphor all the losses, both real and imaginary, that the child has already suffered (birth trauma, maternal breast, excrement, etc.)."[67] Metz develops the discussion, proposing that fear of loss of the organ leads to a fascination with a fetish. He writes: "The fetish always represents the penis, it is always a substitute for it, whether metaphorically (= it masks the absence) or metonymically (= it is contiguous with its empty place)."[68] Metz then attempts to see how this psychic drama manifests itself in "the cinematic perspective."[69] He discusses ways in which audiences receive the filmic illusion, in part accepting the happenings shown on the screen as "real" while at the same time knowing they are not. Metz goes on next to a brief, and unrelated, discussion of how cinematic subcodes "inscribe disavowal." Now comes the announcement, "As for the fetish itself, in its cinematic manifestations, who could fail to see that it consists fundamentally of the equipment (= its 'technique'), or of the cinema as a whole as equipment and as technique?"[70] Why should this be so? Well, "the fetish, like the apparatus of the cinema, is a *prop*, the prop that disavows a lack and in doing so affirms it without wishing to." So "the cinema fetishist is the person who is enchanted with what the machine is capable of."[71]

In miniature this demonstrates some of the problems facing the reader of Metz's book: problems of logic – because it is so often lacking; problems of evidence – because it is so often inadequate; problems of language – because it is jargon-ridden; and above all, problems of credulity – for who can credit this sort of nonsense?[72]

Bearing these factors in mind, let us now turn cautiously and critically to what Metz has to say about the psychoanalytic dimensions of metaphor and metonymy.

Metz is pleased to find a further homology that corresponds to that between metaphor–metonymy and the paradigmatic–syntagmatic. The pair of terms providing this new homology are condensation–displacement. (For reasons that should now be apparent, it is not possible to reproduce all the twists and turns of Metz's discussion. His use of psychoanalytic jargon, amounting at times to little less than terminological obfuscation, is particularly trying. But I will do my best to bring out salient features of his argument.)

Metz defines condensation as a "matrix of semantic convergence": It is a nodal point where various meanings coalesce, it is "a short circuit of disparate intensities."[73] Displacement is the transfer of energy from one focus to another. (I suppose an example might be from the penis or its absence to cinema technique.) How Freud spoke of condensation and displacement has to be understood, and so Metz considers various passages where he discusses them. Metz concludes, approvingly, that Freud came regularly to associate condensation and displacement with the "primary process" – that is, with the action of the unconscious, which leaves its stamp, in varying degrees, on all conscious activity (this latter being the "secondary process").

The prime function, Freud had suggested, of condensation and displacement is to smuggle things past the censor. They are, in effect, modes of disguising contraband mental material. This leads Metz into a lengthy discussion of the nature of the "censor." The censor protects the secondary process from that which would alarm it, but if censorship were perfect, as in an absolutist state, it would manage to conceal the fact that censorship was occurring. Only because the censorship is not absolute is it recognizable.[74] Its own self-contradictions reveal its activities, as conflicting items in the press might reveal what the authorities wish to hide. Furthermore, censorship is not to be thought of like a frontier that lets some through and bars others; rather, it lets through everything, but only after transformation, alteration, refraction.

In addition to his use of the technical language of psychoanalysis, Metz is prodigal in his employment of metaphors to describe psychic processes. Indeed, Metz himself calls attention to many of Freud's own metaphors. In particular, he notes how Freud's fundamental theory is set out in terms of two different-styled models, each with its own grouping of metaphors: the first model, that of "blind forces," being based on the "mechanics" scientifically fashionable in his day; the second on "symbolics," which provides descriptions associated with linguistic accounts. Freud's dependence on mixed sets of metaphor does not, however, lead Metz to question the literal reliability of Freud's explanations.

Metz concludes that the transfer of something from the primary process to the secondary is not unlike the changes brought about when translating from one language into another. He insists that any attempt to comprehend the workings of the primary process can only be done by means of the secondary process, and as the laws governing the two are radically different so our account of the primary process must inevitably misrepresent it. Metz emphasizes this point repeatedly. We can only know the unconscious through consciousness: We can never know it directly.[75]

I believe in some of the discussion on this issue Metz is inchoately sensing a problem, but one that he never quite brings into the open: If condensation is to be related to metaphor, and displacement to metonymy, first we have to know enough about their workings in the unconscious to identify crucial likenesses (something his argument makes difficult) to the workings of the rhetorical figures. But ab initio we are faced with one major disparity. *By definition,* within the Freudian system, the role of condensation and displacement is one of concealment. It becomes the analyst's function, consequently, to unravel the symbolic disguise, to trace it back, to sort out its components, to identify the disparities yoked together by condensation, or given masks by displacement. But if the function of condensation and displacement is to suppress expression, surely the opposite is the case with metaphor and metonymy, for they give expression to thought and feeling. What fascinates us about them is not normally where they began, but how apt and resonantly meaningful they are.

"Well," someone might say, wishing to counter this objection, "surely there are times when metaphor and metonymy are used to disguise what is being said, so only the alert or initiated will understand, whereas the dull or the ignorant will miss the point. Indeed, has not a school of literary criticism put forward something very like this, claiming that literature actually wraps meanings up so that the reader has to seek out explanations for himself?"[76] Yes, I would acknowledge all this. But the use of puns, fables, and allegories, as well as metaphors and metonymies, to deceive religious, social, or political censors still assumes that literary devices are in essence expressive, even if external circumstances may now and then force them to be obliquely or even circumspectly so. (Even then the roundaboutness itself often becomes a way of thumbing one's nose at the censors. Mae West, ostensibly subservient to the Hays office, is all the more Mae West abristle with sexual innuendo.) My point remains: The basic purpose of rhetorical figures is to *express* meanings, not *suppress* them.

As I said, this disparity is never actually brought to the surface by

Metz. But it is one that any Freudian account of metaphor and metonymy should face, particularly as there are rival theories of dreams – such as C. S. Hall's[77] – that see dreams as agents of expression. I suppose the most well-known alternative account is that of Jung, who held that the unconscious provides us with symbolic commentaries to warn or advise us. Metz does not even pause to consider any of these competing accounts.

Another facet of Metz's procedure requires critical consideration. As I remarked before, Metz is insistent on the impossibility of knowing the primary process directly. If its nature is so difficult to apprehend, being outside the realm of conscious experience, it would seem desirable that accounts of it by the secondary process be duly cautious; but Metz, in his descriptions of it, seems possessed by a remarkable confidence. I am not now merely thinking of passages where Metz invites us to imagine how the unconscious envisages the conscious[78] – these may be taken as mere flights of fancy, as cases of rhetoric going too far – but rather of those occasions when he asserts firm conclusions about how the unconscious "thinks." For example, he assures us that the "absence of the principle of non-contradiction"[79] plays a vital part in the processes of the secondary. How can he be sure that it is so totally absent there? We have, on the one hand, Metz claiming that we cannot "grasp it [the unconscious] by making it conscious," that we cannot "get hold of it,"[80] although how anything so intangible could become the basis of explanation is not clear. On the other hand, we have him dogmatizing as follows – and it must be remembered, when reading the passage, that displacement and condensation have been associated throughout with the primary:

In truth, displacement and condensation are not "qualities", still less "devices" of meaning. They are meaning itself (Kristeva's "*significance*"). Displacement is meaning as transit (as a flight from meaning), condensation is meaning as encounter (as meaning rediooovorod for the space of an instant), The horizontal and the vertical dimensions of meaning. And Jacques Lacan's two formulae which spring to mind again, inevitably: Condensation: "the structure of the superimposition of the signifiers, which metaphor takes as its field." Displacement: "that veering off of signification that we see in metonymy".[81]

Meaning itself! Metz is so sure what meaning is, and where it is to be found. (What a pity it is so hard to catch his meaning.) But it appears he does not consider meaning to be situated in the realm of conscious thought, with its principles such as the principle of noncontradiction.

Does Metz have much to teach us about cinematic metaphor itself? In my view, not a great deal. For one thing, he does not look at many actual examples – in all only about a dozen are mentioned in the fourth part of his book. On the very rare occasion when he examines one of these, he does what most critics do: He discusses the meanings that are generated by the play between tenor and vehicle. Here, for instance, is his lengthiest analysis of a cinematic metaphor:

There is a sequence in *Citizen Kane,* the film by Orson Welles, in which Kane's former butler is getting ready to tell the investigator about the sudden departure of the hero's second wife, Susan. He has just said: "Yeh, but I knew how to handle him. Like that time his wife left him." An ultra-rapid dissolve ushers in the close-up of a shrieking cockatoo (a little textual trauma: nothing has led us to expect it) which immediately flies away from the verandah where it was perched, revealing Susan who is crossing it hurriedly to leave Xanadu (the metonymic pretext, as you see, is extremely thin). It is the metaphor of flying away – which applies to Susan also, as when you say that "the bird has flown" – of a sudden, cacophonous, compulsive soaring, over-compensating in the idea of something completely unpremeditated (= the gesture of the bird) for the long years of weakness and of putting up with it which the film has previously evoked: a real syntagmatic jolt for the spectator, as for the husband whom we see shortly afterwards, after a moment of reeling confusion, in an attack of impotent rage, wrecking the room of the woman who has left. And then the cockatoo, although it looks stupid (like Susan again) seems through the bad-tempered violence of its cry wanting to provoke Kane, and taunt him; it is something of the hero's very power, of his capacity to dominate, which has just flown away: a discreet surfacing of the phallic resonance which our culture associates with the theme of the bird. Via this multiplicity of superimposed associations (I have mentioned only a few), the metaphor accomplishes something of the work of condensation.[82]

Although one might wish to qualify some points here – for example, the associations attaching to a cockatoo are not those attaching to a cock – it is a reasonable exposition of the metaphor. A pity there is not more discussion of this nature in the book. (Though could not all this have been said without jargon, perhaps even without the preconceptions that give rise to the jargon?)

Of course, as I remarked earlier, Metz conceives his task as one of analyzing "operations" rather than localized figures. I am not wholly sure what he means by this,[83] but I think his treatment of the lap-dissolve is intended as a paradigm of operational analysis. And it is in this discussion that Metz brings together all his twinned pairs of terms, and attempts to show how they may be used in concert.

He now has four twinned pairs:

metaphor–metonymy
paradigmatic–syntagmatic
condensation–displacement
primary process–secondary process.

A taxonomic arrangement of them is possible. First, however, Metz suggests that whereas paradigmatic and syntagmatic are mutually exclusive concepts, all the others are polar pairings, and it makes sense to consider whether something partakes more, say, of metaphor than of metonymy. The weighting of the most active member of a pair can be placed. This said, Metz gives his proposed procedure.

It seems to me that real progress could be made (at the present time) if critics were to undertake the task of situating filmic figures in relation to four independent axes: any one figure is secondarised to a greater or lesser extent; closer to metaphor, or closer to metonymy, or a clear mixture of the two; manifests condensation especially, or displacement especially, or an intimate combination of the two operations; is syntagmatic or paradigmatic.[84]

I shall summarize what happens when Metz considers how the lap-dissolve stands in relation to the four axes.

Is the lap-dissolve condensation or displacement? Metz decides it is both. Insofar as two images are mingling and coming to coexist, it is condensation; insofar as one image is displacing another, we have displacement. If this seems self-evident and trite, and clearly deriving from the definitions originally provided of condensation and displacement, then that is because I have stripped away the jargon Metz uses.

Is the lap-dissolve primary or secondary? Since we cannot experience the primary, this might seem a meaningless question to some – a twentieth-century equivalent, perhaps, to medieval arguments about the number of angels that can dance on the head of a pin. But Metz takes it seriously. The lap-dissolve, he proposes on the one hand, has secondary features because there is a time when the two images are distinguishable (as in the principle of separation), and also because it belongs to an acknowledged code of film punctuation. On the other hand, two signifiers are combined, and this combination partakes of the primary process and the way it fabricates dream imagery.

But what, asks Metz, if someone protests about this answer, invoking "the regimented way of the dissolve and the total obviousness of what is going on"? The response Metz gives to this is revealing. First, he falls back on a ploy Freudians are now notorious for using, one that leads people not to take Freudians seriously: He says that the objector can be "only speaking the language of defence, of resistance." Next he says that "a certain vigour of the secondary is often evidence of the primary." How do we know this is so of the dissolve? Well, it "explains the fact that the dissolve was used for such a long time, and so frequently." But supposing we wanted to come back at this and ask: Why then is the lap-dissolve so little used now? Has the primary given up invigorating it? Is the unconscious subject to fashions? Metz does not seem to have thought the argument through that far.

Syntagmatic or paradigmatic? Again, the answer only reveals the triteness of Metz's discussion. Since the dissolve is a way of linking two shots (i.e., making them contiguous), and since the syntagm is the name for contiguous organization, it follows that the dissolve is syntagmatic!

Metaphor, metonymy, or both? Quoting Metz:

It all depends, here, on the relationship between the initial image and final image. Insofar as they come together for reasons to do with the plot, or on the basis of some stable proximity known both to the film-maker and the spectator, the movement forward is metonymic; if it plays on a similarity or a contrast, it is metaphorical.[85]

In other words, we have to look at the images themselves, see how they relate, and then consider which of our original definitions is most appropriate in this particular case. (This resort to specific content and context, of course, makes nonsense of the claim that we can discuss "operations" in themselves.)

As if to dodge the banality of his first answer to the question, Metz provides a second, and different, answer. The "lap-dissolve, though it isn't purely metonymic, shows a remarkable *capacity to metonymise.*" Why? Because it tends "to create a preexisting relationship after the event." How? By bringing together two images it restricts "the spectator's freedom to think that the two elements it associates might not be contiguous in some referent."[86] But surely it would be simpler, and truer, just to say that the association of two images created by the prolonged transition of the lap-dissolve invites the spectator to seek connections between them? And that often the connections thus discovered are founded on more elaborate relationships than merely that of contiguity?[87]

To sum up, Christian Metz has produced an extremely elaborate and ingenious theory of cinematic metaphor. But does it have much substance? Certainly, one of its difficulties is that it relies heavily on Freudian dogmas. Query these, and much of the edifice crumbles. But even if all these were to be conceded, a fundamental difficulty would remain. It pertains to the nature of theory in regard to the arts.

Theories of all kinds are subject to a variety of tests to see whether they are valid or sound. The tests entail considerations such as the following:

Is the theory logically coherent and consistent?

Is it supported by relevant and significant evidence?

Is it elegant – which usually devolves into asking whether it is clearly expounded, and whether it is frugal in its employment of means to ends?

Has it predictive power?

Does it open promising lines of further research?

(and so on)

Where a theory relates to the arts there is one test that becomes very important: Does the theory illumine our understanding of the art it refers to, or – the issues are inseparable – does it enrich our experience of works that form the very basis of the art? The issues are inseparable because our knowledge of works of art is only acquired by experiencing them, and our grasp of genre, mode, or genus derives directly (and cannot be divorced) from that experiencing.[88] It follows that a theory must be *dispositional* – that is, it must affect how we perceive the works, and how we reflect upon our experience of them subsequently. Theories may meet this test to different degrees, and in many ways. The writing of a great theorist – Aristotle or Coleridge, say – may well permanently transform our reception of art. Or the influence may be more fleeting, yet still succeed in drawing our attention to something neglected in our previous appreciations. We may even reject a theory, only to find it has redirected where we look and how we feel.[89] Sometimes it may do little more than crystallize what was only sensed before, giving form and edge to inklings we took for granted. Pope's line is appropriate here: "What oft was Thought, but ne'er so well Exprest."

How does Metz's theory fare by such a test? Poorly, I fear. I do not mean that his work is devoid of insights into cinema art – for there are scattered observations to be found – but simply that such insights as there are do not derive from the theory constructed. Conversely, the theory itself does not emerge from any such insights. It originates not in a focus on cinema art, but in a fascination with linguistic and psychoanalytic notions, which themselves have little commerce with art. Hence the theory is developed at such remove from the actual experiencing of cinematic figures that it can offer virtually no purchase on such experience. It is theory evolved for the sake of theory, not for insight into art.[90] (Of course, it might be argued that Metz's intention is not so much to illuminate art, as to advance linguistic and psychoanalytic projects. The other tests then would be more applicable. I have already said enough to indicate why I do not think the theory would fare too well in that regard either.) Alas, although the means Metz employs are complex, the results are trite.

Metz takes his own enterprise very seriously.[91] By contrast, Roy Clifton is modest about his endeavor. But to my mind there can be little doubt which has the most to tell us about the fecundity and profusion of cinematic figures.

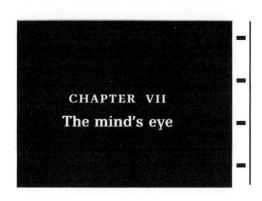

CHAPTER VII
The mind's eye

The mind is insatiable for meaning, drawn
from, or projected into, the world of appearances, for unearthing hidden analogies
which connect the unknown with the familiar, and show the familiar in an unexpected
light. It weaves the raw material of experience into patterns, and connects them with
other patterns; the fact that something reminds me of something else can itself become a potent source of emotion.
— Arthur Koestler[1]

Make visible what, without you, might perhaps never have been seen.
— Robert Bresson[2]

Introduction

Chapter V presented a number of cinematic metaphors, arranged according to types. Certainly, form may call attention to metaphors, and
some metaphors may be clustered together because they seem to share
a common structure. But often, depending on how a metaphor is read,
there will be dispute about how it should be classified. The rhetorical
theory, by placing too much stress on form, tends to suggest that it is
by such means that all metaphors are detected and subsequently interpreted. In Chapter II it was demonstrated that this was a fallacy, and
it was shown how metaphorical meanings can arise in unexpected
ways. Hence a definitive topology of metaphors is no more than a pipe
dream. Classification often depends on interpretation, and not vice
versa.

Another danger of the rhetorical theory is that it may lead to the belief that metaphors are merely stylistic and that they are desirable
solely because they are ornamental. Because ornaments are what we

97

add or remove, one consequence of this is to separate metaphor from the fundamental fabric of works of art. I have tried to oppose this tendency, in my analyses of metaphors throughout this book, by relating them to the larger context of the works in which they appear. Inevitably such exposition of metaphors raises issues relating to the totality of works of art, to their coherence, and the nature of their organization.

The imaginative theory of metaphor, by its emphasis on the making of patterns and the search for interplicit meanings, avoids many of the pitfalls of the rhetorical theory. In its focus on what Coleridge called the "esemplastic" powers of the mind, it directs attention to interrelationship and integration, and to the creation of emergent totalities. But the imaginative theory may also be the cause of misunderstandings and fallacies. By its concern with mental activity it can suggest that this is something purely internal and subjective. Extreme versions of the theory can descend into outright solipsism, and even milder variants may adopt a skeptical view of the degree to which people are able to share thoughts and feelings. How can one mind understand another? How can one person pass on to another his personal way of seeing connections and finding meanings? Even the notion that metaphor calls forth the creative powers of the person encountering it may lead to the conclusion that the maker does nothing and the recipient does it all. Such absurdities can be quite as harmful as the worst reductions of the rhetorical theory.

For this reason alone we need the two accounts of metaphor: They help to balance and correct one another. Yet even to say this may be misunderstood as positing a cleaving dualism. The situation need not be envisaged that way. The principle of complementarity claims no more than that we have two descriptions of metaphor, indeed two metaphors for metaphor, with each naturally drawing attention to different aspects. Either account by itself is inadequate; taken together a completer picture is possible. Where the rhetorical theory is concerned with signs and their localized organization, the imaginative theory is concerned with how we make sense of signs. One attends to formal properties, the other attends to mental operations. What makes the operations feasible are the signs, and the signs exist by reason of the operations.

A common error is to think that signs belong to the public domain, whereas mental operations do not – that they are private and idiosyncratic. Reflection soon shows this dichotomy to be false. What makes a sign a sign, and not just a noise, a squiggle, or a blotch is that it has intentional significance. It belongs to a system, and by virtue of that system is recognized to be a phoneme, or a B-flat, or a letter of the alphabet, or a word, or an image in a painting, or a photograph. The sign is no more, and no less, publicly accessible than the system it depends on for its existence as a sign. The system, which makes the sign's existence possible, and establishes how it may be operated with other signs, is no more private or inaccessible than the sign itself. But the system is a mental construction that is acquired through a socializing and socialized process (including learning what is a sign and what is not), and creates the possibility of further mental operations, including ones that may amend the system itself.

What I have simply referred to as the system will be immediately understood by some to be what linguists, following Saussure, have called *langue*. The mental operations I have spoken of they will take as the equivalent of the codes that semioticians claim govern the identification, utilization, and interpretation of signs. But Saussurean semiotics as a mode of explaining signs and meaning notoriously suffers from self-made difficulties. First, the dependence of langue on synchronic considerations only makes it impossible to explain certain kinds of creative changes in a language.[3] Second, the term *code* both conceals and misleads on important matters. It plays down the heterogeneity of the operations it is supposed to name, making it seem that laws, rules, principles, conventions, tones, registers, styles, moods, empathies, intuitions, and other means whereby we glean the purport of something, all function alike. Too much is swept under the one mat. At the same time the word carries the implication that all these things are equally susceptible to explicit formulation. The term code would impress upon us things we know are not true, and its use should be avoided as much as possible.

The reminder of these flaws in Saussurean semiotic theory, however, helps to focus our attention on the special importance of metaphor. For the study of metaphorical working does not need to rely on the notion of codes. Further, it inevitably focuses on the interplay between novelty and system, and consequently helps bridge the artificial division between the historical and the ahistorical that Saussurean structuralism assumes.[4]

That metaphor is a significant cause of words changing their meaning has long been acknowledged. Accounts of those changes, however, have usually been given in terms of the rhetorical theory. We have also seen, in Chapter VI, when applying a version of the rhetorical theory to cinematic metaphors, what fecundity of metaphors (and, it may be added, wealth of figurative meanings) is to be found, even within the structured restrictions of the formulas employed to identify the metaphors. What is needed now is a look at the way figurative meanings are related not so much to configurations of signs as to the modes of thought that produce them.

Two theories that endeavored particularly to explain how cinematic metaphors are generated and understood were discussed in the previous chapter. Both may be said to be more akin to imaginative accounts of metaphor than to rhetorical accounts. I refer, of course, to Metz's Freudian enterprise and to Eisenstein's proposals about inner speech. A further look at some of the problems and deficiencies of these theories will help us understand what an imaginative theory of cinematic metaphors should encompass.

Fallacies of the psychoanalytic approach

There have been many attempts, including some by Freud himself, to relate psychoanalysis to the study of art.[5] Some of the comments I shall now make apply to aspects of these as well as to Metz's version, but on the whole I shall be focusing on the ideas advanced by Metz.

Metz adopts a Lacanian reading of Freud. By doing so he plays down the causal element in many of Freud's concepts and arguments. But, as Metz himself shows, Freud regularly resorted to employing two main types of metaphor – the one set deriving from mechanics, the other from linguistics.[6] That is, Freud hovered between two incompatible modes of explanation – the causal and the intentional. For example, Freud's discussion of condensation and displacement stresses a causal mechanism at work. Suppressed *forces* interact with a *filtering* process and produce dreams. These forces constitute *wishes,* which the *censoring agency* disguises so as not to wake the dreamer. Analysis employs *free association,* enabling the patient to face suppressed *memories.* In the Freudian account causal and intentional terms are inextricably muddled together, and the result is a terrible hodgepodge. It is rather like explaining a move in chess by saying it was made because White's hand pushed the bishop there *and* threatened a mate in two moves. It is confusing one language game with another. What this critique leads to is the recognition that intentional behavior needs to be understood in terms of reasons. An imaginative account of metaphor must *offer explanations in terms of meanings, not in terms of causal factors.*

Any attempt to utilize Freud's theory for aesthetic purposes inherits another handicap. Although Freud believed in the universal application of his psychological scheme, it grew out of his attempts to treat neuroses. So, incorporated in his system from the very beginning was a sense of malaise and irrationality. It colored his account of the primary process and of the operations connected with it. We have observed how Metz, following Freud in his explanation of condensation and displacement, is led to seeing them as concealments of meaning rather than as expressions of meaning. Metaphors, however, are so prevalent, so ubiquitous in human discourse that any attempt to link them in the main with maladjustment and ailments of the mind must be far off the mark. An imaginative theory of metaphor must start from the premise that it is *dealing with something quite normal and everyday in human behavior.*

Another unfortunate legacy comes from Freud. He placed great emphasis on the essential irrationality and pleasure-seeking nature of the primary process, in contrast to the secondary process that he identified with rationality and the reality principle. If the making of metaphors is associated with the primary process, *so conceived,* the danger is that metaphor too will be tarred with the same brush: It will be regarded as a mode of discourse that is unreasonable and that seeks to evade reality. A psychoanalytic account of metaphor may easily then reinforce the long-held distrust of metaphor for its power to unsettle our fixed views of things and mold them anew. It is true that Metz, in his version of Freudian theory, does not regard metaphor as unhealthy, but that may be because he welcomes irrationality. I do not believe that an account of metaphor has to assume that the metaphorical process itself is irrational – though, of course, particular metaphors may be irrational in their import.

Even if it should be accepted that the unconscious plays a role in the creation of metaphors, it does not follow that this in itself implies that metaphorical conjunctions and the ensuing meanings are against reason. Indeed, this would only follow if it was entailed in the way the unconscious was defined. Freud, of course, never discovered the unconscious – evidence of its existence was long known.[7] What he did was to construct a particular model of it. It can well be objected that his model has serious shortcomings. In particular, there are many types of unconscious behavior of which it takes no account and for which it offers little explanation: pleasant memories, long buried; unrecognized assumptions; skills so made part of us, we take their possession for granted; inherited prowesses, biological or genetic; tacit knowledge; intuitive gropings and flashes.[8] Cognitive psychology is beginning to expand the understanding of our mental processes, and to reveal aspects of the mind's behavior not dreamed of in Freudian psychology.[9] It has even begun to publish some interesting results of empirical enquiries into the workings of metaphor,[10] at least one of which I shall have more to say about later. Metz restricts the scope of his psychological enquiry into cinematic metaphor far too narrowly by relying solely on Freud's model of the primary process.

Freud, for instance, connects condensation and displacement with childhood memories and suppressed wishes. Consequently the meanings of dream images relate to the dreamer's personal history. He also posits that many of the traumas people experience may be traced back to common origins – to Oedipal conflicts, for example. But it is to commit the genetic fallacy to identify the meaning of a work of art with its origins. Certainly, with Freud's own example before them, this is what some Freudian critics have chosen to do. One cannot accuse Metz of this.[11] But on the few occasions when he looks at specific cinematic metaphors, he is never able to bring his exposition of the condensed meaning found in them (which relates to the story and themes of the film) into line with Freud's definition of condensation (which relates to the private past of an individual).

We have already seen in virtually all our analyses of metaphor that the whole is more than the sum of the parts. An imaginative theory of metaphor must *focus on emergent meanings then, and on the public accessibility of such meanings.*

There is one other major flaw in the psychoanalytic account of metaphor, a flaw particularly to be discerned in Metz's book. He gives considerable emphasis to the difficulties the secondary process has in comprehending the primary. But, since explanation belongs to consciousness, what is the point in trying to explain metaphor, about which we know quite a lot, in terms of unconscious operations, about which we necessarily know less. This reverses the proper direction of explanation, which is from the better understood to the less understood. It also is likely to lead to the pursuit of absurd problems (such as asking whether editing devices belong most to the primary or the secondary – which is about as sensible as asking how unconscious are punctuation marks). So, once again, even if it is granted that the unconscious may have a role to play in the creation of metaphors, it does not follow that our investigations should begin there. We would expect a valid imaginative theory of metaphor to *focus then on what people can be observed to do when they make and interpret metaphors.*

The critique of the psychoanalytic account of metaphor has thus been useful: It has made possible the sketching of some guidelines for an imaginative theory.

More on Eisenstein

According to Herbert Eagle, in *Russian Formalist Film Theory,*[12] Eisenstein utilized the theories of the psychologist Lev Vygotsky in expounding his ideas on "inner speech." I can find no evidence of this. Their two theories are quite divergent, and Eagle misrepresents what Vygotsky says when he claims that Vygotsky believed that human mental processes ("inner speech") depend on apprehending in total images.[13]

Lev Vygotsky wished to study the inner workings of thought and speech, that aspect turned to the person rather than to the outer world. Seeking the hidden, he started from the known and observable, and then conducted experiments to test the hypotheses he made. Taking his cue from early work of Piaget, he investigated how children acquired oral and then written speech, and in particular what happens when they begin to talk, as it were, to themselves, and commence the process of internalizing speech. He concluded that there were stages to this development, which led to corresponding layers of consciousness. Intermediate between vocal speech and the final phase and innermost level of thought itself comes inner speech. This mode exists on its own plane, with its own laws, some of which he attempted to define. Although the links between words and meanings are not severed to the extent they are in pure thought, inner speech functions differently from vocal speech. For example, *sense* becomes more important than *meaning* – that is, where *meaning* is the stable element linked to a word, *sense* is the sum of all the psychological associations that may accrue around it. (This might be illustrated by saying that while the meaning of *honest* is constant, the sense of it changes considerably as Antony reiterates that "Brutus is an honest man.") "In inner speech, the predominance of sense over meaning, of sentence over word, and of context over sentence is the rule," asserts Vygotsky.[14] And he mentions other characteristics such as *agglutination* (where several words are merged into one) and *saturation* (where there is "an influx of sense").

Just as inner speech is an autonomous speech function, so Vygotsky sees thought itself as a further independent plane of consciousness. He talks about its affective-volitional aspects, as well as its freedom from word-meaning. Interestingly, he says that "the theatre faced the problem of the thought behind the words before psychology did," and cites Stanislavsky's practice with the subtext of dramatic dialogue.[15] All these observations, calling attention as they do to the significance of overall context, are stimulating, and still seem pertinent to an attempt to relate inner thought to the making and understanding of metaphors.

Vygotsky's aims, it should be noted, are directed toward investigating the relationship between words and thought. Our enquiry, however, because it is concerned with film, must go beyond thought's links with the verbal only, and must consider the nature of the very categories that underpin thought and experience.

Vygotsky does not, however, either in connection with thought or with inner speech say that we apprehend in images – as Herbert Eagle thinks he does. This is where Vygotsky is far removed from Eisenstein who did believe that inner speech is "image-sensual." Nor did Eisenstein need to rely upon Vygotsky for the acquisition of the term, for it was current at that time. It was to Lévy-Bruhl that Eisenstein was chiefly indebted, not least for the notion that this type of speech is more primitive or regressive than "thematic-logical" discourse. (No such implication is to be found in Vygotsky's book.) As with Freud, this leads to an undesirable and certainly unwarranted dichotomy between public rationality and personal irrationality. (Freud, of course, was also influenced by Lévy-Bruhl in some of the arguments he used.)

Eisenstein formulates the true nature of art as being a unity of dualities:

The affectiveness of a work of art is built upon the fact that there takes place in it a dual process: an impetuous progressive rise along the lines of the highest explicit steps of consciousness and a simultaneous penetration by means of structure of the form into the layers of profoundest sensual thinking.[16]

He associates the tensions produced by these coexisting tendencies with "the dialectic," and praises a synthesizing harmony.

By allowing one or other element to predominate the art-work remains unfulfilled. A drive towards the thematic-logical side renders the work dry, logical, didactic. But over-stress on the side of the sensual form of thinking with insufficient account taken of the thematic-logical tendency – this is equally fatal for the work: the work becomes condemned to sensual chaos, elementalness, raving. Only in the "dually united" interpenetration of these tendencies resides the true tension-laden unity of form and content.[17]

What is novel about Eisenstein's formulation of these issues is his identification of inner speech with that which is image-sensual. As a gifted filmmaker, Eisenstein himself might well have had an inclination to think in images. But he presents no evidence to support the suggestion that this is the very substance of inner speech. Even the examples he gives from the mythic nature of "early forms of thought" do not provide this, since they deal with modes of associating things, not with conceiving in images. At best, then, this identification merely sets out a personal bias; at worst, it makes a special, and unwarranted, plea for cinema as the art closest to the fountainhead of inner speech. It is therefore difficult to feel that this part of Eisenstein's theory possesses weight or leads anywhere.

Much else that Eisenstein says is not new. As I noted in Chapter IV, his "dialectic" is subsumed in an organic theory of art – a traditional theory that can be traced back to Aristotle. Even the warning just cited about the dangers of permitting one tendency to overwhelm the other can be seen as a call for a balance of Apollonian and Dionysian elements. I believe that Brian Lewis, in his dissertation *Jean Mitry and the Aesthetics of the Cinema,* is fundamentally right in suggesting Eisenstein is one of the twentieth-century heirs of Romantic and symbolist conceptions of art.[18] Lewis argues that Eisenstein strongly influenced Mitry in this, and that both of them may be seen as belonging to an extended *famille d'esprits,* a family of like-minded theorists and critics who share a common belief in the importance to mankind of "symbolic" expressions in contradistinction to "discursive" or "allegorical" modes of expression.[19] In saying this Lewis intends no denigration of Eisenstein (or Mitry), nor do I. Indeed, I would go further. At least since Goethe this has been the mainstream of art theory and criticism, and it has generated the most productive insights into art. It still does. Countermovements, such as Marxist, semiotic, or deconstructionist approaches, have generated lots of jargon and ideology, but have been quite meager in displaying any fresh understanding of art. Certainly they have produced no critics or critical theorists so far of the caliber of the leading representatives of the *famille d'esprits*.

A major representative of this tradition is undoubtedly Ernst Cassirer, and in Chapter IV I drew attention to some parallels between Eisenstein's discussion of "early thought processes" and Cassirer's account of "mythical" thinking. Indeed, where their concerns overlap, what Cassirer has to say often adds greater perspective, and sometimes correction, to Eisenstein's explorations.

For example, Cassirer explicitly repudiates the notion that "mythical" thinking relates to a kind of prelogical thinking peculiar to our early ancestors. He points out that anthropological and ethnological evidence shows that primitive societies are quite as practical and logical in many things as modern society is, and that conversely modern life and culture manifest many mythical assumptions and practices.[20] He does, however, concur with Eisenstein in arguing that there are categories of mythical thinking that conflict with logical relations and the scientific approach. In particular, Cassirer cites the part not only standing for the whole but positively being the whole;[21] how also a thing is present as a whole, as soon as anything similar to it is given;[22] and of myth binding particulars together in the unity of an image, a mythical figure.[23] Further, Cassirer is also at one with Eisenstein in emphasizing the affective nature of mythical apprehension: "The real substratum of myth is not a substratum of thought but of feeling."[24]

Although I do not wish to be taken as concurring with everything that Cassirer says, I believe he touches on issues seminal to an imaginative theory of metaphor. Therefore I wish to extrapolate some points from his writings and to give my own sense of their importance.

One issue frequently returned to in Cassirer's work is the role of language in human development. From an evolutionary perspective the acquisition of speech is a crucial development, and Cassirer regards humankind as above all an *animal symbolicum*. In discussing a related issue – whether speech metaphors produce mythical understanding, or whether (as Max Müller proposed) the mythic view of things gives rise to metaphor – Cassirer rejects these questions as specious, arguing that both metaphor and myth spring from the same basic mental activity.[25] For what is language but a transference of cognitive or emotional experience into a sign or symbol? This entails both *displacement* (one thing coming to stand for something other), and *condensation* (a locus of perception wrung from the multiplicity and diffusion of experience).[26] The major implication, as I understand it, from this is that the act of speech, of symbolizing, is the primal metaphorical act. Far from metaphorical thinking representing some pathology of human behavior, it would seem to be the very condition that makes language possible, and consequently all that follows from language: thought, culture, civilization – even cinema itself. Not only would the technology of cinema be impossible without a symbol system, but the very comprehension of the indexical or iconic signs that constitute photographic images presupposes the mental leap that relates sign to referent. An imaginative theory of metaphor, then, does well to ground itself in this fundamental acknowledgment.

Such acknowledgment, of course, still leaves much to be answered. For example, it tells us little about the distinction we make within speech between metaphorical and nonmetaphorical utterances, or why we make such a distinction. Nor does it tell us why artistic structures are so dependent on metaphorical organization. But one line of thought pursued by Cassirer may help us to understand why artworks often resort to nonlogical connections.

Cassirer holds mythic and artistic thinking to be related, but he argues that as they evolve they develop away from one another. One characteristic, however, that Cassirer ascribes to mythic thinking remains, I believe, a fundamental characteristic of art as well. Myth, says Cassirer, strives for "unity of the world" – that is, for comprehension of a whole in which everything is assigned a meaning, and in which everything is intelligible.[27] This also is an axiom of art. In an artistic work everything must fit, and have its reason for being there. As a practical rule of thumb this has long been known and practiced. Coleridge's schoolmaster, from whom he acquired his training in classical texts, taught him there was a reason for every word, and for the position of every word, and that even the wildest ode had a logic of its own "as severe as that of science, and more difficult, more complex."[28] This is more than sensible exhortation. It is the fundamental axiom that underlies all that readers and viewers do when they approach a work of art, and seek to understand its unity and coherence.

The artist's obsession with binding things together in a coherent totality is quite as great as the reader's or viewer's. One cannot, indeed, encounter Eisenstein's discussion of montage without feeling the intensity of his fixation on linkage. Eisenstein also suggests that the artist's commitment to this is so strong that irrational, even atavistic, connections will be drawn upon (though, as we saw before, he felt this set up a conflict between rational aspirations and psychic regression).[29] Again, this is not a novel observation. Aristotle makes it when he cites the statue of Mylos at Argos: It fell upon Mylos's murderer while he was a spectator at a festival. Such events, remarks Aristotle, seem not to be due to mere chance. So plots constructed on the principle of design rather than accident are the best, he concludes.

It would seem that the fundamental human need is for life to be intelligible. Myth aims to satisfy this need by placing our perceptions and actions within a meaningful cosmic order. Art aims to satisfy it by offering us symbolic works in which comprehensive design reigns. For the artist the achievement of that comprehensive design is everything. This credo will often incorporate the view that art celebrates affinities and synchronicities, chords and correspondences beyond the grasp of logic, and in so doing answers to our deepest yearnings for and intimations of wholeness. It also asserts that the greatest enemies of art are accident and senselessness.[30]

Hence, Eisenstein's proclamation that montage is "a means of achieving *a unity of a higher order – a means through the montage image of achieving an organic embodiment of a single idea conception, embracing all elements, parts, details of the film-work.*"[31] Hence, too, his insistence on organicism, and his declaration in another essay that a "work has a completely individual affect on its perceivers, not only because it is raised to the level of natural phenomena [i.e., it obeys the same law of structure as organic phenomena], but also because the laws of its construction are simultaneously the laws governing those who perceive the work, inasmuch as this audience is also part of organic nature."[32] Hence, also, his conviction that inner speech was the key to understanding the laws governing art – not merely because he conceived it as based on images, but above all because he deemed it to be affective–sensual, generating "new qualities" by its facility for "emotional fusion."

Although I am profoundly sympathetic to Eisenstein's reaffirmation of the symbolist view of art, and in particular to his hypothesis that the same laws of artistic meaning bind together makers and viewers alike, I cannot but feel some disappointment that his thesis is urged in such general terms. When he comes down to the concrete and to specifics, when indeed he is at his most original as a theorist of cinematic practice, what he writes about are not so much the governing mental operations as the techniques and artistic strategies of filmmaking. On the potency and potentiality of montage he has no equal. These considerations, however, are formalist in nature. They belong more to a rhetoric of the cinema than to an exposition of the principles and, as it were, the ordinances governing the artistic imagination.

On schemata

So far one thing has emerged as paramount. It is that the mind seeks for meaning and sense. How the mind does this has now become one of the major concerns of cognitive psychology. Though doubtless more will emerge as the research proceeds, some findings are already proving of great interest. I would like to single out one study in particular that relates the interpretation of metaphors to the comprehension of meaning conveyed not literally but obliquely through a text. David E. Rumelhart, in "Some Problems with the Notion of Literal Meanings," writes:

I have over the past several years, been involved in a study of the processes whereby people interpret stories. It was here that it became clearest to me that literal meanings – in the sense implied by the advocates of compositional theories – and conveyed meanings deviated in even the most mundane cases. It also became clear to me that a schema-based notion of the comprehension process is the most viable alternative account. A careful look at almost any story and the interpretations given to it make this abundantly clear. Consider the following brief passage:

Business had been slow since the oil crisis.
Nobody seemed to want anything really elegant anymore. Suddenly the door opened
and a well-dressed man entered the showroom. John put on his friendliest and most
sincere expression and walked toward the
man.

Although the example is merely a fragment, most people generate a rather clear interpretation of this story. Apparently, John is a car salesman fallen on hard times. He probably sells rather large elegant cars – most likely Cadillacs. Suddenly a good prospect enters the showroom where John works. John wants to make the sale. To do this he must make a good impression on the man. Therefore he tries to appear friendly and sincere. He also wants to talk to the man to deliver his sales pitch. Thus, he makes his way over to the man . . .

How do people arrive at such an interpretation? Clearly, people do not arrive at it all at once. As the sentences are read, schemata are activated, evaluated, and refined or discarded. When people are asked to describe their various hypotheses as they read the story, a remarkably consistent pattern of hypothesis generation and evaluation emerges.[33]

That cinemagoers interpret the events on the screen in much the same sort of way cannot be doubted. (There is an amusing illustration of this in Scott Fitzgerald's *The Last Tycoon* where Stahr, the producer, demonstrates to a novelist the studio has hired how to write a film script.)[34] Indeed, the kind of interpreting that is considered here is *situation-focused* rather than *language-focused,* and therefore as applicable to film as to written narrative. Adopting this approach helps us to escape the confines that semantic- or semiotic-based theories, with their roots in syntax and vocabulary, inevitably impose.

The crucial notion is that of *schemata*. This most fruitful concept has become as seminal for helping us understand how we make sense of what we perceive as how we make sense of situations and contexts we interpret. It has already made its mark in such varied fields as the psychology of seeing, the history of art, and the philosophy of science.[35] Its merit lies in the way it brings together the, hitherto separated, ideas of received configurations and of hypothesizing and testing.[36]

On the one hand the term looks back to the way in which we draw upon past experiences as models for comprehending what we encounter. In this sense it overlaps with much that a term like *code* is intended to cover, but it avoids the implication, strongly carried by the semiotic word, that what we think or perceive is *determined* by conventions, assumptions, rules, manners, or clichés. It also avoids the implication that a schema must preexist the occasion that calls it forth, whereas there is a marked suggestion in *code* that this is always the case. *Schema* stresses the hypothetical, speculative, and explorative way in which we may utilize either what we have personally experienced before or received indirectly.

On the other hand the term looks forward from the occasion that presents us with a problem, on through a process of trial and adjustment, to a resolution of the problem. A schema may be as fleeting as the fractional hesitation before we identify an old friend, or as considered as a scientific hypothesis. It permits the possibility of our entertaining an illusion, as well as the possibility of our improving our grasp of reality. It straddles both recognition and learning. As a tool for investigating the making and comprehension of metaphors, the notion of schemata, then, has many advantages. It is worth spelling out some of these in relation to issues raised earlier in this chapter.

I have suggested that a satisfactory imaginative theory would have to show how metaphorical thinking can be accounted for as a natural and ordinary activity, and not as something uncommon and pathological. This, as I shall argue, is now made possible. I criticized the Freudian/Metzian account of metaphor as relying too much upon what is unknowable as the basis for explaining things. There is, however, no mystification attached to the schema of schema itself. Its employment is frequently fully conscious, and open to investigation. At the same time, the use of schemata as a means of explaining cognitive processes does not rule out the possibility of unconscious factors influencing our thoughts. Many of the memories, or presuppositions, or situational configurations drawn upon for schemata will undoubtedly be preconscious or unconscious in origin. The notion of schema itself does not prejudge the sources that particular schemata derive from – these would have to be examined in their own right (doubtless by the application of further, particular schemata – a Freudian and a Jungian will bring quite different schemata to bear on the analysis of a dream).

The affective nature of artworks (an issue raised by Eisenstein in some of the passages quoted earlier) also falls within the scope of this mode of explanation. Clearly emotion can be a means of fusing many disparate impressions into one schema, as Shakespeare seems to have been aware when he wrote,

Or in the night, imagining some fear,
How easy is a bush supposed a bear.

A good theory of cognition should, as this does, show how thought and feeling may run together. It will also show how errors, as well as insights, can be generated.

The nature of the situation will determine the type of schemata produced. Thus the notion of schema presupposes a range of types, and even of levels, of schemata. For example, the types of schemata that relate to the perception of depth in cases of retinal disparity[37] will be quite different from those relating to perceptions such as that of the bear that a fearful person on a dark night believes he has seen. Thus, studies of schemata might well focus on different types in different areas of cognition. Schemata entailing "seeing as" might be said to belong to a different category of schemata involving mere "seeing." (Both the data encountered and the sources of the schemata employed need to be considered when establishing categories.)

As the reference to "seeing as" might suggest, the notion of schema is quite compatible with dispositional assertions. Critical comments that aim to illuminate a particular work of art can well be interpreted as the critic's explicit schemata, which invite a reexperiencing of the work, with aspects highlighted. They will probably entail our modifying our grasp of the work and thus may also lead to us carrying over an influence that will affect the schemata we employ in considering future works. What applies to critical reassessments applies also to the influence of new works. They too create schemata that affect our future reading. Here we have a justification for T. S. Eliot's famous remark in "Tradition and the Individual Talent" to the effect that new works modify our sense of previous works and their order among themselves.[38]

Schemata may be traced in all categories of cognitive behavior. Their presence in both the formation and interpretation of works of art provides the means whereby we can account for the bond between what the artist intends and what the spectator understands. Indeed, this mode of explanation helps us to escape from the subjectivities that purely mentalist accounts would impose. For schemata can be as available to public consideration as hypotheses. What one mind can hypothesize, so can another. Behavior can provide clues whereby the hypothesis being acted upon may be deduced by other people. The same applies to schemata. Indeed, in works of art genre, style, and mood often indicate more reliably than the expressed intentions of the artist what schemata are appropriate and should be brought to bear upon the work. Also, particularly where there are shared heritages and cultures, strategies for forming schemata are likely to be common and comprehensible. Across cultures the issues may be more problematic, but even to say this is to acknowledge that our concerns pertain to public domains and not to essentially personal and private ones.

But one important qualification needs to be made. Hypotheses as such do not have to be explicit, but normally they are and can be made so. Schemata, however, are more often *tacit,* although in some cases they may be rendered explicit. In using this term I am, of course, referring to the implications given it by Michael Polanyi[39] – in particular, his suggestion that all focal knowledge is dependent on subsidiary awarenesses that are less determinate. Not only will the sources we draw on for constructing schemata be indeterminate in this sense, but also frequently the schemata themselves will be. Especially will this be so where the schemata are innate and preconscious – as with our making sense of speech by the application of grammatical schemata we may not even know we possess – or where the integration they achieve results so instantaneously in new and emergent properties that the schemata cannot be separated from what they produce.[40]

Tacit awareness also relates to the distinction between knowledge how and knowledge that.[41] We may know how to ride a bicycle without being able to give the mathematics of it. Our possession of many skills entails a tacit knowing how. At the simpler levels – identifying a familiar shape, for example – the formation of schemata is certainly an activity, but it may entail little or no skill. We tend to feel skill is involved where there is a possibility of the cultivation and improvement of the activity. At more complex levels the formation of schemata will certainly entail skill. We can train ourselves, for instance, to be better readers, more sensitive to recognizing interpretative clues. Much of this will, however, be tacit, and be none the worse for that.[42] Tacit awareness is always demonstrable, even if not always explicable.

The recognition that schemata are often tacit helps to account for an important feature of the creative act. Often the artist does not know exactly what he is making until it is made. Often, perhaps particularly in the collaborative arts, what occurs in the process helps discover the goal. This does not necessarily mean artists do not know what they are doing: It just means that the schemata guiding their choices are tacit, perhaps even intuitively so. Tacit schemata may even be shared, as they clearly are on occasions by collaborators in the performing arts where the different modes of contribution (acting, design, music, editing) can mesh together to extraordinary effect.

Schemata also function to bring about organizational hierarchies, as when a listener draws upon linguistic schemata to process the phonemes of the speech, the words and their grammar, the meanings of the sentences, and the illocutionary force.

I hope enough has been said to demonstrate that the notion of schema provides us with an explanatory tool of some sophistication and power. But its application to metaphor is of main interest to us. How does Rumelhart relate the use of schemata in comprehending conveyed meanings to the problem of metaphors?

He concludes that the way we understand metaphors is essentially similar to the way we understand conveyed meanings, but there is a difference in the outcome:

[Most metaphor works] by reference to analogies that are known to relate the two domains [that is, of tenor and vehicle]. Consider, as an example, the metaphor...

Encyclopedias are gold mines.

How are we to understand it? According to the schema theory of comprehension...the task for the comprehender is to find a schema within which this utterance is coherent.... In general, predication suggests that the characteristic properties of the predicate concept are to be applied to the subject concept. In this case, we find that the "gold mine" schema fits only partially, although certain of the primary characteristics of gold mines can be shown to be true of encyclopedias.... other characteristics (such as being underground) do not hold. I suspect that it is the unevenness of account – certain primary features of the gold mine schema fit very well, others not at all – that leads to the metaphorical flavor of statements such as this. The interpretation process, I believe, is no different here than for literal predication, the outcome is simply different. We say that a statement is literally true when we find an existing schema that accounts fully for the data in question. We say that a statement is metaphorically true when we find that although certain primary aspects of the schema hold, others equally primary do not hold. When no schema can be found which allows for a good fit between any aspects of the schema and the object for which it is said to account, we are simply unable to interpret the input at all.[43]

Rumelhart believes, then, that the same process is to be observed at work in the interpreting of metaphors as in the interpreting of obliquely conveyed meanings. Both cases entail the application of a schema. But where a metaphor is involved, there is a special kind of tension, as it were.

Rumelhart sees the domain of the vehicle as providing the schema.

In the example cited, the various properties associated with gold mines should provide the schema, but only some of them fit. In contrast to this view, which would put all the emphasis on the vehicle, I would wish to maintain the interplicitness of tenor and vehicle. Not only must some of the associated properties of "gold mines" be considered, but also our experience of reading encyclopedias. The metaphor does not merely assert the cliché that the learning contained in encyclopedias is precious[44] but, more important, conveys the sense that when reading encyclopedias discoveries may come unexpectedly, and that we feel there is always more buried there than we have actually delved out. In an earlier chapter I have called this the *interpretand* of the metaphor. It is the product of tenor and vehicle together. What is important is not so much the vehicle as schema, but the schema that accounts for the interplay of tenor and vehicle.

Indeed, Rumelhart does seem to come round to this same viewpoint in his final sentence. But in the way he puts it there also seems to be an implication, if I am catching his drift, that where no schema can be found (i.e., preexists) to account for tenor and vehicle together, then interpretation fails. We do not, in other words, invent a schema if one is not to hand. On the contrary, I believe we often do. Consequently a metaphor entails more than merely promoting certain salient features of the vehicle as predicates of the tenor. It entails shifting the categories by which we account for our experience, sometimes only fleetingly or provisionally, sometimes radically and more permanently. This has been argued elsewhere in this book, and the argument will be pursued further in the next section.

Lakoff and Johnson on metaphor

Recent decades have witnessed an extraordinary increase in the number of studies published on metaphor.[45] I have touched on only one contribution from the field of cognitive psychology. Scientists from other fields have also displayed interest, in the main because of metaphor's connection with the creation of scientific models. Perhaps some of the most innovative approaches have come from philosophers.[46] I shall mention two philosophic approaches, in each case again using them as jumping-off points for comments of my own.

The first I wish to draw attention to is the experientialist account of metaphor as expounded by George Lakoff and Mark Johnson in *Metaphors We Live By.*[47] They take metaphor to entail understanding and experiencing something in terms of some other thing. A major accomplishment of the book is their demonstration that metaphors are all-pervasive in our lives, influencing at every level our thoughts, attitudes, and actions. As important is their construction of a theory that delineates the role of metaphor in the forming and re-forming of our categories of thought and experience.

Against the view that experiences and objects have inherent properties and are understood solely in terms of those properties, the authors argue that inherent properties only in part account for how we comprehend things. Just as important is the way our concepts, and consequently our experience, are structured in terms of metaphors. Many important concepts, for example, are either abstract or not clearly delineated (the emotions generally, ideas, our apprehension of time – these sorts of things are cited). To get a grasp on them we turn to concepts we understand in clearer terms (spatial orientation, objects, etc.). Simple physical concepts – up–down, in–out, object, substance – derived from our fundamental bodily experience of the world form the basis of many elementary metaphors, and make possible a more complex metaphorical development. The authors are at pains to emphasize that metaphors we hold to be true are grounded in systematic correlations with our experience. (They acknowledge that the philosophy they are evolving is indebted to the insights of pragmatism and phenomenology as well as to the later philosophy of Wittgenstein.)

Many of the metaphors Lakoff and Johnson discuss are what they call *conventional* metaphors, that is, metaphors that structure the ordinary conceptual system of our culture. (Indeed, they imply there is a correspondence between a culture's most important values and the metaphors it adopts.) They are less interested in individual "dead" metaphors as in clusters of conventional metaphors that form a cognitive gestalt and that, perhaps without our fully realizing it, systematically affect the way we think about and experience things. An illustration of this would be the various clusters of hackneyed terms that represent different attitudes to love: LOVE IS MADNESS, LOVE IS WAR, LOVE IS A JOURNEY, and so on. To employ any one of these is to highlight certain features of love while suppressing others. Sometimes, as in the formulation of scientific theories, we attempt to employ consistent sets of metaphors, so that inferences we draw will not conflict. But often we reject consistency in our employment of metaphors. It seems that successful functioning in our daily lives requires a constant shifting of metaphors.

Lakoff and Johnson also discuss new metaphors and their effect:

New metaphors have the power to create a new reality. This can begin to happen when we start to comprehend our experience in terms of a metaphor, and it becomes a deeper reality when we begin to act in terms of it. If a new metaphor enters the conceptual system that we base our actions on, it will alter the conceptual system and the perceptions and actions that the system gives rise to. Much of cultural change arises from the introduction of new metaphorical concepts and the loss of old ones. For example, the Westernization of cultures throughout the world is partly a matter of introducing the TIME IS MONEY metaphor into those cultures.[48]

It follows that the authors reject many traditional ways of thinking about metaphor. The comparison theory, for instance, is discarded because of its failure to see that metaphors *constitute* similarities instead of merely depending on them.[49] In doing so, they begin to develop a philosophy of their own, which they name experientialism. It incorporates its own view of category formation and of validating the truth of statements. In particular, Lakoff and Johnson seek to establish an account of understanding and truth that will avoid the errors of either objectivist or subjectivist epistemologies. The book is far-reaching in its implications, and it is not possible in a brief synopsis to do justice to the argument.

The relevance of Lakoff and Johnson's book to an imaginative theory of metaphor will be apparent. Many of the things they say fulfill the criteria I have proposed an imaginative theory should meet. I have said that a satisfactory theory must explain the essential normality of metaphorical thinking – that metaphors should not be treated as linguistic aberrations, or as pathological maneuvers of the irrational mind; that an explanation should be given of emergent meanings, and it should be shown why such meanings are public and not merely subjective. Lakoff and Johnson's approach, which regards metaphor as a matter of imaginative rationality, goes a long way to meeting such demands. Their explanation of metaphor as a cognitive activity and not merely a linguistic device avoids the deficiencies of a purely semiotic account, and their explanation of categories of thought allows for the coming into existence of new understanding and emergent meanings. One need not be in agreement with everything they put forward to be able to see that Lakoff and Johnson have presented a fascinating and powerful model. Their account of categorization is central to their own exposition, and particularly pertinent to the construction of an imaginative theory. It is too complex to set out in full here, but certain points may be extrapolated for consideration.[50]

We categorize our experience in order to make sense of it. Categories are thus experiential gestalts – experience organized into structured wholes, and related to other structured wholes. They are partly the direct product of our experience as beings, with particular receptors and faculties placed in the physical environment that is the world; partly they are the product of our evolved needs and purposes as social beings. That is, they are interactional. Additionally, many of these gestalts are complex ones that are structured partially in terms of other gestalts. These are what Lakoff and Johnson call metaphorical structured concepts. For example, they cite LOVE as a concept that is mostly structured in metaphorical terms. The same thing may be categorized in different ways in different situations. Any categorization highlights certain properties, downplays others, and hides still others. Hence when we wish to focus on some aspect and conceal others, we choose the categories our statements shall employ.

Because the dimensions of categories arise out of our interactions with the world, the properties given by these dimensions are not properties of objects in themselves but are interactional properties. They are not fixed but may be narrowed, expanded, or adjusted according to our purposes. And according to the way we restructure them in terms of other gestalts. Consequently, metaphors that organize one domain in terms of another are a regular means by which we form and re-form our categories.

An explanation of metaphor in terms of the categories of thought holds a special interest for any investigation into cinematic metaphors. This is because it bypasses one of the main objections brought against the existence of cinematic metaphors – namely, that metaphor is a linguistic notion only, and therefore not applicable to a medium so largely dependent on visual images. For if metaphors occur at the level of thought, then metaphors are bound to occur in films as well as in written texts. Any shot will itself be structured according to what the director wishes to emphasize, downplay, or rule out of consideration. In the very planning and shooting, the categories and the metaphors that help construct many of the categories are necessarily involved.

This has to be the case. But an opponent of cinematic metaphor might still argue that to say this is to do no more than state the obvious without dealing with the real point at issue. If, for example, one of the categories by which we highlight certain properties of love is that of LOVE IS MADNESS, then certainly we can expect some screwball comedies in which people do crazy things for love. But where are the cinematic metaphors in this? Naturally, if people believe in certain categories, characters in films are likely to behave in accordance with those categories. That is not the same as saying that their behavior is being depicted by means of cinematic metaphor.

This is where the distinction between conventional and new metaphors is important. Our tendency is to accept conventional metaphors as if they were literal representations. So it is hardly likely we will notice any metaphorical element – that is, *unless our attention is drawn to it,* as when someone points out to us that the series of events in a film all enact the same metaphor, LOVE IS MADNESS. Thus the critical analysis of films may well entail detecting the metaphorical aspect-seeing of filmic incidents (as in literary criticism where, e.g., it is the custom to point out recurrent metaphorical patterning such as the scene-after-scene portrayal of people spying upon one another in *Hamlet*). What is said of recurrent incidents may also be said of other significant elements in films – for example, the way the moody lighting in film noir reflects a treacherous world full of shadows out of which an unseen destiny may step at any moment.

Thus, an analysis of the categories created by conventional metaphors in films is likely to take us into the realm of narrative, genre, and style, rather than into the study of marked and localized metaphors. With new metaphors, however, the opposite is likely to be true. As we are being asked to rethink our accepted categories, so a jolting novelty or strangeness is likely to be apparent. Thus, in Kubrick's *2001: A Space Odyssey*, we are made to see the link between ape-age and space-age technology when a bone transforms itself into a spaceship. But if the shock cut makes these connections in thought possible, it is because thought itself is pervaded by metaphor and restructured by metaphor, and consequently there exists the possibility both of manufacturing cinematic metaphors and of their being interpreted. A theory of categorization functioning largely through metaphor, such as Lakoff and Johnson expound, goes a long way toward showing how cinematic metaphors are created and understood.

A further interesting aspect of Lakoff and Johnson's account of categories and their formation is that it is compatible with the notion of schemata that we discussed in the previous section. For if categories are gestalts, experiences organized interactionally into structured wholes, they must function as schemata are said to do. Like schemata they may be said to be dispositional, shaping how we apprehend new experiences. Further, if categories can be restructured and their dimensions changed, they have something of the hypothetical nature that we accorded to schemata. Both notions then, that of schemata and that of categories, envisage the integration of elements into emergent properties. Consequently, it seems reasonable to claim that schemata are to be understood as provisional categories.

Therefore, an imaginative theory of metaphor would do well to draw upon both notions, emphasizing that our perceptions and compartments of knowledge are not fixed and immutable but are open to revision and restructuring by means of metaphor. The interaction of different domains brings about new schemata, new categories. Further, this process is not some pathological condition of the mind, but the very way we as human beings organize our experience and cognitions, and reorganize them to meet and be alert to new contingencies.

One final point remains before the conclusion of this section. I have said that new metaphors call attention to themselves more than conventional ones. This would seem to make novelty the crucial factor; however, it may also be a question of where attention is directed.

Michael Polanyi points out that all attention comprises both focal and subsidiary awareness, the latter being inevitably tacit. As we assimilate things so that they become an integral part of the way we function, our awareness of them becomes subsidiary.[51] An example is that of driving a motorcar. Proficient drivers do not focus on changing gear, they just do it. I suggest the same applies to our handling of metaphors. It is not so much that they are conventional or we accept them as though they are conventions – rather it is that we allow our awareness of them to become subsidiary. We accept them existentially as they dwell in us, and become inseparable from our thoughts, perceptions, and actions. They are schemata made tacit, and converted into tools for dealing with the world. Even novel metaphors may acquire this status, depending on the context in which they are encountered. Indeed, the title "dead" may be misleading when applied to metaphors: Some metaphors may be all the more influential when subliminal and seemingly quiescent.

A sequence in John Ford's *The Grapes of Wrath* may be cited to illustrate the power of tacit metaphor. The Joad family is being evicted and their home is being bulldozed. The man who drives the tractor, masked behind his protective goggles, seems to be as mass-produced as his machine, one with it and part of it. But when he pushes his goggles aside to argue with the Joads, he is only another poor Oakie trying to find a way to feed his family. The notion that men are being converted into machines and are losing their humanity is a recurrent theme of the film – the scene with the traffic cop reiterates it later – but the metaphors by which this theme is conveyed are probably all the more telling because for the most part they are assimilated tacitly.

Muthos and metaphor

The second philosophical approach to metaphor I wish to touch on is that of Paul Ricoeur. It is appropriate that some of his ideas should be set beside those of George Lakoff and Mark Johnson, and not merely because they acknowledge him as an influence on their thought. They all share a belief in metaphor as a source of knowledge. Metaphor contributes, they believe, to "the logic of discovery."[52] Again, my interest in Ricoeur's philosophy, as discussed here, is partial: I wish to direct attention only to those aspects that are particularly pertinent to the kind of imaginative theory of cinematic metaphor I am seeking to outline.

La Métaphore vive is a seminal work on metaphor, wide ranging and immensely learned, a major contribution to the topic. In the main, however, the book is concerned with verbal discourse.[53] In this, to some degree, it contrasts with Lakoff and Johnson's approach, which

is more concerned with metaphor in relation to thought. Through a series of eight studies Ricoeur explores the way metaphor has been
expounded, thus surveying and relating various methodological approaches, while developing his own philosophy of metaphor. His strategy is to open out the context in which metaphor may be comprehended. He considers its role in regard to the word, to the sentence,
and to discourse. He moves through rhetoric to semantics and on to
hermeneutics. He discusses the *form* of metaphor as a word-focused
figure of speech; its *sense* as a founding of new semantic possibilities; finally, its *reference* as the power it possesses to "redescribe" reality. Although he does not claim to seek to replace rhetoric with semantics and the latter with hermeneutics, seeing each stage as having
merits within its limitations, there is no doubt that the hermeneutic
perspective represents the more inclusive view of the issues, and that
an integrated understanding of metaphor in all its ramifications is his
goal. The issues I shall pick out come largely from the hermeneutic
part of Ricoeur's investigations.

Metaphorical meaning, Ricoeur argues, is not the enigma itself —
that is, the problem set up by trying to reconcile the domains of tenor
and vehicle — but the solution of the enigma (or what we called earlier
the *interpretand* of a metaphor). At the same time, "seeing X as Y" encompasses the idea that "X is not Y." Thus the notion of seeing as, or
perhaps more generally of reconsidering a tenor in terms of the vehicle, permits both a tension ("X is not Y") and a fusion ("X seems
Y").[54] This formulation could be said to be another way of accounting
for the acknowledged hypothetical nature of a metaphor's *interpretand,*
what makes it both tentative and exploratory.

Ricoeur defines hermeneutics as "the theory that regulates the transition from structure of the work to world of the work."[55] That is, with
regards to metaphor, both its internal organization and the means by
which it refers to the world must be explicated. Denotation is considered to be direct reference to a state of affairs. Ricoeur proposes that
discourse should be understood as possessing two kinds of reference.
First-level reference is direct description, and belongs to the logic of
justification or proof; it is what we are speaking of when we say something is literally true. Second-level reference is suspended reference: It
is concerned not with description but redescription, and belongs to
"the logic of discovery." In order to reconstruct what we know, metaphor puts in abeyance the literal references that would otherwise be
made by tenor and vehicle, permitting us to entertain the possibility of
a recategorization of the world. This is what figurative reference, or
metaphorical truth, is.

Ricoeur argues that what occurs with metaphor is to be observed on
a larger and more significant scale in artistic works. Here one finds a

metaphorical network that has a "systematic deployability"[56] much like that possessed by scientific models. In works of fiction language divests itself of its function of direct description in order to comment on the world by transforming the way we envisage it. Ricoeur here has recourse to Aristotle who, in his account of tragic *poiêsis* links *mimesis* and *muthos.* Ricoeur suggests that *muthos* should be interpreted as the "organization into a network" that characterizes the suspension of first-order reference; and that *mimesis* should be understood not as the copying of reality but as the second-order reference that entails re-describing it.[57]

Although Ricoeur's discussion, as I have mentioned, is mainly concerned with written fiction, what he says has special relevance for the study of cinematic metaphor. The reason lies in the indexical nature of film images. In Chapter III I noted the way film testifies to the existence of objects in a manner that language does not: Film images are the imprints or moldings in light of actual objects. But though we need to acknowledge what the objects are that a film depicts, our sense of the causal and denotative aspect of the images is a highly qualified one. Certainly there are occasions where direct referentiality, even in fictional films, may fascinate us. We may think: So that is what Rome as an open city looked like in 1945; or, so that is how the newsroom of the *Washington Post* was laid out at the time of Watergate. For historians the indexical and documentary aspect of a film may even be paramount. (In Appendix 1 there is further discussion of some of these issues.) It is indeed easy to see why film's "ontological plenitude" led to the development of a realist school of film criticism. But those critics still acknowledged that in films, as in other arts, the significance of the whole is more important than the fidelity of the parts. They discussed the *muthos* as the means to the *mimesis* – as we all must.

Perhaps the most economical way to demonstrate the primacy of *muthos* is to take the case of films citing authentic and shocking images, such as the photography of the Jewish boy in the Warsaw Ghetto that is contemplated in Bergman's *Persona,* or the execution that newsreel cameras recorded and Antonioni incorporated in *The Passenger.* Because of the horrors they signify, and in these instances because of their notoriety, they do force literal denotation on the viewer. But they also force something else: a demand that the surrounding narrative, by its integrity or compassion or moral perspective, must earn the right to employ such images. Otherwise the films will be dismissed as exploitive. It is to the merit of Bergman and Antonioni that their films can assimilate such sequences without creating any disparity between the serious purport of the images and the probity of the surrounding fictions. Artists worthy to be called by that name know that the more painful the subject matter, the more important becomes the way it is treated within the overall cohesiveness of the work — hence, for example, the highly wrought structure of Resnais's *Nuit et brouillard,* which depicts Auschwitz. John Grierson was right to demand of documentary that it be "the creative treatment of actuality." For the moment a film aspires to being something more than the most literal recording of an event, it must face the problems imaginative organization lays upon it.

There is another consideration with regard to the indexical nature of film images. Although in one sense there is a genuine causal link between what is shot and the shot itself, the shot itself is never neutral. It will represent only selected aspects of the object. The object is brought before us, as it were, under a description. It may be shown front on, or side face; in full light, or in shadow; statically or with a zoom. Something has been highlighted; something has been suppressed. We are given, as it were, a schema of the noumenon. Furthermore, in feature films the events are mostly invented and staged. They may even be "faked," like the night scenes of the prairie in *Red River,* which were actually shot in daylight (a device that led Truffaut to call his film about the real and unreal paradoxes of filmmaking *Day for Night* [*La Nuit américaine*]). All this said, and in the light of the discussion carried out in the last section, can we even speak of the "literal truth" of an image?

If we do, it is likely to be for two main reasons. First, we wish for convenience to make some distinction between literal and figurative discourse, so that aspects can be highlighted. Or, second, we are drawing attention to a psychological attitude with which a film is being received, normally to that condition of suspension of disbelief that fiction films invite.

Ricoeur's reason for juxtaposing the literal against the metaphorical is the first, and he does not see this contrast as completely hard and fast. The literal is merely what is current, or usual. With words, the literal sense is the one that is lexicalized.

Is a similar, pragmatic distinction possible with films? I think so. One cannot, of course, have a lexicon of film images. But one certainly can have standard ways of filming things. When something is filmed in a standard manner, and nothing in the surrounding context of the shot indicates otherwise, our tendency is to accept the shot as primarily denotative. An image of a telephone depicts the object itself. Speaking in this way provides a means of defining a localized and marked cinematic metaphor as one where we realize a literal reading will not do, and an appropriate schema must be sought. Thus even in asserting (as Lakoff and Johnson do) that many of the categories with which we operate are interactional and sustained by tacit metaphors, and that such categories influence how film images are made and read, it is not necessary to forgo the distinction between literal and figurative.[58] But we do need to recognize that what we regard as the literal purport of such shots will be drawn upon and be assimilated into a metaphorical reference created by the *muthos* of the film.

The organization of the *muthos* is crucial then. Unfortunately, Ricoeur says very little about this. He merely asserts that the creation of a plot, a tale, makes it take on the characteristics of metaphorical models as employed in science, and that this "metaphoricity consists in describing a less known domain – human reality – in the light of relationships within a fictitious but better known domain," which is that of the tale itself.[59] That a work is a vehicle for redeploying our perception of the world I have already suggested in Chapter II. But can we see any other links between metaphor and tales? Does the actual construction of a plot in any way entail a metaphorical process? If we think of a plot as simply a string of incidents one following another, then the answer would be no. But if we see these incidents as fused together as an organic whole – in the way that Aristotle himself suggests – then we may see how frequently plots depend on figurative procedures. For the function of plot is not merely to relate events, it is to give those events meaning. It is only when the meaningfulness of the whole is grasped that it becomes possible to understand the world in terms of it.[60]

Now there are a number of ways in which events may be meaningfully related. Some of these, as we saw earlier in our discussion of Eisenstein and Cassirer, are connected to mythic modes of thought. There are also, as Aristotle again pointed out in connection with tragic drama, certain technical devices (e.g., reversal and irony) that help constitute meaningful linkage. Some of these may be viewed, like the principle of contrast, as aids to both artist and spectator to help in their formulation of the schemata that bind together the incidents. But most important for our purpose here are the operations of *displacement* and *condensation* (together with *hidden analogy* and *concretization,* which may be regarded as further modes of the functioning of displacement and condensation).

Although these operations have been associated by Freud and his followers with the primary process and the dreamwork, they are so fundamental to all narration and storytelling that they must be seen as agents of the secondary process. They belong to the culture of narrative itself. (Indeed, how else could Freud have become aware of them?) Stories are deliberately and critically organized. They do not possess the passivity of dreams, nor are they egoistic as dreams are. For as Freud says, "It has been my experience – and to this I have found no exceptions – that every dream treats of oneself. Dreams are absolutely egoistic."[61] Stories, however, treat of humanity at large.

They are public in character and content, and the means whereby they are organized are comprehended and utilized by all in the same way.

Despite this, story films have often been compared with dreams.[62] So it is tempting to illustrate how displacement and condensation function in the construction of the *muthos* of films by considering a film that partakes in some respects of the quality of dreams. Consider, for example, a film like *The Conversation,* which develops rather like a nightmare. One could comment on the condensation to be found in the protagonist's name, Harry Caul; or on the displacement provided by the lavatory basin, which overflows with blood; or on the concretization of mental – and moral – illness to be discerned in the concluding sequence in Caul's home. But, because we have been discussing first- and second-order reference, it is more appropriate to take a film apparently very literal in its organization and far removed from figurative devices. A better choice then than *The Conversation* is a neorealist film such as de Sica's *The Bicycle Thief* (*Ladri di biciclette*). We shall consider therefore some of the metaphors involved in the construction of its narration and mise-en-scène.

In an early sequence Maria Ricci (Lianella Carell) pawns the bed-sheets in order to get the bicycle her husband must have if he is to take up the job of billposter. Her eyes (and the camera) follow the pawnbroker as he carries her bundle to place it among shelves stacked with hundreds and hundreds of similar bundles. Certainly this is a vivid concretization of widespread poverty and desperation; but it is only one of many shots wherein the individual object or person seems lost amid a host of fellows. When Antonio (Lamberto Maggiorani) and his friends go to the bicycle market the morning after the theft of his own, the impossibility of identifying his machine, whole or dismantled, is manifested by the sheer multitude of bicycles and of parts confronting them. The film indeed opens with an anonymous group of men waiting for employment, out of which Antonio emerges to claim the job of billposter; and it closes with Antonio and his son Bruno (Enzo Staiola) being swallowed up in the crowd. One of the effects of reiterations such as these is to establish an analogy between people and objects: Identity is easily lost in mass. Thus the experience of urban alienation – a minor theme of the film – is rendered by means of images of pawned beddings and assorted bicycle parts. A human anguish is conveyed by means of telling displacements. But these displacements also entail condensations for, when the film is contemplated in retrospect, such images can be understood as encapsulating many meanings, the most notable being poverty, alienation, personal sacrifice, and society's indifference.

Both displacement and condensation are major strategies of *The Bi-*

cycle Thief. Ostensibly the film is "a slice of life," a simple chronicle of a few hours in the lives of persons arbitrarily picked, as it were, from among thousands in the streets. In keeping with such a type of narration, the film is crowded with many casual and accidental incidents that would appear to have no direct bearing on either the narrative or its themes. That we experience them as such when viewing the film is a tribute to the success of the style. The pattern of incidents, however, does contribute to a subtle coherence. For one thing, the film is far from restricted to portraying external events only. Much of it is concerned with Antonio's inner life: his thoughts, feelings, and moral struggles. These are often revealed indirectly. The film is more allegory than it is anecdote. At the core of the film is the loss of love through obsession. Antonio becomes so fixated on recovering his stolen bicycle that he does not realize what he is doing to himself: how he is nurturing injury, becoming hard, acting irrationally, laying himself open to humiliation, demeaning his own humanity – above all, damaging his relationship with Bruno. Many of the incidents are covert demonstrations of this.

One commentator on De Sica's film misses this thread because he takes too narrowly political a line. John F. Scott, believing that the central argument of the film is the way the social and political systems conspire against the man who tries to lift himself out of his poverty by his own effort, concludes that too many incidents are unattached to "the central axis of the film."[63] He cites Bruno's encounter with the homosexual who tries to entice him with an expensive toy, and also Bruno's near-drowning. Although the political layer is there, it is less important than the theme of paternal responsibility and care. Antonio is more than the passive figure that Scott thinks he is. Antonio's obsession leads him to neglect Bruno. At one time Bruno is accosted by the homosexual, at another he is nearly run down by a car in the street. Antonio hardly even sees these incidents. But his realization that Bruno may have drowned, and that his own behavior was largely to blame, forces Antonio to acknowledge his guilt and leads him to attempt a reconciliation with his son. Scenes that appear merely random and contingent actually have an oblique and cumulative function in the *muthos* of the film.

Doubtless the collaboration of two figures each with his own approach to offer – Zavattini fascinated by mundane reality, De Sica with his sense of poetry – helped bring about the film's fine balance between felt life and resonant fable. In their subsequent comments on the film the two revealed the deliberation and conscious organization that went into the making of it. "We discussed with De Sica the content of every scene and established the meaning of every image," remarked Zavattini.[64] De Sica told an interviewer:

I had no intention of presenting Antonio as a kind of "Everyman" or a personi-
fication of what is called today "the underprivileged." To me he was an individual, with his individual joys and worries, with his individual story. In
presenting the one tragic Sunday of his long and varied life, I attempted to
transpose reality into the poetic plane. This indeed seemed to me one of the
important features of my work, because without such an attempt a film of this
kind would simply be a newsreel. I don't see any future in neo-realism if it
does not surmount the barrier separating the documentary from drama and
poetry.[65]

The Bicycle Thief serves to illustrate then that, even in a neorealist
drama, narrative organization and mise-en-scène depend on metaphorical structuring.

It should be noted, however, that in commenting on the film, a principle additional to displacement and condensation was assumed, one
that is, I contend, fundamental to all thinking, and particularly operative in the making and interpreting of artistic works. Thus, it is a principle that cannot be omitted from an imaginative theory of metaphor.
Arthur Koestler has seen this principle as a key to understanding how
human communications function and one indeed that is ubiquitous in
the organization of all living systems.[66] I refer of course to the *principle of hierarchy*. On the basis of such a principle, issues are clustered
together according to significance, ranked in order of importance, and
the lower order of meaning made to serve the higher. Without such a
mechanism we would not be able to order our speech any more than
our art. For hierarchical organization is one of the cornerstones of linguistic science, being employed to explain how phonetic levels are
subordinate to syntactic, and these in turn to semantic. My contention
is that it is a basic mechanism of the mind for processing and arrang-
ing data coherently. It is through such an agency that schemata are
formed, and by means of it emergent properties are made possible.

Interpreting a work of art relies heavily upon this principle, for
much of the activity consists in trying to understand how parts are
structured and related to one another. For the artist's shaping of his
material, and the spectator's groping for the form and meaning of the
work are closely allied. The principle of hierarchy explains why the
more organized a work of art is, the more it calls forth from its viewer
a corresponding effort of organizing and ordering. One may say of
films as of other artworks, the more poetic they are the greater their
complexity and cohesion. Eisenstein draws upon the notion of hierarchy when expounding the organic laws of art that filmmakers obey;
filmgoers tacitly employ it when responding to the film before them.
But that response we can see is not passive. For it is one of the paradoxes of aesthetics that the more highly structured a work is, the more
it calls forth the mind's creatively cooperative powers.[67]

The notion that works and interpretations of works are structured hierarchically calls attention to the way both making and understanding are *processes*. Of course, at some stage an artist must relinquish his work: The film has its release date and is handed on to the public. The public, given repeated access to the work, will read it anew each time. Further connections are spotted, other constellations crystallize, hitherto unrecognized nuances become pervasive. Thus finality of interpretation is never arrived at. Elucidation is always provisional, and always is an invitation to a better synthesis.

In writing of *muthos* and its manifestation in film, I have attempted to show how its very coherence is dependent on principles that we have seen elsewhere as central to metaphorical thinking. This is not to deny, of course, the role of other agencies in the shaping of a film's narrative or its thematic structure – for example, the way patterns may be suggested and connections established by the employment of tacit genre conventions. But recourse to such aesthetic and cultural resources is still dependent on more innate powers, and it is these I have wished to delineate.

Conclusion

I have argued that in order to understand metaphor we need an account of the psychological process whereby metaphors are conceived and comprehended. Such an account I have designated an imaginative theory of metaphor, and I have attempted to sketch what it must be. Central to it is the notion of *seeing as* – that is, the reconsideration of one thing in terms of some other taken from a different domain. To perceive or conceive of one thing in terms of another is to restructure and amend the tenor of the metaphor in terms of the vehicle; and it has been urged that this is an interplicit action in which properties attributed to both tenor and vehicle interact to produce an emergent concept. A person attempting to interpret the metaphor seeks this concept, and posits schemata that satisfy the conditions set up by seeing the tenor in terms of the vehicle. The schemata are normally novel – that is, not covered by current concepts and categories. This tends to be the case even where the experience defined thus by the metaphor has been inchoately apprehended before. Normally, also, these novel schemata do not become established as a standard category, but remain tentative and exploratory. They create, as it were, that free play of the faculties that Kant speaks of in the *Critique of Judgment* as a mark of the imagination at work. Where the schemata do become established as a standard category, we have a dead metaphor, one that has come to be taken as a literal description.

Certain advantages flow from this explanation of metaphor, and some implications are also entailed in it. There are explanations, for example, that have attempted to hold metaphor to the level of language, or at least to the domain of signs.[68] Consequently, they have sought – without success – to define the rules whereby metaphors may be identified. The imaginative theory, by proposing that metaphors function at the level of category formation, avoids this consequence, and indeed enables us to explain why a definitive topology of metaphorical forms is impossible. Something that by its very nature challenges and breaks regulatory boundaries can never be pinned down by rules. It follows that the best a rhetorical theory can ever hope to do is to call attention only to those forms that recur with some frequency. No categorization of metaphors can ever claim either completeness or constancy, and the reasons for this are implicit in the imaginative account.

Another advantage is that the imaginative account is compatible with what cognitive psychology has begun to reveal about how we grasp and form concepts. Thus metaphor becomes viewed as part and parcel of normal cognitive behavior and is liberated from the charge that it is an esoteric or illegitimate mode of thinking. Further, by taking the interpretation of a metaphor to be a schema or schemata, the comprehension of metaphor is allied to the procedures of hypothesizing and testing. As with the establishment of a hypothesis and the setting up of observations to confirm or negate it, the construction and assessment of schemata can be brought into the open. What a metaphor means can be explicated, debated, and challenged. In this, the imaginative account possesses a merit sadly lacking in explanations such as the psychoanalytic, where what we know something about is to be explained in terms of what, by definition, we can know nothing about.

The notion of schemata is employed in many contexts, and in particular it is brought into explanations of such phenomena as stereoscopic vision. That is, the notion is applicable to experiential situations as well as more conceptual ones. This is decidedly an advantage when the notion is incorporated into an account of metaphor, for the term is able to take in the affective and experiential aspects of metaphor as well as the intellectual aspects.

An implication of the imaginative account as it is put forward here is that it does stress the uniqueness of each metaphor. The schemata to which one metaphor gives rise will not be the same as those brought forth by any other metaphor. (For example, "O my Luve's like a red, red rose" and "Now she is like the white tree-rose" must each be taken on its own terms.)[69] This itself carries a further implication. To see a work of art incorporating metaphors (and what work of art does not?) for what it is, we have to unravel the metaphors. This means that the uniqueness of a text must be grasped before we can even talk about its "textuality." Recent theoretical approaches to literature and film, which try to bypass interpretation of the text in order to pursue "textuality," invalidate themselves by ignoring this prior, critical responsibility.

Schemata, it has been emphasized, are dispositional. They lead us on to look more closely, and to verify what we think. In this they are akin to scientific hypotheses. And like scientific hypotheses they are useless unless they allow for evidence not only to confirm but also to negate them. Self-fulfilling prophecies are no good. There has to be a tension between what is sought after and what it is possible to find. Where metaphor is concerned, this tension is in part provided by the disparity between tenor and vehicle. Then in turn any schemata that seem to satisfy these conditions must be assessed as to whether they fit the context in which the metaphor is placed. This includes not only the metaphor's place in the whole work of art itself, though this is one of the most important considerations, but also how the metaphor relates to the wider artistic context of genre, style, period, and oeuvres of the artist. Ultimately, the schemata must also be tested by their reference, their *applicatio,* to life itself. Thus, at each stage, the schemata are not only dispositional, they are also provisional. One is always comparing one interpretation with a modified or slightly different version, to see which is the apter. This is why works of art, if they have integrity, never exhaust exposition, and always invite reinterpretation and reappraisal. There is so much there, both in terms of inner organization and "second-order reference," to be contemplated.

It will be recalled that the phrase just quoted is Paul Ricoeur's, and employed by him to explain how works of art "refer." He aligned Aristotle's *muthos* with "organization into a network," and *mimesis,* he argued, entails not the "copying" of things but rather their redescription. In this sense *mimesis* itself is dispositional, and in saying that I am also implying that an important aspect of appreciating works of art is the testing of their validity against our deepest convictions and must sensitive intimations.[70] But while I have indicated my support for Ricoeur's contention that *muthos* is essentially metaphoric in character, I have indicated a further reason not, I think, sufficiently stressed by him: *The implicative network he speaks of is itself largely created by metaphorical operations.* To point toward these operations I appropriated the terms condensation and displacement. But I am using them in a different way to Freud's employment of them, because they are not to be taken as necessarily referring to the – virtually unknowable – workings of the primary process. (Indeed, Freud could not himself have even used these terms unless they were comprehensible from the activities of the secondary process.) Rather I am employing them to describe the way metaphors regularly function when they present one thing in terms of another, and when they fuse multiplicity into unity. In connection with the creation of the *muthos* I also drew attention to another important principle: that of hierarchical arrangement. (Indeed, in an earlier chapter I had already suggested that to make sense of cinematic narrative it was necessary to think of planes of discourse, and to conceive of these as arranged in some hierarchical order.) By these means I have tried to show that metaphors are not merely localized figures, but are operational at every level in a work of art, and are essential to the establishment of its organic unity.

There are two problems I have scarcely touched on. I will mention them now, and suggest that their resolution is already implicit in the imaginative theory of metaphor as it has been adumbrated.

First, can any two items from different domains be brought together to create a meaningful metaphor? My answer to that is yes. But it will depend on the establishing of a suitable context for the metaphor, so that the one item can be reconceived in relation to the other. The importance of context for integrating tenor and vehicle has been emphasized frequently throughout the book, as well as in pages just preceding this.[71] As is well known, even a nonsense sentence, such as "Colorless green ideas sleep furiously," can be given figurative meaning when sited in an appropriate environment. (Indeed, somewhere I have come upon the suggestion that Chomsky's phrase gives quite a good description of some undergraduates' essays.)

Second, can we say what makes for a good or bad metaphor? Here, in the main, the answer must be no. There can no more be a recipe for constructing good metaphors than there are for cracking good jokes or making good works of art. Each has to be judged according to its own merits. That said, there are certain qualities we look for in good metaphors: that a metaphor should be apt; that it should take us by surprise; that it should be memorable; that it should have resonance; that it should bring us to new awareness; that it should live in us. We look for all or some of these. Doubtless, too, at different times certain qualities will be more highly prized in metaphors than others, as fashions shift or sensibility alters. But that metaphor is an invaluable aid to thought and insight generally, and integral to artistic endeavor of all kinds, has been the purport of this chapter and much that has gone before.

This book began as an investigation of cinematic metaphors. To vindicate their importance and explain how many of them worked, it became necessary to go well beyond metaphor as a verbal device. Metaphor had to be understood both as an operation of thought and as an artistic occurrence. Some of the forms in which metaphors frequently recur needed to be noted, and generalized as formulas that would be as applicable to films as to literary works. I hope that what has been demonstrated beyond question has been the actual existence of cinematic figures.

There was one approach to cinematic metaphor I had thought of adopting, but chose not to. It was to have asked what was specific to the medium of film, what possibilities did it possess that a literary medium did not, which made it capable of engendering purely cinematic metaphors. I rejected this strategy for several reasons. First, I was not (and am still not) convinced of the purity of any medium. All the arts borrow from one another, and lend to one another. Second, there are difficulties inherent to an essentialist account of the cinematic medium. Third, it might have cut down the range of metaphors I could cite.[72] For example, some visual metaphors derive from verbal counterparts, but their transition to a new context often changes their effect. "Up against a blank wall" is little more than a verbal cliché. But when Nicolas Roeg uses an urban wall to depict the father's despair and drive to suicide at the beginning of *Walkabout* (as discussed in Chapter V), it does not come over in the least way as hackneyed.[73] Finally, I did not want to get involved in discussions as to what is cinematic and what is not, particularly as there is good reason to feel that cinema as yet is still in the process of marking out its terrain.

Yet such an approach would not have been without its own interest, as clearly there are some effects special to cinema that would be nigh impossible to render in any other medium. One need only take, for example, the texture of the visual image on the screen, and how it can be utilized for metaphorical effect. Three filmic scenes spring to mind. The final sequence of *The Wild Bunch* depicts the American bandits marching through the Mexican encampment for the final shoot-out. They are filmed in long focus, which magnifies them against the motley around them. They march together in rank, which gives them solidity and purpose, but this is undermined by the long-focus lens, which gives the effect of retarded progression. Furthermore, the hot air between camera and figures being filmed makes the image blur and quiver. Heroism is made insubstantial even as it is depicted. Peckinpah's master, Akiru Kurosawa, also employs the long lens for texturally figurative effects. In *Throne of Blood* (*Kumonosu-jo*) the long lens achieves, in the opening sequence, a flattened pointillism that helps evoke a primitiveness and remoteness befitting the legendary. Whereas in Ingmar Bergman's *The Passion of Anna* (*En passion*) the increasing graininess of the final shot enacts the disintegration of the character played by Max von Sydow. In sequences such as these the cinematic medium is being used to advantage.

In the course of writing this book, however, I have come to realize that the kind of cinematic metaphors that most interest me are not necessarily especially cinematic, or even ones that are in themselves vivid and remarkable. Rather they are metaphors that do not stand out from the *muthos* of the film, but are part of the very warp and woof of it. These metaphors are often at once elusive, and pervasive. Subordinate to the tale told, they yet seem central to its very conception. For it is by means of them the cinematic fable achieves its potency and resonance. One might say only an imaginative theory of metaphor can begin to account for them. But they are not easy to write about as metaphors, for they are inseparable from the art that embodies them. What they portend takes us to the heart of the filmmaker's view of things, of how he sees the world, and frames his response to it. I am thinking of the way Bresson, for example, makes us look closely at material things, and at mundane events and gestures, so that the unseen and unspoken grace may be felt in its apparent absence – as the essential transfiguration of martyrdom is paradoxically purveyed through the final shot in *The Trial of Joan of Arc* (*Le Procès de Jeanne d'Arc*), which holds on the burnt and blackened stake only. I am thinking of the way Monument Valley becomes more than just a scenically beautiful backdrop to Ford's frontier dramas, of how that landscape, carved and emboldened by the ravages of aeons, dignifies man's recurrent strifes and rituals. I am thinking too of the way Renoir, in film after film, contrasts men's self-inflicted barriers with the free flow of life itself.

Indeed, perhaps it is fitting I should end with mentioning Renoir, for his art epitomizes the kind of cinematic metaphor I most admire: unobtrusive and unforgettable. These are my last two examples of metaphor. Think of the hunt in *The Rules of the Game* (*La Règle du Jeu*), and how disturbingly reverberative it becomes in its context, hinting at the carnage of World War I, and of such contributory causes for it as obsession with class, social vanity, and indifference to life itself. Or think of the character of Ballochet (Claude Rich) in *The Elusive Corporal* (*Le Caporal épinglé*): the inspector of gas meters who yearns to escape from the ignominies and servitudes of life. In one of the film's moments of finest pathos, Ballochet speaks of his cowardice and his aspirations. How does Renoir present it? Ballochet sits upon the lavatory seat. Here, linked to the ground and to one's corporeal functions, he talks of his ardent desire to fly and to have been a fighter pilot. A tragic dilemma is, unobtrusively, articulated by the mise-en-scène.

The greatest metaphors, cinematic and literary alike, encapsulate the most-telling truths.

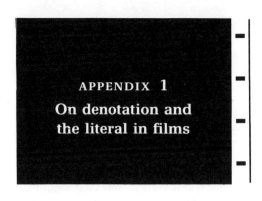

APPENDIX 1

On denotation and
the literal in films

It should be noted that the term *denotation* is ambiguous when it is used in the context of film images, for it may cover two different situations. In one case it may refer to the way a film image reveals, or claims to reveal, the existence of a real object or event that was recorded by the camera. In the other case it may refer to the bringing before us of an object or event we are to accept as depicted by the image, though whether it does or does not exist in reality is not an issue. The distinction is acknowledged in the difference we draw between documentary and feature films. In documentaries, though the makers may be distorting the facts or even lying to us, it is important that the images be taken as directly relating to the real things, and as substantiatable by them. (Indeed, Woody Allen's *Zelig* – where Zelig himself appears on the papal balcony, and behind Hitler on the platform of a Nazi rally – might be taken as the definitive put-down to any belief in the unchallengeable authenticity of film images.) Normally with feature films, however, referential accuracy is irrelevant. Although there may still be some edification or interest to be derived from direct denotation, mostly we see this as being subordinated to the ends of fiction. A bargain of "make-believe" is tacit, and we interpret accordingly. Consequently there is a shift in how we read images as "literal." In documentaries a shot is literal if it does not deviate too markedly from our normal vision of things and the customary way cinema represents this. In features the same holds true, but also we are inclined to accept as literal that which appears to be at home in the domain of the narrative and does not in any way challenge the categories established as belonging to it. Apparitions quite acceptable as literal though fictitious in a fantasy film become figurative when appearing in a psychological drama such as *Juliet of the Spirits* (*Giulietta degli spiriti*).

It is important to know when to test a film over the claims it implicitly makes about its direct or suspended relation to reality.[1] Although it may be useful to maintain the dichotomy between the literal and the figurative even where films are concerned, certain considerations should never be forgotten. Even with direct filmic denotation, where the indexical link between image and phenomena in the real world is strongest, we have a seeing of the object in a certain way, a describing of it, not a neutral copying or reflecting. Despite the indexical bond then, film documentaries share with verbal reports the assumptions and bias of the authors and their culture.

133

Both films and verbal reports are shaped by prior categories and concepts.

Words, however, are general – film images are characteristically specific. The word *telephone* denotes a class of objects – the film image denotes a particular member of the class.[2] The writer has to strive for specificity; the filmmaker does not. Whatever categories he has imported into his film manifest themselves through the particular. The categories as reproduced are thus fused with and modified by what is individual and unique. Hence film images, while signs, are not normally signs in the Saussurian sense: In their individuality they cannot be reduced to mere counters in a system, and their signification (in Saussure's sense) is never only conventional. For a film image is the locus of a meeting between categories the filmmaker would impose and a recalcitrant reality surly to such bondage. Much of the charm of Truffaut's *Day for Night* (*La Nuit américaine*), his film about filmmaking, comes from showing how, while film production attempts to cheat on or manipulate reality outside itself, the contingencies of that reality inevitably impress themselves upon the production and the film itself. In any film image, then, there is a tension and a density that arises from the encounter of our preconceptions with the otherness of the world.

It follows that one film image, even of the same object, is never quite synonomous with another. Consequently, too, how that image will combine with other images and how it will then function can never be wholly predicted. This means that the search for codes that would chart what syntagmatic or paradigmatic organizations of film images are possible is clearly misguided, and based upon a misunderstanding of the nature of cinematic signs. At most, one can only speak of tendencies, or likelihoods, based on one's previous experience of films. Where films are concerned one can speak of parole, not langue – of unfolding practice, never of fixed system.

I have argued that the imaginative account of metaphor, taken together with the rhetorical delineation of figurative devices, is sounder, more explanatory and fruitful in application than any other account of cinematic metaphor attempted so far. Further, I have suggested that by applying the concept of metaphor to film a more general view of metaphorical working is made possible. Perhaps the best way of highlighting the merits of the approach adopted in this book is to set the imaginative account alongside a very different view of metaphor – indeed one not so far discussed here.

John Searle's analysis of metaphor has attracted a great deal of interest. It is wide enough in scope, and original enough in approach, to act as a good touchstone.[1] For Searle, metaphor involves a discrepancy between sentence meaning and speaker's utterance meaning, and the meaning of the metaphor is to be located in the speaker's utterance meaning. So for Searle metaphor in essence involves a sentence, "S is P," but the hearer is to understand the meaning as S is R, and $S \neq R$, and R is the speaker's intended meaning.

Normally when the speech act of assertion is employed sentence meaning and speaker's meaning are the same, and the same truth conditions apply equally to both. Discussing this, Searle does draw attention to the fact that in order to determine the truth conditions of the sentence a background of factual assumptions not explicitly realized in the semantic structure of the sentence must be understood. (In our terms this means that both speaker and hearer are drawing upon a set of shared schemata when uttering and comprehending the sentence.) Where a metaphor is involved, however, not only will R instead of P be a predicate of S, but the truth conditions pertaining to the two predications will be different.

The central problem of metaphor for Searle then is how "an expression with its literal meaning and corresponding truth conditions can, in various ways specific to metaphor, call to mind another meaning and corresponding set of truth conditions." (It might be noted that this is putting the cart before the horse. A metaphor must be coined by a speaker before a hearer needs to interpret it. What prompts the speaker to resort to metaphor in the first place? This surely is the more germane question.)

In unfolding his answer to the problem as he has defined it, Searle sets out some interesting ideas. He presents a stimulating critique of the two major types of account, namely the comparison theory of metaphor and of the inter-

135

action theory – though I shall question the validity of his argument against the latter shortly. More directly pertinent to our enquiry is Searle's attempt to define the principles underpinning our interpretation of metaphor. Searle distinguishes between the meaning of an expression and the process or strategy employed by the hearer to arrive at that meaning. Where metaphor is concerned Searle envisages the hearer going through three steps to interpret the metaphor:

1. identifying that there is a metaphor present that requires interpretation;
2. applying a set of principles for computing possible values of R;
3. having a set of principles or strategies for restricting the range of R.

(We might note in passing that I have attempted to define Searle's step 1 through establishing the set of frequently employed rhetorical cues; and that my imaginative theory of metaphor is meant to *underpin* the processes Searle discusses in his steps 2 and 3. So there is some overlap between us in topics explored.)

In explicating what is entailed under step 1, Searle suggests that such cues as "obvious falsehood, semantic nonsense, violations of semantic speech acts of one kind or another" trigger the recognition that a metaphor is being communicated. But he acknowledges that the presence of such cues is not a necessary condition and there may be other means employed for recognizing metaphors (e.g., expectation that a Romantic poet might be prone to the use of metaphor). In other words, no complete set of cues can ever be identified, though certain cues might be listed as frequently employed ones.

In dealing with step 2, Searle makes a similar acknowledgment: Not all the principles for identifying the range of possible R's are known to him, but again he attempts to mention some of the more prevalent (e.g., "look for salient, well-known, and distinctive features of P things" which might be applicable).

Step 3 involves cutting down the range to those features that actually may be regarded as applicable. Some attributes identified under step 2 will be found to be irrelevant (e.g., that the sun is for the most part gaseous is not helpful in interpreting "Juliet is the sun") whereas others have a valid bearing on S. Searle sees the interaction theory of metaphor as having been evolved to deal with step 3 but he still has doubts about the theory itself.

Searle interprets the interactionist theory to be saying that the juxtaposition of S and P in the original sentence establishes an association between P and R that did not exist previously. Searle challenges this view. He claims R is simply specifiable from P, and must be in the range of features of P. S only restricts the range of P and does not create an R not in that range.

Yet Searle himself in crucial sections of his own argument asserts that there is a feature of R not subsumed under the range of P, namely that R is figurative and as such is not paraphrasable without loss. This is incompatible with saying that R is within the range of features of P taken by itself. The features of P sought for under step 2 must involve what is salient, well known, and distinctive about P. If certain features of P, say P_n and P_{n+y}, are the features that make R possible, they must themselves be either metaphorical or literal features of P. If they are metaphorical features, then their figurative purport would predate the combination "S is P" and metaphorical meaning would therefore not be dependent on a speaker's intention. If they are literal, then how can R be metaphorical and yet be within the range of literal features of P?

The difficulties Searle has in explaining this emerge in his attack on the comparison theory of metaphor. Searle argues, rightly I believe, that there need be no literal similarity between S and P. How then, given P, do we arrive at R? How, for instance, given "Sally is a block of ice," do we move from "block of ice" to a figurative meaning such as "unresponsive"? Searle's explanation is weak. He says that, by step 2 we must look for salient, well-known, and distinctive features of P. But is lack of feeling such a feature of a block of ice? Surely not. Searle tries to get round this by saying that "simply as a matter of perceptions, sensibilities, and linguistic practices, people find the notion of coldness associated in their minds with lack of emotion."[2] But surely this is only so when we think of human emotions – that is, P can only be said to possess this feature when conjoined with an S involving a person. So S interacts with P to produce R, and we are back to the interaction theory from which Searle is trying to escape.[3]

Evasiveness of some kind is surely present in Searle's Principle 4:

Things which are P are not R, nor are they like R things, nor are they believed to be R; nonetheless it is a fact about our sensibility, whether culturally or naturally determined, that we just do perceive a connection, so that P is associated in our minds with R properties.

Or in other words, it happens because it happens.

The only sensible course would seem to be to accept, with the interaction theory, that when P_n and P_{n+y} are attributed to S literal attributes or associations become transformed into (new) figurative attributes because two alien domains are interplicit.

Searle's account is attended by other deficiencies. The distinction between literal and figurative plays an important role in the discussion, but at no stage is the distinction adequately explained or clarified. In arguing that "S is R" must be a meaning belonging to the speaker's utterance and not to sentence utterance, he omits to explain why as such it is necessarily metaphorical. Nor, at the end of his paper, does his attempt to distinguish between metaphorical utterances and other indirect speech-act utterances such as irony remedy this omission. At one point Searle explains the expressive power of metaphor (which is intrinsically not paraphrasable) by saying that the hearer has to contribute more to the communication than just passive uptake and has to do this by going through another and related semantic content. But irony too gives us two ideas for one, and metaphors may be ironical as well as metaphorical (e.g., Pope's line about young Aeneas who, on his European tour, "Dropt the dull lumber of the Latin store").[4] Something other than relations between subject and sentence and speaker's meanings must be involved. But just what is not delineated.

The claim that metaphor is sited only in, and is only constituted by, speaker's utterance also is too restrictive and ignores important features of metaphor.

At one stage in Searle's critique of the interactionist account he suggests that interactionists assume metaphors occur only in sentences employing other expressions that are literal. This assumption is unwarranted, he rightly says, because not every metaphor is embedded only in literal expressions: Metaphors may be surrounded by other metaphorical expressions. Indeed they often are. But Searle's own discussion is for the most part restricted to sentences employed for the speech act of assertion only – that is, to predications where truth conditions apply. Many metaphors, however, do not occur in such sentences. More important, for a great range of metaphors the notion of truth conditions itself is a very problematic one indeed. I am thinking of that enormous range of metaphors that occurs within works of poetry or fiction. How, for instance, are we to specify the truth conditions for "I wandered lonely as a cloud / That floats on high o'er vales and hills"? Can we even paraphrase, except trivially, a line like "still unravish'd bride of quietness" so as to establish its truth conditions? Something further would have to be said of truth conditions in relation to literary works before one could see Searle's discussion of metaphor as having any relevance to metaphors in poems or novels.

The same stricture must apply even more forcibly to Searle's idea of metaphor occurring in speaker's utterance and not in sentence utterance. Is the relationship between a poet or a novelist and a reader the same as that between speaker and hearer? Many think not.[5] The onus is on Searle to show that speech-act theory as applied to speaker and hearer is applicable to literary artifacts. Given the close connection many see between the way literature generally functions and how metaphors function – that, for instance, they mean, or show, or maybe just suggest more than they state on the surface[6] – an account of metaphor is incomplete unless accompanied by an appropriate account of the way literature refers to or alludes to the world.

Searle's idea of metaphor, linked as it is to sentence utterance and speaker's utterance, does not lend itself to the interpretation of metaphors outside speech acts – and hence probably not to films, unless speech-act theory can somehow be expanded to account for cinematic communication. Until that is done, we are left with a lacuna here. In my case I have been able to use the concept of filmic metaphor to help formulate and test a more general account of metaphor. Despite the limitations of Searle's account of metaphor that I have drawn attention to, the account is ambitious enough and touches upon enough issues to make comparison between it and my own an informative exercise. By presenting such a comparison, in particular by showing how the two accounts offer similar and/or conflicting answers to some fundamental questions about metaphor, some of the strengths of the account of metaphor I have proffered in this book may be foregrounded.

What is a metaphor?

For Searle metaphor is a figurative meaning discovered in a speaker's utterance that differs from his sentence meaning. "Figurative," however, is not adequately characterized.

By the account I have employed a metaphor involves the redescription of one thing in terms of something else belonging to an alien category. The meaning of the metaphor is to be located in the schema or schemata so generated in order to reconcile the incompatibility between the tenor and the vehicle applied to it.

How does metaphorical utterance differ from literal?

Searle says that metaphor can express things that literal utterances do not, but he does not explain why this is so beyond saying that metaphor gives us two ideas for one. Nor does he adequately explain how a speaker's metaphorical utterance is to be distinguished from a speaker's nonmetaphorical utterance when in both cases these bear a meaning that differs from the sentence meaning.

My account has it that a literal utterance accords with our employment of preexisting categories, whereas a figurative expression does not since it involves "a deliberate category mistake."[7] In this way it forces upon us a recognition of features pertaining to the tenor that literal attributions cannot render.

Why are metaphors used?

Both Searle and I consider the most important reason to be that metaphors can express things literal utterances cannot. My explanation for this is that metaphor is a way of rendering some things that fall outside or between our received categories. I believe it to be a major strength of my account that it accords with the effects of metaphor as delineated by writers on literature – particularly by Romantic critics such as Coleridge – while at the same time it is compatible with what cognitive psychologists are now saying about the role of schemata in perception and cognition.

Both Searle and I see metaphor as forcing a certain creativity on the hearer when the hearer carries out the mental activity appropriate to realizing the metaphor. But whereas Searle seems to believe that this is primarily employing a strategy of comprehension – in steps 2 and 3 – I follow those who like Paul Ricoeur envisage it as much more than that, considering that the realizing of a metaphor belongs to "the logic of discovery," which brings about a new way of both describing and perceiving aspects of the world.

How do we recognize metaphors?

Both Searle and I confess we do not know all the ways in which metaphors identify themselves as such, though we both believe there are some cues that are quite common. The more prevalent cues I have attempted to define through establishing a set of rhetorical formulas, and I have shown that such formulas can be observed at work in films as in literary works.

How are metaphors comprehended?

Searle sketches two stages subsequent to the recognition of a metaphor being present. Basically, he does it in terms of the range of predicates and mental associations conjured up by P in the sentence "S is P," and in regard to the limits placed upon that range by the connotations and reference of S itself. My account goes along with most of what Searle says here, but gives more emphasis to the clash of categories with their accompanying cognitive networks.[8] It envisages this as entailing a redescription of aspects of the world.

What is a dead metaphor?

For me a dead metaphor is one that has acquired the status of a literal description and now names an accepted category of objects (e.g., skyscraper). It would appear Searle believes something similar, but he denies that with metaphor there is ever a change in meaning in at least one term of the expression. This denial robs him of any means whereby he can account for how metaphors do, diachronically speaking – as he himself admits – initiate semantic changes in the language.

Why do some metaphors work and others not?

Perhaps this is an unanswerable question, in the same way as "Why are some jokes funny and others not?" All we can say is that a metaphor just does work, or just does not, as the case may be. Searle, I imagine, like myself would have to say it depends on how a particular P stands in relation to a particular S. But Searle seems to regard the intention of the speaker as being a key factor. For my part I would see the context too as playing a crucial role in the functioning of a metaphor. Searle, despite his primary emphasis on the speaker's intention, seems to do this too: He offers, for example, "quadrilaterality drinks procrastination" as an acceptable metaphorical description of any postwar four-power disarmament conference, even though that was not Bertrand Russell's intention when he minted the phrase.[9]

Why do we say something is lost when a metaphor is paraphrased?

Searle clearly considers this to be the case, but I cannot see that he provides any justification for thinking so, other than in the very last paragraph of his paper – and I have commented already on the vagueness of that. In the account I have pursued, the clash of categories and the ensuing attempt to reconcile disparate networks lead to the formation of schemata. These are cognitive or perceptual hypotheses that we try out. They provide us with a mental set toward the object we are contemplating rather than with a specified number of assertions about it. Paraphrases on the other hand must particularize; normally they employ literal terms (except in rare cases where we may use a simpler or more commonplace metaphor to explain a complex one); and they are cut and dried in their application of categories. They lack the tentativeness, the openness to other possibilities, and the "free play of the imagination" (to appropriate Kant's expression) that characterize the experience of metaphor itself.

Notes

I. Introduction

1. François Truffaut, *Hitchcock* (London: Panther Books, 1969), pp. 359–60.

2. "Screen Writer: *Taxi Driver's* Paul Schrader," interviewed by Richard Thompson, *Film Comment* 12, no. 2 (March–April 1976), p. 17.

3. James F. Scott, *Film: The Medium and the Maker* (New York: Holt, Rinehart & Winston, 1975), p. 113.

4. W. Bedell Stanford, *Greek Metaphor* (Oxford: Basil Blackwell, 1936), p. 95n. The film discussed is *Song of Ceylon,* dir. Basil Wright, and the reviewer is Graham Greene.

5. Calvin B. Pryluck, "The Film Metaphor Metaphor: The Use of Language-Based Models in Film Study," *Literature/Film Quarterly* 3, no. 2 (Spring 1975), pp. 119–30.

6. Rudolf Arnheim, *Film* (London: Faber, 1933), p. 265.

7. George Bluestone, *Novels into Film* (Baltimore: The Johns Hopkins Press, 1957), pp. 19–20.

8. For example, John Middleton Murry: "[Metaphor] is the means by which the less familiar is assimilated to the more familiar, the unknown to the known." *Selected Criticism 1916–1957* (Oxford: Oxford University Press, 1960), pp. 65–6.

9. See Nicholas Vardac, "Realism and Romance: D. W. Griffith," in *Focus on D. W. Griffith,* ed. Harry M. Geduld (Englewood Cliffs, N.J.: Prentice-Hall, 1971), pp. 70–9; Yon Barna, *Eisenstein* (London: Secker & Warburg, 1973), chap. 3 and p. 132.

10. See J. Dudley Andrew, *The Major Film Theories* (Oxford: Oxford University Press, 1976), pp. 129–31 and 235–6.

11. See, for example, Marcus B. Hester on "seeing as": *The Meaning of Poetic Metaphor* (The Hague: Mouton, 1967), pp. 181–7; and Winifred Nowottny, *The Language Poets Use* (London: Athlone Press, 1965).

12. I am thinking of the fascinating use of Chomskian analysis for the exposition of musical metaphors; see Leonard Bernstein, *The Unanswered Question* (Cambridge, Mass.: Harvard University Press, 1976), chap. 3: "Musical Semantics."

13. See Hester, *Poetic Metaphor,* p. 196.

14. See also J. Dudley Andrew, *Concepts in Film Theory* (Oxford: Oxford University Press, 1984), particularly chaps. 9 and 10, which present a critique of recent semiotic and structuralist approaches to cinema.

II. The concept of poetic metaphor

1. Percy Bysshe Shelley, "A Defence of Poetry," in *English Critical Texts,* ed. D. J. Enright and Ernst de Chickera (London: Oxford University Press, 1962), p. 227.

2. I. A. Richards, *The Philosophy of Rhetoric* (Oxford: Oxford University Press, 1936), p. 96.

3. Some writers dispute the notion that simile is a species of metaphor, arguing that it functions differently. E.g. W. Bedell Stanford, *Greek Metaphors* (Oxford: Basil Blackwell, 1936), pp. 28–9; see also David M. Miller, *The Net of Hephaestus: A Study of Modern Criticism and Metaphysical Metaphor* (The Hague: Mouton, 1971), p. 30. Most writers, however, including Aristotle and Richards, regard the differences as inessential. This view is adopted here. An analysis later in this chapter shows that a simile can be quite as complex as a metaphor.

4. This has become known as the "interactionist" account of metaphor. It is the account that accords best with the experience of understanding metaphors in poetry.

5. See Edward Sapir, *Language* (New York: Harcourt & Brace, 1921), and Benjamin Lee Whorf, *Language, Thought, and Reality,* ed. J. Carroll (Cambridge, Mass.: MIT Press, 1956). The Sapir–Whorf hypothesis, that language rather than preexisting reality establishes human categories of experience, is still a subject greatly debated. For a philosophic comment on the problems of testing the hypothesis, see David E. Cooper, *Philosophy and the Nature of Language* (London: Longman, 1973), chap. 5. Howard Gardner, *The Mind's New Science* (New York: Basic Books, 1985), summarizes the recent views of cognitive psychologists on these issues.

6. See Terence Hawkes, *Metaphor* (London: Methuen, 1972), p. 31.

7. Wallace Stevens, *Opus Posthumous* (New York: Alfred A. Knopf, 1957), p. 179.

8. See Stanford, *Greek Metaphor,* p. 105.

9. See Richards: "In general, there are very few metaphors in which disparity between tenor and vehicle are not as much operative as the similarities" (*Rhetoric,* p. 127).

10. Quoted by Peter Dixon in *Rhetoric* (London: Methuen, 1971), p. 37.

11. For an account of Shakespeare's use of schemes and tropes, see Bertram Joseph, *Acting Shakespeare* (London: Routledge & Kegan Paul, 1960), p. 196. For a fuller description of rhetorical figures, a useful book is Lee A. Sonnino, *A Handbook of Sixteenth Century Rhetoric* (London: Routledge & Kegan Paul, 1968).

12. See David Lodge, "The Language of Modernist Fiction: Metaphor and Metonymy," in *Modernism,* ed. Malcolm Bradbury and James McFarlane (Harmondsworth: Penguin Books, 1976), pp. 481–6. Roman Jacobson's, "Two Aspects of Language and Two Types of Aphasic Disturbances," was the paper

that became so influential in redirecting attention to metonymy. Unfortunately it also led to setting up metaphor and metonymy as polar opposites. Jakobson's paper is reprinted in *Selected Writings II: Word and Language* (The Hague: Mouton, 1971), pp. 239–52. See also René Wellek and Austin Warren, *Theory of Literature* (Harmondsworth: Penguin Books, 1976), pp. 194–5; and Stephen Ullman, *Language and Style* (Oxford: Basil Blackwell, 1964), p. 117.

13. See Wellek and Warren, *Literature,* p. 195.

14. Philip Wheelwright, *Metaphor and Reality* (Bloomington: Indiana University Press, 1975).

15. Ibid., p. 81.

16. Stanley Cavell, for instance, still seems to think that the use of the word *like* changes how the rhetoric functions; see Stanley Cavell, *Must We Mean What We Say?* (Cambridge: Cambridge University Press, 1976), p. 79. See also n. 3 above.

17. Wheelwright, *Metaphor,* pp. 80–3; S. T. Coleridge, *Biographia Literaria,* 2 vols., ed. J. Shawcross (reprinted with corrections, Oxford: Oxford University Press, 1907), chap. 10; T. S. Eliot, "The Metaphysical Poets," in *Selected Essays* (London: Faber, 1932), p. 287.

18. See Wheelwright, *Metaphor,* pp. 80–2; Northrop Frye, *Anatomy of Criticism* (Princeton: Princeton University Press, 1971), p. 123; and Wellek and Warren, *Literature,* pp. 187–211.

19. C. Day Lewis, *The Poetic Image* (London: Jonathon Cape, 1947), p. 18.

20. "[A symbol] is characterized by a translucence of the General in the Especial, or of the Eternal through and in the Temporal. It always partakes of the Reality it renders intelligible; and while it annunciates the whole, abides itself as a living part in the unity of which it is the representative." S. T. Coleridge, *The Statesman's Manual,* in *The Collected Works of Samuel Taylor Coleridge, no 6: Lay Sermons* (London: Routledge & Kegan Paul, 1972), p. 30.

21. T. S. Eliot, "Hamlet," in *Selected Essays,* pp. 124–5.

22. E.g.: "This leads to the recognition of the important point (often overlooked in syntax as well as in semantics) that acceptability and deviation are gradable, not absolutely yes-or-no concepts.... we point out that a sentence which is contradictory or otherwise absurd on one interpretation may become sensible through the operation of rules of transfer of meaning: acceptability therefore becomes a question of the ease with which a lexical rule may provide us with an alternative interpretation, if the face-value or literal value is ruled out as a violation." Geoffrey N. Leech, *Semantics* (Harmondsworth: Penguin Books, 1974), pp. 230–1. See also Geoffrey N. Leech, *A Linguistic Guide to English Poetry* (London: Longman, 1969), chap. 9, "Figurative Language."

23. In an earlier draft of this chapter, published in *U.C.T. Studies in English,* no. 6 (1978), analyses of chiming metaphors in Shakespeare's dramatic verse were provided.

24. The phrase was introduced by G. Wilson Knight in *The Wheel of Fire* (London: Oxford University Press, 1930), p. 15.

25. This paragraph is indebted to ideas expounded by W. K. Wimsatt, Jr. See *The Verbal Icon* (London: Methuen, 1979), particularly p. 217.

26. William Empson, *The Structure of Complex Words* (London: Chatto & Windus, 1951), chap. 18.

27. Leonard Bernstein bases his analysis of musical metaphors on the notion of such transformations: *The Unanswered Question* (Cambridge, Mass.: Harvard University Press, 1976), chap. 3.

28. "The reader pieces out the metaphor by something supplied or constructed from his own experience, according to the specifications given linguistically by the utterance in which the metaphor occurs." Winifred Nowottny, *The Language Poets Use* (London: Athlone Press, 1965), p. 59. See also Graham Dunstan Martin, *Language, Truth and Poetry* (Edinburgh: University Press, 1975), pp. 209–10.

29. See Marcus B. Hester, *The Meaning of Poetic Metaphor* (The Hague: Mouton, 1967), pp. 199f.

30. Christine Brooke-Rose, *A Grammar of Metaphor* (London: Secker & Warburg, 1958), introduction.

III. Language, metaphor, and the film image

1. Gilbert Ryle, *Dilemmas: The Tarner Lectures 1953* (Cambridge: Cambridge University Press, 1954), p. 66.

2. Cf. Calvin B. Pryluck, "The Film Metaphor Metaphor: The Use of Language-Based Models in Film Study," *Literature/Film Quarterly* 3, no. 2 (Spring 1975), pp. 117–23.

3. See Irvin Rock's discussion of how we perceive representational images: *Perception* (New York: Scientific American Books, 1984), particularly chaps. 4 and 7; for a fuller discussion of various accounts of representation in the cinema and why so many of them are misguided, see Noël Carroll, *Mystifying Movies: Fads and Fallacies in Contemporary Film Theory* (New York: Columbia University Press, 1988), esp. pp. 106–46. See also the discussion of the priority of object perception in the cinema in David Bordwell, *Narration in the Fiction Film* (London: Methuen, 1985), pp. 100–54.

4. Peter Wollen, *Signs and Meaning in the Cinema* (London: Secker & Warburg, 1969), pp. 102f.

5. André Bazin, *What Is Cinema?* trans. Hugh Gray (Berkeley: University of California Press, 1967), p. 12. See the critique of Bazin's account, however, in Noël Carroll, *Philosophical Problems of Classical Film Theory* (Princeton: Princeton University Press, 1988), chap. 2.

6. Christian Metz, *Film Language,* trans. Michael Taylor (New York: Oxford University Press, 1974), p. 8.

7. Ibid., p. 6. For an opposing view, see Stanley Cavell, *The World Viewed: Reflections on the Ontology of Film* (New York: Viking Press, 1971), p. 26.

8. Coleridge, *Literaria Biographia,* 2 vols., ed. J. Shawcross (Oxford: Oxford University Press, 1907), chap. 13.

9. Pryluck, "Film Metaphor," pp. 119–20. "A number of writers have criticized the whole idea of 'film metaphor' on the partially valid basis that the photographic image in film is a literal representation of objects and events. These objects and events, the argument goes, have intrinsic meanings which militate against the images being interpreted figuratively." He mentions Siegfried Kracauer, Rudolf Arnheim, and George Bluestone.

10. Jean Mitry, *Esthétique et psychologie du cinéma,* 2 vols. (Paris: Editions Universitaires, 1963, 1965).

11. Christian Metz, "Current Problems of Film Theory: Mitry's *Esthétique et Psychologie du Cinéma,* Vol. II," in *Movies and Methods,* ed. Bill Nichols (Berkeley: University of California Press, 1976), pp. 569–70. Metz's full review of Mitry's work was first published in *Screen* 14, nos. 1–2, pp. 40–87.

12. I. A. Richards, *The Philosophy of Rhetoric* (Oxford: Oxford University Press, 1936), p. 94.

13. Cf. *Biographia Literaria,* chap. 10. Also see previous discussion in Chapter II.

14. G. D. Martin, *Language, Truth and Poetry* (Edinburgh: University Press, 1975), p. 209; see also p. 66.

15. Ibid., p. 213.

16. Ibid., pp. 208–9. Max Black's "interaction view of metaphor" is very similar. See Max Black, "Metaphor," in *Contemporary Studies in Aesthetics,* ed. Francis J. Coleman (New York: McGraw-Hill, 1968), pp. 216–32. The article was first published in *Proceedings of the Aristotelean Society* 55 (1954–55).

17. Marcus B. Hester, *The Meaning of Poetic Metaphor* (The Hague: Mouton, 1967), p. 169.

18. Ibid., p. 183.

19. Ibid. Another writer on metaphor, who follows this line of thought and explores some of its epistemological implications, is Philip Wheelwright in *Metaphor and Reality* (Bloomington: Indiana University Press, 1962); see particularly chap. 8: "The Sense of Reality."

20. Ludwig Wittgenstein, *Philosophical Investigations,* trans. G. E. M. Anscombe (Oxford: Basil Blackwell, 1958), p. 202.

21. Ibid., p. 213.

22. Yves de Laurot, "From Logos to Lens," in *Movies and Methods,* p. 581; originally published in *Cinéaste* in 1970. Yves de Laurot gives a narrower definition of metaphor than many referred to in this book: "Traditionally, metaphor has been defined as a junction between two phenomena or objects that are similar in essence though dissimilar in appearance. The way we [i.e., he and his associates of Cinema Engagé] use it, one even tends toward the fulfillment in the other. In other words, by prolepsis, we perceive the essence in the appearance, the latent in the real" (p. 579). (De Laurot's appeal to essence might be described, in the jargon of left-wing structuralism, as an attempt to "naturalize" the revolutionary viewpoint and so – illegitimately – persuade the reader to accept its "privileged" status.)

23. Ibid., p. 581.

24. Cf. James Monaco, *How to Read a Film* (New York: Oxford University Press, 1977), pp. 149–64.

25. This account corresponds closely to Max Black's "interaction view" of metaphor previously mentioned.

26. Rudolf Arnheim, *Film as Art* (London: Faber, 1958), pp. 122–3.

27. This usage should not be confused with the usage of the term by film semioticians; see, for instance, John Fiske and John Hartley, *Reading Television* (London: Methuen, 1978), pp. 40–7. It is employed more or less as a synonym for "meaning" or "meaning as process." See also *The Cinema Book,* ed. Pam Cook (London: British Film Institute, 1985). For Saussure, signification results from the arbitrary, but conventionally established, assignment of a given signifier to a given signified. Ferdinand de Saussure, *Course in General Linguistics,* trans. Wade Baskin (London: Fontana/Collins, 1974), pp. 114–22.

28. Pier Paulo Pasolini, "The Cinema of Poetry," in *Movies and Methods,* p. 545.

29. Cf. Metz, *Film Language,* and *Language and Cinema,* trans. Donna Jean Umiker-Seboek (The Hague: Mouton, 1974). See also J. Dudley Andrew, *The Major Film Theories* (Oxford: Oxford University Press, 1976), chap. 8.

30. "Signs that are wholly arbitrary realize better than the others the ideal of the semiological process." Saussure, *General Linguistics,* p. 68.

31. Noël Burch, *Theory of Film Practice* (London: Secker & Warburg, 1973).

32. Linguists refer to the paradigmatic (or selectional) and the syntagmatic (or combinatory) axes of linguistic structure. In effect, what is being suggested is that the signification of film images is created on both axes through selecting the image that is to represent the object, and through placing that image in a context of other images.

IV. Planes of discourse in cinema

1. Eric Rhode, *A History of the Cinema from Its Origins to 1970* (London: Allen Lane, 1976), p. 41.

2. See the discussion in Chapter III.

3. F. de Saussure, *Course in General Linguistics* (London: Fontana/Collins, 1974), pp. 65f.

4. The word *code,* fashionable in certain linguistic circles at present, is not a fortunately chosen term: Some implications inherent in it are questionable. Cf. Ian Robinson, *The New Grammarians' Funeral* (Cambridge: Cambridge University Press, 1975), pp. 74–9. In general, it is better to use specific terms in its place, such as *syntactic rules, semantic rules, artistic conventions, genre expectations, social customs, manners, rituals, beliefs, proverbs,* etc. Of course, a term such as *convention* is itself not without ambiguities – as I point out in *A Reading of the Canterbury Tales* (Cambridge: Cambridge University Press, 1968), pp. 34f. – but it does not lend itself to mystification to the extent *code* does.

5. Jonathan Culler, *Saussure* (Brighton: Harvester Press, 1976), pp. 100–1.

6. Ibid., pp. 104–5.

7. Andrzej Wajda, *The Wajda Trilogy,* trans. and intr. Boleslaw Sulik (London: Lorrimer, 1973), pp. 21–5.

8. For a study of the relation between finance, audiences, and filmmaking policy, see John Izod, *Hollywood and the Box Office 1895–1986* (London: Macmillan, 1988).

9. I am referring here to what is sometimes called "mainstream cinema" – i.e., cinema practice developed mainly in America and influencing popular European cinema. For discussion of other modes of cinematic narrative, see David Bordwell, *Narration in the Fiction Film* (London: Methuen, 1985).

10. James F. Scott, *Film: The Medium and the Maker* (New York: Holt, Rinehart & Winston, 1975), p. 314.

11. To convince a skeptic one might have to point to similar shots in Ford's films where the metaphor is more immediately apparent, such as the shot of Lincoln riding toward the thunderstorm at the end of *Young Mr. Lincoln.* Only a sensitivity to larger patterns and characteristics of style makes identification of some tropes possible.

12. See Lincoln F. Johnson, *Film: Space Time Light and Sound* (New York: Holt, Rinehart & Winston, 1974), for a discussion of this sequence in *The Red Desert;* see particularly pp. 150 and 163–4.

13. William Empson, *The Structure of Complex Words* (London: Chatlo & Windus, 1951), p. 341.

14. Ibid., p. 347.

15. Ibid., pp. 347–8 (italics added).

16. A version of the ballad is published in *The Oxford Book of Ballads,* ed. James Kinsley (Oxford: Oxford University Press, 1969), pp. 68–9.

17. David Lodge, *The Modes of Modern Writing: Metaphor, Metonymy, and the Typology of Modern Literature* (London: Edward Arnold, 1977), pp. 107, 159, 200.

18. For a fuller analysis of the film, I recommend Joseph McBride and Michael Wilmington, *John Ford* (London: Secker & Warburg, 1974), pp. 110–24.

V. Varieties of cinematic metaphor

1. Max Black, *Models and Metaphors* (Ithaca, N.Y.: Cornell University Press, 1962), pp. 28–9.

2. E. H. Gombrich, *The Sense of Order* (London: Phaidon Press, 1979), p. 129.

3. See the quotation from Metz on Mitry in Chapter III. Actually, the point was made earlier by Raymond Spottiswoode in *A Grammar of the Film* (Berkeley: University of Berkeley Press, 1950), pp. 252–4. He proposed that one of the variants of a wipe should by convention be made to stand for "like" – a suggestion that has never been adopted.

4. See, for example, I. A. Richards, *The Philosophy of Rhetoric* (Oxford: Oxford University Press, 1936), p. 127.

5. Robin Wood, *Hitchcock's Films* (London: Zwemmer, 1965), p. 118.

6. François Truffaut, *Hitchcock* (London: Panther Books, 1969), pp. 369–70.

7. Amusingly illustrated by the discussion Stahr has with Boxley in F. Scott Fitzgerald's *The Last Tycoon* (Harmondsworth: Penguin Books, 1965), pp. 39–41. Calvin C. Pryluck cites evidence to show that people are capable of inferring connections between extremely diverse objects; see *Sources of Meaning in Motion Pictures and Television* (New York: Arno Press, 1976), pp. 136–7.

8. The shot to which I am referring is illustrated on p. 273 of Stanley J. Solomon, *The Classic Cinema: Essays in Criticism* (New York: Harcourt Brace Jovanovich, 1973).

9. David Lodge, *The Modes of Modern Writing* (London: Edward Arnold, 1977), p. 76.

10. James Monaco, *How to Read a Film* (New York: Oxford University Press, 1977), p. 140. On the same page he mentions as metonymy the shot from *The Red Desert* (*Deserto Rosso*), which I gave as an example of a juxtaposition metaphor. This illustrates the difficulty of attempting a classificatory scheme. There are bound to be overlaps, borderline cases, and disagreements according to how a trope is itself interpreted. (The same situation exists in literary criticism.) As Monaco says, "The terms 'synecdoche' and 'metonymy'...are, of course, imprecise. They are theoretical tools that may be useful for analysis: they are not strict definitions" (ibid., p. 140).
11. Cf. "Some Visual Motifs of *Film Noir*" by J. A. Place and S. L. Petersen, available in *Movies and Methods*, ed. Bill Nichols (Berkeley: University of California Press, 1976), pp. 325–38.
12. Cf. Robin Wood's discussion of this sequence in *Hitchcock's Films*, pp. 117–8.
13. *The Basic Writings of Sigmund Freud*, trans. and ed. A. A. Brill (New York: Random House, 1938), p. 642. Freud gives this, in *Wit and Its Relation to the Unconscious*, as an example of condensation.
14. Wood, *Hitchcock's Films*, p. 121 (italics added).

VI. Theories of cinematic metaphor

1. E. M. Forster, *Howard's End* (London: Edward Arnold, 1960), title page.
2. There is a chapter on metaphor in Louis D. Gianetti, *Godard and Others: Essays on Film Form* (London: Tantivy Press, 1975); a chapter on "Imagery" in Roy Huss and Norman Silverstein, *The Film Experience* (New York: Harper & Row, 1968); a section, "The Angel of Poetry Hovering," in Raymond Durgnat, *Films and Feelings* (London: Faber, 1967); a paper by the Russian formalist, Boris Ejxenbaum, entitled "Problems of Cinema Stylistics," reprinted in Herbert Eagle, *Russian Formalist Film Theory*, Michigan Slavic Materials, no. 19 (Ann Arbor: University of Michigan, 1981), pp. 55–80. The importance of cinematic metaphor for the study of film is discussed in the last two chapters of J. Dudley Andrew, *Concepts in Film Theory* (Oxford: Oxford University Press, 1984).
3. Sergei Eisenstein, *The Film Sense*, trans. and ed. Jay Leyda (London: Faber, 1943), pp. 34–5. Note that Eisenstein is using *image* in a special way, and that the term is to be understood as meaning something like "a synthesis incorporating the artistic theme." See p. 33.
4. Ibid., p. 59.
5. Sergei Eisenstein, *Film Form*, trans. and ed. Jay Leyda (New York: Harcourt, Brace & World, 1949), p. 30. The italics here, and later, are Eisenstein's own.
6. Ibid., p. 30.
7. Ibid., p. 160.
8. "For us the microcosm of montage had to be understood as a unity, which in the inner stress of contradictions is halved, in order to be re-assembled in a new unity on a new plane, qualitatively higher, its imagery new perceived" (*Film Form*, pp. 235–6).
9. I stress the teaching because Eisenstein's approach appears to have been

very pragmatic, and accounts of his classes reveal a flexibility and openness to a wider range of issues than his published essays by themselves show. See Vladimir Nizhny, *Lessons with Eisenstein,* trans. and ed. Ivor Montagu and Jay Leyda (London: George Allen & Unwin, 1962). Also "Problems of Composition" in Sergei Eisenstein, *Film Essays,* ed. Jay Leyda (London: Dennis Dobson, 1968). Yon Barna, in *Eisenstein* (London: Secker & Warburg, 1973), has some comments on Eisenstein's practice on his film theory.

10. *The Film Sense,* pp. 44–5.

11. *Film Form,* p. 21.

12. Andrew Tudor, in *Theories of Film* (London: Secker & Warburg, 1974), discusses the difficulty of interpreting what Eisenstein means by some of these terms: see esp. pp. 36–8. A synoptic study of Eisenstein on montage is to be found in Jacques Aumont, *Montage Eisenstein,* trans. Lee Hildreth, Constance Penley, and Andrew Ross (London: British Film Institute, 1987). For a brief discussion of Eisenstein's disputes over film theory with Dziga Vertov, see Vlada Petrić, *Constructivism in Film* (Cambridge: Cambridge University Press, 1987), chap. 1.

13. *Film Sense,* p. 14.

14. Ibid.

15. It must be acknowledged that to some extent this essay is a piece of national and socialist propaganda, identifying the discovery of a new cinematic language with the achievements of revolutionary ideology.

16. *Film Form,* p. 241.

17. Ibid., p. 242.

18. Ibid., p. 245.

19. Ibid., p. 248.

20. Ibid., p. 249.

21. Ibid., p. 251.

22. Ibid., p. 254.

23. Siegfried Kracauer, *Theory of Film: The Redemption of Physical Reality* (Oxford: Oxford University Press, 1960), p. 208.

24. John H. Fell, *Film: An Introduction* (New York: Praeger Publishers, 1975), pp. 87–8.

25. See the statement by Boris Shumyatsky, director of the Soviet Film Office in 1937: quoted in Leon Moussinac, *Sergei Eisenstein,* trans. D. Sandy Petrey (New York: Crown Publishers, 1970), pp. 157–60. See also Marie Seton, *Sergei M. Eisenstein* (New York: A. A. Wyn, 1960).

26. Peter Harcourt, *Six European Directors* (Harmondsworth: Penguin Books, 1974), p. 50.

27. Charles Barr, "Cinemascope: Before and After," *Film Quarterly* (Summer 1963); reprinted in *Film Theory and Criticism,* ed. Gerald Mast and Marshall Cohen (Oxford: Oxford University Press, 1974), pp. 131–2.

28. *Film Form,* pp. 122–49. Boris Ejxenbaum made a similar declaration in his 1927 paper, "Problems of Cinema Stylistics": "In order to study the laws of cinema ... it is very important to realize that the perception and understanding of films is inseparably linked to the formation of internal speech, which chains the individual shots together" (in Eagle, *Russian Formalist Film Theory,* p. 62). It is clear, however, that his notion of inner speech, which places the emphasis on verbal categories, does not consort with Eisenstein's view of inner speech as image-sensual. For a critique of Ejxenbaum's argument in relation to cinematic metaphor, see below, Chapter VII, n. 68.

29. The phrase is used on p. 132 of *Film Form.*
30. Ibid.
31. Ibid., p. 141.
32. Ernst Cassirer, *The Philosophy of Symbolic Forms,* vol. 2: *Mythical Thought,* trans. Ralph Mannheim (New Haven: Yale University Press, 1977). Another interesting discussion of myth in relation to metaphor is to be found in Philip Wheelwright, *Metaphor and Reality* (Bloomington: Indiana University Press, 1962). Cliford Geertz has some interesting pertinent ideas on early anthropological views of "primitive thought" in *Local Knowledge: Further Essays in Interpretive Anthropology* (New York: Basic Books, 1983), chap. 7.
33. Cassirer, *Mythical Thought,* pp. 67–8.
34. N. Roy Clifton, *The Figure in Film* (East Brunswick, N.J.: Associated University Presses, 1983).
35. Ibid., p. 19.
36. Ibid., p. 271.
37. Ibid.
38. I am in good company here. It is a modern trend, for, as Jonathan Culler notes in *The Pursuit of Signs* (London: Routledge & Kegan Paul, 1981), metaphor has become "not just the literal or proper name for a trope based on resemblance but also and especially a figure for figurality in general"; see pp. 189–209.
39. Clifton, *The Figure in Film,* p. 74.
40. Ibid.
41. Ibid., p. 86.
42. Ibid.
43. Ibid., p. 87.
44. Ibid., p. 88.
45. Ibid., p. 101 (italics added).
46. Ibid., p. 87.
47. Ibid.
48. See I. A. Richards, *The Philosophy of Rhetoric* (Oxford: Oxford University Press, 1936), pp. 100f.
49. Clifton, *The Figure in Film,* p. 87.
50. Ibid.
51. Richards, *Rhetoric,* p. 96.
52. Ibid., p. 119 (italics added).
53. Christian Metz, *Le Signifiant imaginaire: Psychanalyse et cinéma* (Union Generale d'Editions, 1977); the English version, *Psychoanalysis and Cinema: The Imaginary Signifier,* was translated by Celia Britton, Annwyl Williams, Ben Brewster, and Alfred Guzzetti, and published by Macmillan in 1982. This is the translation I have used and refer to throughout.
54. Ibid., p. 209.
55. Ibid., p. 214.
56. Ibid., p. 217.
57. See Chapter II, n. 12.

58. For any reader still hazy about syntagmatic and paradigmatic, let me offer a brief explanation. Linguistic structures might be seen as being ordered in two ways. First, we might consider how words (or their phonetic equivalents) are arranged as a sequence. Thus, in English, a common syntagmatic structure would be the serial arrangement: subject, verb, object, as in "The cat chased the mouse." Because this may be thought of as a sequence occurring as a spatial or temporal line, it is often called the horizontal axis of organization. Second, we might think of the organization in terms of what could be substituted for the words present without altering the syntactic sequence and without creating a meaningless sentence. Thus other nouns could replace "cat" or "mouse," other verbs could replace "chased." So we would get sentences such as, "The dog chewed the bone," or "The boy climbed the fence." The classes of comparable elements that could be selected for the purpose of substitution belong to the paradigmatic system. This is often posited as a vertical axis of organization. Since syntagmatic relations are based upon things being set beside one another (i.e., on contiguity), whereas paradigmatic relations are based on like or comparable things being substituted for one another, it seemed reasonable to think of metonymy (which is based on contiguity) as a syntagmatic device, and to think of metaphor (which entails substitution or the associating of like things) as a paradigmatic device. There is, however, one serious consequence that would seem to be entailed in thinking this way. By definition, syntagmatic organization is conceived of as being distinct from paradigmatic, and vice versa. So it would seem to follow that metaphor and metonymy must, in the way they work, be just as distinct from one another. This conclusion, however, is much disputed; and it would probably be true to say that the present consensus is still that metaphor and metonymy are interrelated, and often interlocked, figures. It is the view I have myself adopted in this book.

Roland Barthes, for instance, takes a similar line: "We prefer here to evade Jakobson's opposition between metaphor and metonymy for if metonymy by its origins is a figure of contiguity, it nevertheless functions finally as a substitute of the signifier, that is as a metaphor." *Image–Music–Text*, selected and trans. Stephen Heath (London: Fontana/Collins, 1977), p. 50.

59. Richards, *Rhetoric*, p. 94.

60. Metz, *Psychoanalysis and Cinema*, p. 151.

61. Ibid., p. 280.

62. Ibid., p. 288.

63. *The Language Poets Use* (London: Athlone Press, 1965).

64. Metz, *Psychoanalysis and Cinema*, pp. 288–9.

65. Jakobson, *Selected Writings II: Word and Language* (The Hague: Mouton, 1971), p. 358.

66. I had in mind Trilling's use of these notions in essays such as the one on Keats in *The Opposing Self* (London: Secker & Warburg, 1955), pp. 3–49. But, of course, Lionel Trilling has also written about Freud's ideas and their relevance to the study of literature; see "Freud and Literature" and "Art and Neurosis" in *The Liberal Imagination* (London: Macmillan, 1948). His admiration for Freud goes together with a critical acuity that identifies, in relation to art, some of Freud's more misleading dicta.

67. Metz, *Psychoanalysis and Cinema*, pp. 69–70.

68. Ibid., p. 71.

69. Ibid., p. 72.

70. Ibid., p. 74.

71. Ibid.

72. Freud, of course, by his own example, encouraged his followers to utter absurdities, and his critics often cite his own with glee. I particularly like one of Frank Cioffi's choices. He writes, "Unlike the chap on Margate Sands, Freud can connect anything with anything. This is Freud's explanation of why a young girl had to place all the clocks in her room, including her wristwatch, out of earshot before she could go to sleep: 'The ticking of a clock is comparable to the throbbing of the clitoris in sexual excitation.' " Cioffi remarks that he has never known a woman who has not found this risible. *London Review of Books* (2–15 June 1983), p. 14.

73. Metz, *Psychoanalysis and Cinema*, p. 242.

74. Ibid., p. 256.

75. Ibid., p. 257.

76. I have in mind here some proponents of the "stylistic" study of poetry, who see in linguistic deviation a ploy for the avoidance of plain meaning so that more complex meanings have to be sought. See, for example, Geoffrey N. Leech, *A Linguistic Guide to English Poetry* (London: Longman, 1969).

77. Calvin S. Hall, *The Meaning of Dreams* (New York: Harper, 1953). Perhaps it is worth adding that Seymour Fisher and Roger P. Greenberg, two psychologists by no means hostile to psychoanalysis, categorically deny the validity of Freud's account of censorship. They write: "One can say without hesitation there is no support in the scientific literature for the 'sleep preservation' theory" (p. 62), and further, "It is certainly not true that the manifest dream content is a camouflaging shell that does not contain significant [explicit] information about the psychological state and emotional orientation of the dreamer" (p. 64). See *The Scientific Credibility of Freud's Theories and Therapy* (Brighton: Harvester Press, 1977). Eberwein notes that "the greatest challenge to Freud's theory of dream formation has come as the result of dream research done recently by physiologists, psychologists, and psychiatrists," and a little later he remarks that, as a result of these recent studies, scientists have found themselves "reversing Freud's claim that the function of the dream was to preserve sleep. In fact, the opposite seemed to be true: the function of sleep was to permit individuals to dream." See Robert T. Eberwein, *Film and the Dream Screen: A Sleep and a Forgetting* (Princeton: Princeton University Press, 1984), pp. 13 and 15.

78. Metz, *Psychoanalysis and Cinema*, p. 262, for instance.

79. Ibid., p. 263.

80. Ibid., p. 262.

81. Ibid., p. 270.

82. Ibid., pp. 271–2. Metz also briefly discusses the surgeon's pince-nez in *The Battleship Potemkin* (p. 200) but does not refer to Eisenstein's own comments on it cited earlier in this chapter. Thus the opportunity to compare what Freud and Eisenstein say about myth in relation to metaphorical meaning is not taken up.

83. See, however, Carroll's discussion of Metz's resort to psychoanalytic theories: *Mystifying Movies* (New York: Columbia University Press, 1988), chap. 1.
84. Metz, *Psychoanalysis and Cinema*, p. 275. The discussion appears in chap. 23, pp. 274–80.
85. Ibid., pp. 278–9.
86. Ibid., p. 279.
87. Several film critics have noted how metaphors are articulated by lap-dissolves; see, for example, Monaco's discussion of a dissolve from *North by Northwest* in *How to Read a Film* (Oxford: Oxford University Press, 1977), p. 191; and Johnson's of one from Ingmar Bergman's *Sawdust and Tinsel* in *Film: Space Time Light and Sound* (New York: Holt, Rinehart & Winston, 1974), pp. 42–3. Metz makes no reference to such discussions.
88. The requirement that acquaintance with art must be by personal experience, and that art cannot be received at second hand, is long established. I suppose the classical exposition is Kant's in the *Critique of Judgement,* trans. J. C. Meredith (Oxford: Clarendon Press, 1928). The corollary that criticism is dispositional has been taken up and affirmed by many aestheticians; recent works discussing this view include Arnold Isenberg, *Aesthetics and the Theory of Criticism* (Chicago: University of Chicago Press, 1973); Roger Scruton, *Art and Imagination* (London: Methuen, 1974); and Joseph Margolis, *Art and Philosophy* (Brighton: Harvester Press, 1980).
89. Carroll, for instance, in his *Philosophical Problems of Classical Film Theory* (Princeton: Princeton University Press, 1988), writes, "What fails as theory may excel as criticism" (p. 171). He finds the film theories of Rudolf Arnheim, André Bazin, and V. F. Perkins wanting, but clearly admires the critical insights their writings exhibit.
90. Carroll accuses Metz and others of producing what he calls "top down" theory. See *Mystifying Movies,* pp. 230–4.
91. The following passage may be cited as an example of how seriously, and with what pretensions, Metz regards his labors: "One of the most obvious characteristics of film (and in this it differs from other arts) is that it combines words and images (visual images), 'representations of words' and 'representations of things', material which is directly perceived and relational orderings, so that one might expect it, in advance, to be connected centrally and as it were via multiple points of attachment, to the most vital of the 'meshings' of the primary and secondary, and therefore to raise the central problem, or at least one of the central problems, of all semiology. It follows that there is more at stake than just the complexities, daunting enough in themselves, which surround the notions of condensation–displacement and metaphor–metonymy. And yet these notions lead fairly directly into the vast hinterland, and this is the route that I now propose to follow" (*Psychoanalysis and Cinema*, p. 231). The passage – so portentous in tone and vacuous in content – is only too representative of much that has passed itself off as film theory in recent years.

VII. The mind's eye

1. Arthur Koestler, *The Act of Creation* (London: Hutchinson, 1964), p. 390.
2. Robert Bresson, *Notes on the Cinematographer,* trans. Jonathon Griffin with an introduction by J. M. G. le Clezio (London: Quartet Books, 1986), p. 72.

3. Roman Jakobson, for example, notes the (too absolute) separation between langue and parole. "Without a confrontation of the code with the message, no insight into the creative power of language can be achieved." "Lingustics" in *Main Trends of Research in the Social and Human Sciences I: The Social Sciences* (The Hague: Mouton, 1970), p. 458. For a further critique of Saussure's approach see G. P. Baker and P. M. S. Hacker, *Language, Sense and Nonsense* (Oxford: Basil Blackwell, 1984), chap. 8.

4. J. Dudley Andrew makes a similar point. See *Concepts in Film Theory* (Oxford: Oxford University Press, 1984), esp. pp. 169–70.

5. See, for example, Lionel Trilling, *The Liberal Imagination* (London: Macmillan, 1948); Jack J. Spector, *The Aesthetics of Freud: A Study in Psychoanalysis and Art* (London: Allen Lane, Penguin Press, 1972); Anton Ehrenzweig, *The Hidden Order of Art: A Study in the Psychology of Artistic Imagination* (London: Weidenfeld & Nicholson, 1967); also Richard Wollheim, "Freud and the Understanding of Art," in *On Art and the Mind* (London: Allen Lane, 1973); and E. H. Gombrich, "Freud's Aesthetics," *Encounter* 26, no. 1 (January 1966), pp. 30–40. A psychoanalytic account of poetic metaphor is put forward in Robert Rogers, *Metaphor: A Psychoanalytic View* (Berkeley: University of California Press, 1978).

6. Christian Metz, *Psychoanalysis and Cinema* (London: Macmillan, 1982), pp. 232–4. The same point is made by Paul Ricoeur, who does attempt, however, to present some justification for Freud's mixing of language games. See Paul Ricoeur, *Hermeneutics and the Human Sciences,* ed. and trans. John B. Thompson (Cambridge: Cambridge University Press, 1981), chap. 10.

7. Koestler cites some of these earlier references to the unconscious: see *The Act of Creation,* pp. 148–66.

8. Ibid., pp. 199–207.

9. A good and readily available introduction to this field is Neil Bolton, *The Psychology of Thinking* (London: Methuen, 1972). See also Howard Gardner, *Frames of Mind* (London: Heinemann, 1984). One of the books most relevant to issues discussed in this chapter, because of its explication of the notions of concept and category, is Jerome S. Bruner, Jacqueline J. Goodnow, and George A. Austin, *A Study of Thinking* (New York: John Wiley & Sons, 1956).

10. See, for example, the papers by David E. Rumelhart, Allan Paivo, Bruce Fraser, Andrew Ortony, George A. Miller, and Michael J. Reddy in *Metaphor and Thought,* ed. Andrew Ortony (Cambridge: Cambridge University Press, 1979); also Roger Tourangeau, "Metaphor and Cognitive Structure," in *Metaphor: Problems and Perspectives,* ed. David S. Miall (London: Harvester Press, 1982), pp. 14–35; also Howard Gardner and Ellen Winner, "The Development of Metaphoric Competence: Implications for Humanistic Disciplines," in *On Metaphor,* ed. Sheldon Sacks (Chicago: University of Chicago Press, 1978), pp. 121–40.

11. E.g. *Leonardo da Vinci: A Memory of His Childhood* (1910); reprinted in *The Pelican Freud Library: vol. 14, Art and Literature* (Harmondsworth: Penguin Books, 1985). Eysenck gives a brief but lucid account of this debacle. See Hans Eysenck, *Decline and Fall of the Freudian Empire* (Harmondsworth: Penguin Books, 1985), chap. 7; for fuller analysis see Meyer Schapiro, "Leonardo and Freud: An Art Historical Study," *Journal of the History of Ideas* (April 1956), pp. 147–78; also D. E. Stannard, *Shrinking History* (Oxford: Oxford University Press, 1980).

Charles Altman, in "Psychoanalysis and Cinema," delineates the various ways recent French theorists, including Metz, have tried to establish the identity of cinema by finding cinema reflected in psychoanalysis. He mentions how they appropriate psychoanalysis with all the fervor of converts, and he criticizes their approaches for being analogical and programmatic. He is also amusing about their jargon-laden language, which he calls "Frenchspeak." In Bill Nichols, ed., *Movies and Methods*, vol. II (Berkeley: University of California Press, 1985), pp. 517–31.

12. Herbert Eagle, *Russian Formalist Film Theory*, Michigan Slavic Materials, no. 19 (Ann Arbor: University of Michigan, 1981). The notion of inner speech may be traced as far back as Plato. Russian psychologists such as L. S. Vygotsky and A. R. Luria took a renewed interest in it, and systematically studied this mode of behavior. For an account of the research, much of it contemporary with Eisenstein's speculations, see A. N. Sokolov, *Inner Speech and Thought*, trans. George T. Onischenko, ed. Donald B. Lindsley (New York: Plenum Press, 1972), particularly chap. 2.

In recent years some film theorists associated with the journal *Screen* and its approach to film studies have taken up the inner-speech debate; see, for example, Paul Willeman, "Cinematic Discourse: The Problem of Inner Speech," in *Cinema and Language,* ed. Stephen Heath and Patricia Mellencamp (Frederick, Md.: University Publications of America, 1983), pp. 141–67. Indeed, Willeman's paper illustrates the characteristic features of the group's approach, including the employment of language as knotted as Frenchspeak. In his hands inner speech becomes another arcane entity, which, like the Marxist historical forces and Freudian primary process, is employed as a device for setting them above non-Marxist/Freudian/*Screen* students of cinema who do not have their access to such mysteries. That the thrust of their thinking is committedly political may be discerned in remarks such as the following where Willeman denounces what he terms "ideologism":

"Although still confined to some marginal academic groups in Great Britain, ideologism could develop into a serious threat, especially in the area of film theory, a relatively new discipline that is particularly vulnerable in its struggle to establish itself as a legitimate field of endeavor and to displace the traditions of literary criticism which still massively occupy the terrain of film studies. Ideologism proclaims the total autonomy of the discursive vis-à-vis the political and the economic; it abolishes the need to think of politics in terms other than those of opportunist manipulation, and it effectively abandons any notion of ideological struggle in favor of philosophical meditation and academic careerism" (p. 166).

13. L. S. Vygotsky, *Thought and Language* (Cambridge, Mass.: MIT Press, 1962).

14. Ibid., p. 147.

15. Ibid., p. 149.

16. *Film Form* (New York: Harcourt, Brace & World, 1949), pp. 144–5.

17. Ibid., p. 145.

18. Brian Lewis, *Jean Mitry and the Aesthetics of the Cinema* (Ann Arbor, Mich.: UMI Research Press, 1984), p. 99.

19. Ibid., p. 107.

20. Ernst Cassirer, *An Essay on Man* (New Haven: Yale University Press, 1962), chap. 7.

21. Ernst Cassirer, *The Philosophy of Symbolic Forms*, vol. 2: *Mythical Thought* (New Haven: Yale University Press, 1977), p. 64.

22. Ibid., p. 68.

23. Ibid., p. 69.

24. *An Essay on Man*, p. 81.

25. Ernst Cassirer, *Language and Myth*, trans. Susanne K. Langer (New York: Dover Publications, 1953), p. 88.

26. I refer to *An Essay on Man*, p. 134.

27. *Mythical Thought*, p. 62.

28. S. T. Coleridge, *Biographia Literaria*, 2 vols., ed. J. Shawcross (Oxford: Oxford University Press, 1907), chap. 1.

29. My own feeling is that Eisenstein's formulation of this tension points to a flaw in his art. Too often the complexity of relationships in Eisenstein's films is to be discerned in the plastic and rhythmic elements, but somehow not satisfactorily carried over and married to the drama and thought, which, by contrast, are simplistic.

30. Even where artists have recourse to aleatory techniques, there is no necessary conflict with this principle. The utilization of chance arrangements or the incorporation of accidents (as with the dancer who tripped as she ran off stage in Balanchine's *Serenade*) is no more than taking advantage of the unexpected, which provokes the mind's esemplastic powers to see how chance events may be incorporated. Significantly, the appreciation of "chance-dance" does not depend upon deducing what the chance rules are by which the choreographer finds his or her movements, but on the interest of the movements themselves and the suggestiveness of their interplay.

31. *Film Form*, p. 254. Italics are Eisenstein's.

32. Ibid., p. 161.

33. Rumelhart in Ortony, *Metaphor and Thought*, pp. 86–7.

34. F. Scott Fitzgerald, *The Last Tycoon* (Harmondsworth: Penguin Books, 1974), pp. 39–40.

35. For example, see R. L. Gregory, *Eye and Brain* (London: Weidenfeld & Nicolson, 1977); E. H. Gombrich, *Art and Illusion* (London: Phaidon Press, 1962); also the discussion of scientific hypothesizing in Stephen Toulmin, *The Philosophy of Science* (London: Hutchinson, 1953).

36. Rumelhart, in Ortony, *Metaphor and Thought*, p. 85.

37. Gregory, *Eye and Brain*, pp. 66–75.

38. T. S. Eliot, *Selected Essays* (London: Faber, 1932), p. 15.

39. See particularly Michael Polanyi, *Personal Knowledge* (London: Routledge & Kegan Paul, 1958). A checklist of Polanyi's writings on tacit knowing is to be found in Harry S. Broudy, "Tacit Knowing and Aesthetic Education," in *Aesthetic Concepts and Education*, ed. Ralph A. Smith (Urbana: University of Illinois Press, 1970), pp. 77–106.

40. I have in mind here a passage in Michael Polanyi and Harry Prosch, *Meaning* (Chicago: University of Chicago Press, 1975), p. 62: "Our dwelling in the particulars, the subsidiary clues, results in their synthesis into a focal object only by means of an act of the imagination – a leap of a logical gap; this does not come about by means of specifiable, explicit, logically operative steps. The depths seen through a stereoscope is a new phenomenal experience, not deducible in its unique phenomenological character from the clues that the process of tacit integration integrates, just as the heliocentric concept of the planets 'seen' by Copernicus was a new conceptual experience not deducible from his available data. We can only point to the existence of tacit integration in our experience. We must be forever unable to give it an explicit specification."

The conversion of still pictures exhibited at twenty-four frames per second into continuous screen movement may also be regarded as an instance of tacit integration.

41. Gilbert Ryle, *The Concept of Mind* (London: Hutchinson, 1949), chap. 2, "Knowing How and Knowing That."

42. Critics need to know when to make their remarks explicit and when to let them be tacit. If they get it wrong, they distort the material they are discussing. Genre criticism in relation to film, for example, often falls into this error. Tacit awareness of film conventions is quickly acquired. Critics, however, who try to spell out every convention are more likely to emphasize the wrong things about a film, and make viewing an artificial and falsely self-conscious activity.

43. Rumelhart, in Ortony, *Metaphor and Thought*, pp. 89–90.

44. This is in essence what Ortony claims that the metaphor means. He cites it as an example of what he terms a "predicate promotion" metaphor – that is, one where predicates relating to the tenor are already there (and known to the hearer) – which he contrasts with a "predicate introduction" metaphor, where predicates are not there and have to be brought in as new predicates. See Ortony, *Metaphor and Thought*, pp. 199–200. Against this, I claim that in the particular case the metaphor is foregrounding and demarcating a realm not previously named, and in so doing it goes beyond any categories previously associated with its tenor and vehicle.

45. See Warren A. Shibles, *Metaphor: An Annotated Bibliography and History* (Whitewater, Wisc.: Language Press, 1971), and J. P. Van Noppen et al., *Metaphor: A Bibliography of Post-1970 Publications* (Amsterdam: John Benjamins, 1985).

46. For example, Max Black, Arthur C. Danto, Donald Davidson, Nelson Goodman, Paul Ricoeur, and J. E. Searle, to name but a few.

47. George Lakoff and Mark Johnson, *Metaphors We Live By* (Chicago: University of Chicago Press, 1980). Since the publication of this book the authors have further developed their ideas and arguments: see George Lakoff, *Women, Fire, and Dangerous Things: What Our Categories Reveal about the Mind* (Chicago: University of Chicago Press, 1987); and Mark Johnson, *The Body in the Mind: The Bodily Basis of Meaning, Imagination, and Reason* (Chicago: University of Chicago Press, 1987).

48. Lakoff and Johnson, *Metaphors We Live By*, p. 145.

49. Others have also said this – e.g., Marcus B. Hester, *The Meaning of Poetic Metaphor* (The Hague: Mouton, 1967), p. 183.

50. I have left out certain things – e.g., the notion that people categorize objects not in set-theoretical terms, but in terms of prototypes and family resemblances. I have also chosen not to take up certain problems arising from Lakoff and Johnson's account of metaphor – e.g., if metaphors become self-fulfilling prophecies by prejudging what evidence will be selected to test their validity (as is suggested in *Metaphors We Live By*, p. 156), how can we ever assess one metaphor as being truer, more perspicacious, or more desirable than another?
51. Polanyi, *Personal Knowledge*, chap. 4.
52. Paul Ricoeur, *The Rule of Metaphor*, trans. Robert Czerny et al. (London: Routledge & Kegan Paul, 1978), p. 240.
53. The role of metaphor in the human sciences is the focus of a subsequent study: see Ricoeur, *Hermeneutics and the Human Sciences*.
54. Ricoeur, *The Rule of Metaphor*, p. 214.
55. Ibid., p. 220.
56. Ibid., p. 243.
57. Ibid., p. 244.
58. For an attempt to discover what people choose to film when they employ cultural categories we do not, see Sol Worth and John Adair, *Through Navajo Eyes* (Bloomington: Indiana University Press, 1972). The book discusses what some Navajo filmed when given cameras and the necessary minimum of practical instruction. The findings of the book tend to confirm the validity of the view I am expressing.
59. Ricoeur, *The Rule of Metaphor*, p. 244.
60. E. H. Hirsch has reminded twentieth-century readers of the important distinction to be drawn between *interpretatio* concerned with the meaning of a text, and *applicatio* concerned with its significance for us and its application to our particular circumstances. See E. H. Hirsch, Jr., *The Aims of Interpretation* (Chicago: University of Chicago Press, 1976), p. 19.
61. *The Basic Writings of Sigmund Freud*, trans. and ed. A. A. Brill (New York: Random House, 1938), p. 349.
62. A list of writers on cinema who have made this analogy would include Hugo Münsterberg, Hugo Mauerhofer, Parker Tyler, and S. K. Langer, as well as such recent theorists as Christian Metz, Jean-Louis Baudry, and Robert T. Eberwein.
63. James F. Scott, *Film: The Medium and the Maker* (New York: Holt, Rinehart & Winston, 1975), p. 194.
64. Cited in Roy Armes, *Patterns of Realism: A Study of Italian Neo-Realist Cinema* (London: Tantivy Press, 1971), p. 153.
65. Ibid., p. 349.
66. See Koestler, *Act of Creation*, pp. 286–7. Of particular interest are his remarks on the dual attributes of "wholeness" and "partness" possessed by all members of living organisms or social bodies. See also E. H. Gombrich, *The Sense of Order* (London: Phaidon Press, 1979), p. 115, for his comment on the role played by "perceptual hierarchies" in our taking in of our environment. It should also be apparent that the principle of hierarchy is often appealed to by Eisenstein in his writings on cinema: e.g. *Film Form*, p. 49.
67. Many commentators, often from quite different standpoints, have testified

to this. May I, as instances, merely cite Rudolf Arnheim, *Visual Thinking* (Berkeley: University of California Press, 1969), p. 90; and Douglas R. Hofstadter, who, comparing the music of Bach and Cage, remarks, "intelligence loves patterns and balks at randomness." See *Gödel, Escher, Bach: An Eternal Golden Braid* (Brighton: Harvester Press, 1979), pp. 174–5.

In this connection it may also be worth calling attention to Arthur C. Danto's suggestive proposal that metaphor may be seen as a kind of elliptical syllogism with a missing term and hence an enthymematic conclusion. See *The Transfiguration of the Commonplace* (Cambridge, Mass.: Harvard University Press, 1981), p. 171.

68. It is refreshing to see someone pointing out the advantages for film studies of a functional account of meaning over the semiological, as Manuel De Landa does in "Wittgenstein in the Movies," in *Cinema Histories Cinema Practices*, ed. Patricia Mellencamp and Philip Rosen (Frederick, Md.: University Publications of America, 1984), pp. 108–19. He argues that an account that relates understanding to contexts and situations instead of to sign structures will have considerable advantage when dealing with sequences in narrative films. What he says complements my own approach.

69. For one thing, Day Lewis's line presupposes awareness of Burns's image, but not vice versa.

70. Again, I have given a slightly different emphasis to what Ricoeur discusses as "appropriation," though I do not disagree with his account of how we understand ourselves by understanding a text. See *Hermeneutics and the Human Sciences*, esp. part 2.

71. The most thorough account of the importance of context for the establishment of metaphors is to be found in Eva Feder Kittay, *Metaphor: Its Cognitive Force and Linguistic Structure* (Oxford: Clarendon Press, 1987). My book had been substantially completed when Kittay's appeared, but I find myself very much in sympathy with her "perspectival" account of metaphor.

72. See Carroll's critique of "essentialism" in *Philosophical Problems of Classical Film Theory* (Princeton: Princeton University Press, 1988).

73. Boris Ejxenbaum believes that in essence the "film metaphor is a kind of visual realization of verbal metaphor," and that "film metaphor is possible only under the conditions of support by verbal metaphor." He believes this is so because "the perception and understanding of films is inseparably linked to the formation of internal speech, which chains the individual shots together." (This essay, dated 1927, has been seized upon by *Screen* theorists to reinforce their approach – e.g., Heath, "Language, Sight and Sound," in Heath and Mellencamp, *Cinema and Language*, pp. 15–20.) Ejxenbaum concedes that one day the cinema may "envision the creation of properly cinematic semantic formulas which would serve as a basis for the construction of independent film metaphor," but states that this "would not change the situation in principle."

Ejxenbaum's arguments suffer from two defects. First, he does not adequately consider how the cinematic version of a verbal metaphor differs in effect from the purely verbal version, and therefore his explanation can offer no account of how a serious cinematic metaphor such as Roeg's functions. (He believes it is merely a matter of "realization," arguing that verbal metaphors do not form clear images in readers' minds, while film images are not realized in the consciousness of film viewers to the point of forming a complete verbal proposition. This explanation relies too much on presupposed subjective uniformities among readers and film viewers.) Second, Ejxenbaum assumes that our categories are essentially verbal in nature – but this is unlikely to be the case. Argyle, for example, questions the notion that the personality is coded verbally, pointing out the extreme difficulty encountered in verbalizing the traits of a personality with whom we are very well acquainted. Further, he calls attention to the importance, and the nonverbal functioning, of rituals: M. Argyle, *Bodily Communication* (London: Methuen, 1975). Spiegal and Machotka present reasons for believing that the categories by which the characteristics and purposes of human movement are grasped are also nonverbal: J. Spiegal and P. Machotka, *Messages of the Body* (New York: Free Press, 1974). Personality, bodily communication, and ritual situations can hardly be regarded as peripheral to the comprehension of films.

Appendix 1. On denotation and the literal in films

1. A stimulating discussion of this and related issues, taking a tack somewhat different from my own, will be found in Ian Jarvie, *Philosophy of the Film* (London: Routledge & Kegan Paul, 1987).
2. But see Carroll, *Philosophical Problems of Classical Film Theory* (Princeton: Princeton University Press, 1988), for a view of how films can be said to depict classes of objects. Context and intention clearly are crucial to the way images are taken.

Appendix 2. Searle on metaphor

1. John Searle, *Expression and Meaning* (Cambridge: Cambridge University Press, 1979), chap. 4; also in Andrew Ortony, ed., *Metaphor and Thought* (Cambridge: Cambridge University Press, 1979), pp. 92–123.
2. Searle, *Expression and Meaning*, p. 97.
3. Another example given by Searle himself helps to demonstrate that R is not derivable from P alone. He quotes, "My love is like a red, red rose," and says of it that this "does not mean there is a class of literal predicates that are true both of my love and red, red roses." It would be reasonable to say that the phrase conveys that the woman is beautiful and also that she is singularly or strikingly passionate. Now beauty is a feature within the general range of P (red, red roses), and so holds literally for her and for P. But passion, being a human attribute, cannot be predicated of red, red roses. Therefore it is not in the range of values of P taken alone. The figurative meaning is dependent on the contribution from the tenor "my love." It is a new R.
   It might also be noted that the figurative meanings are partly created through the rhythm, alliteration, and repetition of "red, red rose" – compare "Now she is like the white tree-rose" (C. Day Lewis) – and that these belong to the sentence rather than any speech act.
4. *Dunciad*, IV, 1, 319.
5. I do not find Searle's preceding chapter on "The logical status of fictional

discourse," with its discussion of "pretended acts of referring," at all helpful in resolving the issues here either. The cognitive nature of literature and metaphor is better handled by Ricoeur and by Kittay. See also Joseph Margolis's critique of the application of speech acts to literature: *Art and Philosophy* (Brighton: Harvester Press, 1980), chap. 11; also Francis Sparshott, *The Theory of the Arts* (Princeton: Princeton University Press, 1982), pp. 83–4; and Anne Shepherd, *Aesthetics* (Oxford: Oxford University Press, 1987), pp. 126–7.
6. Shepherd, *Aesthetics,* p. 120.
7. Gilbert Ryle made the phrase "category-mistake" fashionable, and its application to metaphor has frequently been noted; see Gilbert Ryle, *The Concept of Mind* (London: Hutchinson, 1949), pp. 16–24.
8. Again I would like to draw attention to Kittay's excellent discussion of this and related issues in *Metaphor* (Oxford: Clarendon Press, 1987).
9. A point noted by Samuel R. Levin in his critique of Searle's account of metaphor, "Standard Approaches to Metaphor and a Proposal for Literary Metaphor," in Ortony, *Metaphor and Thought,* pp. 124–35.

Bibliography

Altman, Charles F. "Psychoanalysis and Cinema: The Imaginary Discourse." *Quarterly Review of Film Studies* 2, no. 3 (August 1977), pp. 257–72.

Andrew, J. Dudley. *Concepts in Film Theory.* Oxford: Oxford University Press, 1984.

———. *The Major Film Theories.* Oxford: Oxford University Press, 1976.

Argyle, M. *Bodily Communication.* London: Methuen, 1975.

Aristotle. *The Poetics,* trans. Ingram Bywater. In *Introduction to Aristotle.* New York: Random House, 1947.

———. *The Rhetoric of Aristotle,* trans. J. E. C. Welldon. London: Macmillan, 1886.

Armes, Roy. *The Ambiguous Image.* London: Secker & Warburg, 1976.

———. *Patterns of Realism: A Study of Italian Neo-Realist Cinema.* London: Tantivy Press, 1971.

Arnheim, Rudolf. *Art and Visual Perception.* Berkeley: University of California Press, 1974.

———. *Film.* London: Faber, 1933.

———. *Film as Art.* London: Faber, 1958.

———. *Towards a Psychology of Art.* London: Faber, 1967.

———. *Visual Thinking.* Berkeley: University of California Press, 1969.

Aumont, Jacques. *Montage Eisenstein,* trans. Lee Hildreth, Constance Penley, and Andrew Ross. London: British Film Institute, 1987.

Baker, G. P. and P. M. S. Hacker. *Language, Sense and Nonsense.* Oxford: Basil Blackwell, 1984.

Barna, Yon. *Eisenstein.* London: Secker & Warburg, 1973.

Barr, Charles. "Cinemascope: Before and After." In *Film Theory and Criticism,* ed. Gerald Mast and Marshall Cohen. Oxford: Oxford University Press, 1974, pp. 120–46. First published in *Film Quarterly* (Spring 1963).

Barthes, Roland. *Image–Music–Text,* selected and trans. Stephen Heath. London: Fontana/Collins, 1977.

Bazin, André. *What is Cinema?* trans. Hugh Gray. Berkeley: University of California Press, 1967.

————. *What is Cinema?* Vol. 2, trans. Hugh Gray. Berkeley: University of California Press, 1971.

Bernstein, Leonard. *The Unanswered Question.* Cambridge, Mass.: Harvard University Press, 1976.

Bettetini, Gianfranco. *The Language and Technique of the Film.* The Hague: Mouton, 1973.

Black, Max. "Metaphor." In *Contemporary Studies in Aesthetics,* ed. Francis J. Coleman. New York: McGraw-Hill, 1968. First published in *Proceedings of the Aristotelean Society* 55 (1954–1955).

————. *Models and Metaphors.* Ithaca, N.Y.: Cornell University Press, 1962.

Bluestone, George. *Novels into Film.* Baltimore: The Johns Hopkins Press, 1957.

Bolton, Neil. *The Psychology of Thinking.* London: Methuen, 1972.

Bordwell, David. *Narration in the Fiction Film.* London: Methuen, 1985.

Bradbury, Malcolm, and James McFarlane, eds. *Modernism.* Harmondsworth: Penguin Books, 1976.

Bresson, Robert. *Notes on Cinematography,* trans. Jonathan Griffin. New York: Urizen Books, 1977.

Brooke-Rose, Christine. *A Grammar of Metaphor.* London: Secker & Warburg, 1958.

Broudy, Harry S. "Tacit Knowing and Aesthetic Education." In *Aesthetic Concepts and Education,* ed. Ralph A. Smith, pp. 77–106. Urbana: University of Illinois Press, 1970.

Bruner, Jerome S., Jacqueline Goodnow, and George A. Austin. *A Study of Thinking.* New York: John Wiley & Sons, 1956.

Burch, Noël. *Theory of Film Practice.* London: Secker & Warburg, 1973.

Carroll, Noël. *Mystifying Movies: Fads and Fallacies in Contemporary Film Theory.* New York: Columbia University Press, 1988.

————. *Philosophical Problems of Classical Film Theory.* Princeton: Princeton University Press, 1988.

Cassirer, Ernst. *An Essay on Man.* New Haven: Yale University Press, 1944.

————. *Language and Myth,* trans. Susanne K. Langer. New York: Dover Publications, 1953.

————. *The Philosophy of Symbolic Forms,* vol. 2: *Mythical Thought,* trans. Ralph Mannheim. New Haven: Yale University Press, 1977.

Cavell, Stanley. *Must We Mean What We Say?* Cambridge: Cambridge University Press, 1976.

————. *The World Viewed: Reflections on the Ontology of Film.* New York: Viking Press, 1971.

Clifton, N. Roy. *The Figure in Film.* East Brunswick, N.J.: Associated University Presses, 1983.

Coleman, Francis J., ed. *Contemporary Studies in Aesthetics.* New York: McGraw-Hill, 1968.

Coleridge, S. T. *Biographia Literaria,* 2 vols., ed. J. Shawcross. Reprinted with corrections. Oxford: Oxford University Press, 1907.

———. *The Statesman's Manual,* in *The Collected Works of Samuel Taylor Coleridge, no. 6: Lay Sermons.* London: Routledge & Kegan Paul, 1972.

Cook, Pam, ed. *The Cinema Book.* London: British Film Institute, 1985.

Cooper, David E. *Philosophy and the Nature of Language.* London: Longman, 1973.

Culler, Jonathan. *The Pursuit of Signs.* London: Routledge & Kegan Paul, 1981.

———. *Saussure.* Brighton: Harvester Press, 1976.

———. *Structuralist Poetics.* London: Routledge & Kegan Paul, 1975.

Danto, Arthur C. *The Transfiguration of the Commonplace.* Cambridge, Mass.: Harvard University Press, 1981.

de Laurot, Yves. "From Logos to Lens," in *Movies and Methods,* 2 vols. ed. Bill Nichols, pp. 578–82. Berkeley: University of California Press, 1976, 1985.

Dixon, Peter. *Rhetoric.* London: Methuen, 1971.

Doubrovsky, Serge. *The New Criticism in France,* trans. Derek Coltman. Chicago: University of Chicago Press, 1973.

Durgnat, Raymond. *Films and Feelings.* London: Faber, 1967.

Eagle, Herbert. *Russian Formalist Film Theory.* Michigan Slavic Materials, no. 19. Ann Arbor: University of Michigan, 1981.

Eberwein, Robert T. *Film and the Dream Screen: A Sleep and a Forgetting.* Princeton: Princeton University Press, 1984.

Ehrenzweig, Anton. *The Hidden Order of Art: A Study in the Psychology of Artistic Imagination.* London: Weidenfeld & Nicholson, 1967.

Eisenstein, Sergei. *Film Essays,* ed. Jay Leyda. London: Dennis Dobson, 1968.

———. *Film Form,* trans. and ed. Jay Leyda. New York: Harcourt, Brace & World, 1949.

———. *The Film Sense,* trans. and ed. Jay Leyda. London: Faber, 1943.

———. *Notes of a Film Director.* New York: Dover Publications, 1970.

Eliot, T S *Selected Essays.* London: Faber, 1932.

Empson, William. *Seven Types of Ambiguity.* New York: Moridian Books, 1957.

———. *The Structure of Complex Words.* London: Chatto & Windus, 1951.

Enright, D. J., and Ernst de Chickera, eds. *English Critical Texts.* London: Oxford University Press, 1962.

Eysenck, H. J. *Decline and Fall of the Freudian Empire.* Harmondsworth: Penguin Books, 1986.

Fell, John H. *Film: An Introduction.* New York: Praeger Publishers, 1975.

Fisher, Seymour, and Roger P. Greenberg. *The Scientific Credibility of Freud's Theories and Therapy.* Brighton: Harvester Press, 1977.

Fiske, John, and John Hartley. *Reading Television.* London: Methuen, 1978.

Fitzgerald, F. Scott. *The Last Tycoon.* Harmondsworth: Penguin Books, 1974.

Freud, Sigmund. *The Basic Writings of Sigmund Freud,* trans. and ed. A. A. Brill. New York: Random House, 1938.

———. *Leonardo da Vinci: A Memory of His Childhood.* 1910. Reprinted in *The Pelican Freud Library: vol. 14: Art and Literature.* Harmondsworth: Penguin Books, 1985.

Frye, Northrup. *Anatomy of Criticism.* Princeton: Princeton University Press, 1971.

Gardner, Howard. *Frames of Mind.* London: Heinemann, 1984.

———. *The Mind's New Science.* New York: Basic Books, 1985.

Gardner, Howard, and Ellen Winner. "The Development of Metaphoric Competence: Implications for Humanistic Disciplines," in *On Metaphor,* ed. Sheldon Sacks, pp. 14–35. Chicago: University of Chicago Press, 1979.

Geduld, Harry M., ed. *Focus on D. W. Griffith.* Englewood Cliffs, N.J.: Prentice-Hall, 1971.

Geertz, Clifford. *Local Knowledge: Further Essays in Interpretive Anthropology.* New York: Basic Books, 1983.

Gianetti, Louis D. *Godard and Others: Essays on Film Form.* London: Tantivy Press, 1975.

Gombrich, E. H. *Art and Illusion.* London: Phaidon Press, 1962.

———. "Freud's Aesthetics." *Encounter* 26, no. 1 (January 1966), pp. 30–40.

———. *The Image and the Eye.* London: Phaidon Press, 1982.

———. *The Sense of Order.* London: Phaidon Press, 1979.

Goodman, Nelson. *Languages of Art.* Oxford: Oxford University Press, 1969.

Gregory, R. L. *Eye and Brain.* London: Weidenfeld & Nicholson, 1977.

Hall, Calvin S. *The Meaning of Dreams.* New York: Harper, 1953.

Harcourt, Peter. *Six European Directors.* Harmondsworth: Penguin Books, 1974.

Harmon, Gilbert. "Semiotics and the Cinema: Metz and Wollen." *Quarterly Review of Film Studies* 2, no. 1 (February 1977), pp. 15–24.

Hawkes, Terence. *Metaphor.* London: Methuen, 1972.

Heath, Stephen, and Patricia Mellencamp, ed. *Cinema and Language.* Frederick, Md.: University Publications of America, 1983.

Henle, Paul, ed. *Language, Thought and Culture.* Ann Arbor: University of Michigan Press, 1958.

Hester, Marcus B. *The Meaning of Poetic Metaphor.* The Hague: Mouton, 1967.

Hirsch, E. H., Jr. *The Aims of Interpretation.* Chicago: University of Chicago Press, 1976.

Hofstadter, Douglas R. *Gödel, Escher, Bach: An Eternal Golden Braid.* Brighton: Harvester Press, 1979.

Honeck, Richard P., and Robert R. Hoffman, eds. *Cognition and Figurative Language.* London: Lawrence Erlbaum, 1980.

Hungerland, Isobel. *Poetic Discourse.* Berkeley: University of California Press, 1958.

Huss, Roy, and Norman Silverstein. *The Film Experience.* New York: Harper & Row, 1968.

Isenberg, Arnold. *Aesthetics and the Theory of Criticism.* Chicago: University of Chicago Press, 1973.

Izod, John. *Hollywood and the Box Office 1895–1986.* London: Macmillan, 1988.

Jakobson, Roman. "Linguistics." In *Main Trends of Research in the Social and Human Sciences I: The Social Sciences,* pp. 419–23. The Hague: Mouton, 1970.

———. *Selected Writings II: Word and Language.* The Hague: Mouton, 1971.

Jarvie, Ian. *Philosophy of the Film.* London: Routledge & Kegan Paul, 1987.

Johnson, Lincoln F. *Film: Space Time Light and Sound.* New York: Holt, Rinehart & Winston, 1974.

Johnson, Mark. *The Body in the Mind: The Bodily Basis of Meaning, Imagination, and Reason.* Chicago: University of Chicago Press, 1987.

Joseph, Bertram. *Acting Shakespeare.* London: Routledge & Kegan Paul, 1960.

Jung, C. G. *The Collected Works of C. G. Jung,* vol. 18: *The Symbolic Life,* trans. R. F. C. Hull, ed. Herbert Read et al. London: Routledge & Kegan Paul, 1977.

Kant, Immanual. *Critique of Judgement,* trans. J. C. Meredith. Oxford: Clarendon Press, 1928.

Kittay, Eva Fedor. *Metaphor: Its Cognitive Force and Linguistic Structure.* Oxford: Clarendon Press, 1987.

Knight, G. Wilson. *The Wheel of Fire.* London: Oxford University Press, 1930.

Koestler, Arthur. *The Act of Creation.* London: Hutchinson, 1964.

Kracauer, Siegfried. *Theory of Film: The Redemption of Physical Reality.* Oxford: Oxford University Press, 1960.

Lakoff, George. *Women, Fire, and Dangerous Things: What Our Categories Reveal about the Mind.* Chicago: University of Chicago Press, 1987.

Lakoff, George, and Mark Johnson. *Metaphors We Live By.* Chicago: University of Chicago Press, 1980.

Langer, Susanne K. *Feeling and Form.* London: Routledge & Kegan Paul, 1953.

Leech, Geoffrey N. *A Linguistic Guide to English Poetry.* London: Longman, 1969.

———. *Semantics.* Harmondsworth: Penguin Books, 1974.

Levin, Samuel R. *The Semantics of Metaphor.* Baltimore: Johns Hopkins University Press, 1977.

———. "Standard Approaches to Metaphor and a Proposal for Literary Metaphor," in *Metaphor and Thought,* ed. Andrew Ortony, pp. 124–35. Cambridge: Cambridge University Press, 1979.

Lévy-Bruhl, L. *How Natives Think.* London: Allen & Unwin, 1926.

———. *Primitive Mentality.* London: Allen & Unwin, 1923.

Lewis, Brian. *Jean Mitry and the Aesthetics of the Cinema.* Ann Arbor, Mich.: UMI Research Press, 1984.

Lewis, C. Day. *The Poetic Image*. London: Jonathan Cape, 1947.

Lodge, David. "The Language of Modernist Fiction: Metaphor and Metonymy," in *Modernism*, ed. Malcolm Bradbury and James MacFarlane, pp. 481–6. Harmondsworth: Penguin Books, 1976.

———. *The Modes of Modern Writing: Metaphor, Metonymy, and the Typology of Modern Literature*. London: Edward Arnold, 1977.

Luria, A. R. *The Role of Speech in the Regulation of Normal and Abnormal Behaviour*, ed. J. Tizard. Oxford: Pergamon Press, 1961.

Margolis, Joseph. *Art and Philosophy*. Brighton: Harvester Press, 1980.

Martin, Graham Dunstan. *Language, Truth and Poetry*. Edinburgh: University Press, 1975.

McBride, Joseph, and Michael Wilmington. *John Ford*. London: Secker & Warburg, 1974.

Mast, Gerald, and Marshall Cohen, eds. *Film Theory and Criticism*. Oxford: Oxford University Press, 1974.

Mellencamp, Patricia, and Philip Rosen, eds. *Cinema Histories Cinema Practices*. Frederick, Maryland: University Publications of America, 1984.

Metz, Christian. "On Mitry's Esthétique et Psychologie du Cinéma, Vol. II." *Screen* 14, nos. 1–2 (Spring/Summer 1973), pp. 40–87.

———. *Film Language*, trans. Michael Taylor. New York: Oxford University Press, 1974.

———. *Language and Cinema*, trans. Donna Jean Umiker-Seboek. The Hague: Mouton, 1974.

———. *Psychoanalysis and Cinema*, trans. Celia Britton, Annwyl Williams, Ben Brewster, and Alfred Guzzetti. London: Macmillan, 1982.

Miall, David S., ed. *Metaphor: Problems and Perspectives*. Brighton: Harvester Press, 1982.

Miller, David M. *The Net of Hephaestus: A Study of Modern Criticism and Metaphysical Metaphor*. The Hague: Mouton, 1971.

Mitry, Jean. *Esthétique et Psychologie du Cinéma*. 2 vols. Paris: Editions Universitaires, 1963, 1965.

Monaco, James. *How to Read a Film*. New York: Oxford University Press, 1977.

Moussinac, Leon. *Sergei Eisenstein*, trans. D. Sandy Petrey. New York: Crown Publishers, 1970.

Münsterberg, Hugo. *The Film: A Psychological Study*. New York: Dover, 1970.

Murry, John Middleton. *Selected Criticism 1916–1957*. Oxford: Oxford University Press, 1960.

Nichols, Bill, ed. *Movies and Methods*. 2 vols. Berkeley: University of California Press, 1976, 1985.

Nizhny, Vladimir. *Lessons with Eisenstein*, trans. and ed. Ivor Montagu and Jay Leyda. London: George Allen & Unwin, 1962.

Nowottny, Winifred. *The Language Poets Use*. London: Athlone Press, 1962.

Ortony, Andrew, ed. *Metaphor and Thought*. Cambridge: Cambridge University Press, 1979.

Oxford Book of Ballads, ed. James Kinsley. Oxford: Oxford University Press, 1969.

Pasolini, Pier Paolo. "The Cinema of Poetry," in *Movies and Methods,* 2 vols., ed. Bill Nichols, pp. 542–58. Berkeley: University of California Press, 1976, 1985.

Petrić, Vlada. *Constructivism in Film.* Cambridge: Cambridge University Press, 1987.

Place, J. A., and L. S. Peterson. "Some Visual Motifs of *Film Noir,*" in *Movies and Methods,* 2 vols., ed. Bill Nichols, pp. 325–38. Berkcley: University of California Press, 1976, 1985.

Polanyi, Michael. *Personal Knowledge.* London: Routledge & Kegan Paul, 1958.

———. *The Tacit Dimension.* New York: Anchor Books, Doubleday & Co., 1967.

Polanyi, Michael, and Harry Prosch. *Meaning.* Chicago: University of Chicago Press, 1975.

Pryluck, Calvin B. "The Film Metaphor Metaphor: The Use of Language-Based Models in Film Study." *Literature/Film Quarterly* 3, no. 2 (Spring 1975), pp. 117–23.

———. *Sources of Meaning in Motion Pictures and Television.* New York: Arno Press, 1976.

Rhode, Eric. *A History of the Cinema from Its Origins to 1970.* London: Allen Lane, 1976.

Richards, I. A. *The Philosophy of Rhetoric.* Oxford: Oxford University Press, 1936.

Ricoeur, Paul. *Hermeneutics and the Human Sciences,* ed. and trans. John B. Thompson. Cambridge: Cambridge University Press, 1981.

———. *The Rule of Metaphor,* trans. Robert Czerny et al. London: Routledge & Kegan Paul, 1978.

Robinson, Ian. *The New Grammarians' Funeral.* Cambridge: Cambridge University Press, 1975.

Rock, Irvin. *Perception.* New York: Scientific American Books, 1984.

Rogers, Robert. *Metaphor: A Psychoanalytic View.* Berkeley: University of California Press, 1978.

Ruthven, K. K. *Myth.* London: Methuen, 1976.

Ryle, Gilbert. *The Concept of Mind.* London: Hutchinson, 1949.

———. *Dilemmas: The Tarner Lectures 1953.* Cambridge: Cambridge University Press, 1954.

Sacks, Sheldon, ed. *On Metaphor.* Chicago: University of Chicago Press, 1979.

Sapir, Edward. *Language.* New York: Harcourt & Brace, 1921.

Saussure, Ferdinand de. *Course in General Linguistics,* trans. Wade Baskin. London: Fontana/Collins, 1974.

Schapiro, Meyer. "Leonardo and Freud: An Art Historical Study." *Journal of the History of Ideas* 17, no. 2 (April 1956), pp. 147–78.

Scott, James F. *Film: The Medium and the Maker.* New York: Holt, Rinehart & Winston, 1975.

Scruton, Roger. *Art and Imagination.* London: Methuen, 1974.

Searle, John R. *Expression and Meaning.* Cambridge: Cambridge University Press, 1979.

Seton, Marie. *Sergei M. Eisenstein.* New York: A. A. Wyn, 1960.

Shepherd, Anne. *Aesthetics.* Oxford: Oxford University Press, 1987.

Shibles, Warren A. *Analysis of Metaphor in the Light of W. M. Urban's Theories.* The Hague: Mouton, 1971.

———. *Metaphor: An Annotated Bibliography and History.* Whitewater, Wisc.: Language Press, 1971.

Sokolov, A. N. *Inner Speech and Thought,* trans. George T. Onischenko, and ed. Donald B. Lindsley. New York: Plenum Press, 1972.

Solomon, Stanley J. *The Classic Cinema: Essays in Criticism.* New York: Harcourt Brace Jovanovich, 1973.

Sonnino, Lee A. *A Handbook of Sixteenth Century Rhetoric.* London: Routledge & Kegan Paul, 1968.

Sparshott, Francis. *The Theory of the Arts.* Princeton: Princeton University Press, 1982.

Spector, Jack J. *The Aesthetics of Freud: A Study in Psychoanalysis and Art.* London: Allen Lane, Penguin Press, 1972.

Spiegal, J., and P. Machotka. *Messages of the Body.* New York: Free Press, 1974.

Spottiswoode, Raymond. *A Grammar of the Film.* Berkeley: University of California Press, 1950.

Stanford, W. Bedell. *Greek Metaphor.* Oxford: Blackwell, 1936.

Stannard, D. E. *Shrinking History.* Oxford: Oxford University Press, 1980.

Stern, Gustav. *Meaning and Change of Meaning.* Göteborg: Elanders Boktryckeri Aktiebolag, 1931.

Stevens, Wallace. *Opus Posthumous.* New York: Alfred A. Knopf, 1959.

Thompson, Richard. "Screen Writer: *Taxi Driver's* Paul Schrader." *Film Comment* 12, no. 2 (March–April), p. 17.

Toulmin, Stephen. *The Philosophy of Science.* London: Hutchinson, 1953.

Tourangean, Roger. "Metaphor and Cognitive Structure," in *Metaphor: Problems and Perspectives,* ed. David S. Miall, pp. 14–35. Brighton: Harvester Press, 1982.

Trilling, Lionel. *The Liberal Imagination.* London: Macmillan, 1948.

———. *The Opposing Self.* London: Secker & Warburg, 1955.

Truffaut, François. *Hitchcock.* London: Panther Books, 1969.

Tudor, Andrew. *Theories of Film.* London: Secker & Warburg, 1974.

Turbayne, Colin Murray. *The Myth of Metaphor.* New Haven: Yale University Press, 1962.

Turner, G. W. *Stylistics.* Harmondsworth: Penguin Books, 1973.

Ullman, Stephen. *Language and Style.* Oxford: Basil Blackwell, 1964.

———. *Style in the French Novel.* Oxford: Basil Blackwell, 1964.

Van Noppen, J. P., et al. *Metaphor: A Bibliography of Post-1970 Publications.* Amsterdam: John Benjamins, 1985.

Vardoe, Nicholas. "Realism and Romance: D. W. Griffith," in *Focus on D. W. Griffith,* ed. Harry M. Geduld, pp. 70–9. Englewood Cliffs, N.J.: Prentice-Hall, 1971.

Vickers, Brian. *Classical Rhetoric in English Poetry.* London: Macmillan, 1970.

Vygotsky, L. S. *Thought and Language.* Cambridge, Mass.: MIT Press, 1962.

Wajda, Andrzej. *The Wajda Trilogy,* trans. and introd. Boleslaw Sulik. London: Lorrimer, 1973.

Welleck, René, and Austin Warren. *Theory of Literature.* Harmondsworth: Penguin Books, 1976.

Wheelwright, Philip. *The Burning Fountain.* Bloomington: Indiana University Press, 1972.

———. *Metaphor and Reality.* Bloomington: Indiana University Press, 1975.

Whittock, Trevor. "The Concept of Poetic Metaphor." *U.C.T. Studies in English* 6 (1978), pp. 10–33.

———. *A Reading of the Canterbury Tales.* Cambridge: Cambridge University Press, 1968.

Whorf, Benjamin Lee. *Language, Thought, and Reality,* ed. J. Carroll. Cambridge, Mass.: MIT Press, 1956.

Willeman, Paul. "Cinematic Discourses: The Problem of Inner Speech," in *Cinema and Language,* ed. Stephen Heath and Patricia Mellencamp, pp. 141–67. Frederick, Md.: University Publications of America, 1983.

Wimsatt, W. K., Jr. *The Verbal Icon.* London: Methuen, 1970.

Wittgenstein, Ludwig. *Philosophical Investigations,* G. E. M. Auscombe. Oxford: Basil Blackwell, 1958.

Wollen, Peter. *Signs and Meaning in the Cinema.* London: Secker & Warburg, 1969.

Wollheim, Richard. *On Art and the Mind.* London: Allen Lane, 1973.

Wood, Robin. *Hitchcock's Films.* London: Zwommer, 1965.

Worth, Sol, and John Adair. *Through Navajo Eyes.* Bloomington: Indiana University Press, 1972.

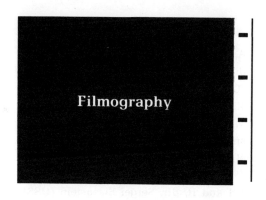

Filmography

All the President's Men, dir. Alan Pakula (USA, 1976)

Andalusian Dog, An (Un Chien andalou), dir. Luis Buñuel (France, 1962)

Ashes and Diamonds (Popiól i diament), dir. Andrzej Wajda (Poland, 1958)

Ballad of a Soldier (Balada o Soldata), dir. Grigori Chukhrai (USSR, 1959)

Battleship Potemkin (Bronenosets Potemkin), dir. Sergei Eisenstein (USSR, 1925)

Best Years of Our Lives, The, dir. William Wyler (USA, 1946)

Bezhin Meadow (Bezhin Lug), dir. Sergei Eisenstein (unfinished; USSR, 1935–7)

Bicycle Thief, The (Ladri di biciclette), dir. Vittorio de Sica (Italy, 1948)

Birds, The, dir. Alfred Hitchcock (USA, 1963)

Birth of a Nation, dir. D. W. Griffith (USA, 1915)

Blow-Up, dir. Michelangelo Antonioni (GB, 1966)

Cabinet of Dr. Caligari, The (Das Kabinett des Dr. Caligari), dir. Robert Wiene (Germany, 1919)

Chinoise, La, dir. Jean-Luc Godard (France, 1967)

Citizen Kane, dir. Orson Welles (USA, 1941)

Clockwork Orange, A, dir. Stanley Kubrick (GB, 1971)

Conversation, The, dir. Francis Ford Coppola (USA, 1974)

Day for Night (La Nuit américaine), dir. François Truffaut (France, 1973)

Dr. Strangelove, dir. Stanley Kubrick (GB, 1963)

Earth (Zemlya), dir. Alexander Petrovitch Dovzhenko (USSR, 1930)

Eclipse, The (L'eclisse), dir. Michelangelo Antonioni (Italy, 1962)

8½, dir. Federico Fellini (Italy, 1963)

Elusive Corporal, The (Le Caporal épingle), dir. Jean Renoir (France, 1962)

400 Blows, The (Les Quatre Cents Coups), dir. François Truffaut (France, 1959)

General, The, dir. Buster Keaton (USA, 1926)

Godfather, The, dir. Francis Ford Coppola (USA, 1972; Part II, 1974)

Gold Rush, The, dir. Charles Chaplin (USA, 1925)

Graduate, The, dir. Mike Nichols (USA, 1968)

Grand Illusion (La Grande Illusion), dir. Jean Renoir (France, 1937)

Grapes of Wrath, The, dir. John Ford (USA, 1940)

Great Dictator, The, dir. Charles Chaplin (USA, 1940)

Happiness (Schaste), dir. Alexander Ivanovitch Medvedkin (USSR, 1934)

Hiroshima, mon amour, dir. Alain Resnais (France, 1959)

If..., dir. Lindsay Anderson (GB, 1968)

Intolerance, dir. D. W. Griffith (USA, 1916)

Ivan the Terrible (Ivan Grozny), Parts I and II, dir. Sergei Eisenstein (USSR, 1944–6)

Juliet of the Spirits (Giulietta degli spiriti), dir. Federico Fellini (Italy, 1964–5)

Kind Hearts and Coronets, dir. Robert Hamer (GB, 1949)

Knife in the Water (Nóż w wodzie), dir. Roman Polanski (Poland, 1962)

Lady Killers, The, dir. Alexander Mackendrick (GB, 1955)

Man Escaped, A (Condamné à mort s'est échappé, Un), dir. Robert Bresson (France, 1956)

Metropolis, dir. Fritz Lang (Germany, 1926)

Miracle Worker, The, dir. Arthur Penn (USA, 1962)

Modern Times, dir. Charles Chaplin (USA, 1936)

North by Northwest, dir. Alfred Hitchcock (USA, 1959)

Nosferatu, dir. F. W. Murnau (Germany, 1922)

Nuit et brouillard, dir. Alain Resnais (France, 1956)

October (Oktiabr), dir. Sergei Eisenstein (USSR, 1927)

Oliver Twist, dir. David Lean (GB, 1948)

Open City (Roma, città aperta), dir. Roberto Rossellini (Italy, 1945)

Passenger, The, dir. Michelangelo Antonioni (USA, 1975)

Passion of Anna, The (En passion), dir. Ingmar Bergman (Sweden, 1969)

Passion of Joan of Arc, The (La Passion de Jeanne d'Arc), dir. Carl Dreyer (France, 1928)

Pather Panchali, dir. Satyajit Ray (Bengal, 1955)

Persona, dir. Ingmar Bergman (Sweden, 1966)

Point Blank, dir. John Boorman (USA, 1967)

Psycho, dir. Alfred Hitchcock (USA, 1960)

Quiet Man, The, dir. John Ford (USA, 1952)

Red Desert, The (Deserto rosso), dir. Michelangelo Antonioni (Italy, 1964)

Red River, dir. Howard Hawks (USA, 1948)

Roaring Twenties, The, dir. Raoul Walsh (USA, 1939)

Royal Wedding, dir. Stanley Donen (USA, 1951)

Rules of the Game, The (La Règle du jeu), dir. Jean Renoir (France, 1939)

Sawdust and Tinsel (Gycklarnas afton), dir. Ingmar Bergman (Sweden, 1953)

Scarface, dir. Howard Hawks (USA, 1932)

Searchers, The, dir. John Ford (USA, 1956)

Seconds, dir. John Frankenheimer (USA, 1966)

Song of Ceylon, dir. Basil Wright (GB, 1935)

Strada, La, dir. Federico Fellini (Italy, 1954)

Strangers on a Train, dir. Alfred Hitchcock (USA, 1951)

Taxi Driver, dir. Martin Scorcese (USA, 1976)

Third Man, The, dir. Carol Reed (GB, 1949)

Throne of Blood (*Kumonosu-jo*), dir. Akira Kurosawa (Japan, 1957)

To Catch a Thief, dir. Alfred Hitchcock (USA, 1955)

Treasure of Sierra Madre, The, dir. John Huston (USA, 1947)

Trial of Joan of Arc, The (*Le Procès de Jeanne d'Arc*), dir. Robert Bresson (France, 1961)

Turning Point, The, dir. Herbert Ross (USA, 1977)

2001: A Space Odyssey, dir. Stanley Kubrick (GB, 1968)

Vertigo, dir. Alfred Hitchcock (USA, 1958)

Vivre sa vie (*My Life to Live*), dir. Jean-Luc Godard (France, 1962)

Walkabout, dir. Nicolas Roeg (Australia, 1971)

Wild Bunch, The, dir. Sam Peckinpah (USA, 1969)

Young Mr. Lincoln, dir. John Ford (USA, 1939)

Zelig, dir. Woody Allen (USA, 1983)

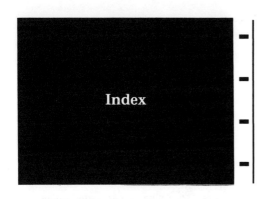

Index